INDONESIA RISING

The **Indonesia Project**, a major international centre for research on the Indonesian economy and society, is housed in the **Crawford School of Economics and Government**'s **Arndt-Corden Department of Economics**. The Crawford School is part of the **ANU College of Asia and the Pacific** at **The Australian National University (ANU).** Established in 1965, the Project is well known and respected in Indonesia and in other places where Indonesia attracts serious scholarly and official interest. Funded by the ANU and the Australian Agency for International Development (AusAID), the Indonesia Project monitors and analyses recent economic developments in Indonesia; informs Australian governments, business and the wider community about those developments and about future prospects; stimulates research on the Indonesian economy; and publishes the respected *Bulletin of Indonesian Economic Studies*.

The College's **Department of Political and Social Change (PSC)** focuses on domestic politics, social processes and state–society relationships in Asia and the Pacific, and has a long-established interest in Indonesia.

Together with PSC, the Project holds the annual Indonesia Update conference, which offers an overview of recent economic and political developments and devotes attention to a significant theme in Indonesia's development. The *Bulletin of Indonesian Economic Studies* publishes the conference's economic and political overviews, while the edited papers related to the conference theme are published in the Indonesia Update Series.

The **Institute of Southeast Asian Studies (ISEAS)** was established as an autonomous organization in 1968. It is a regional centre dedicated to the study of socio-political, security and economic trends and developments in Southeast Asia and its wider geostrategic and economic environment. The Institute's research programmes are the Regional Economic Studies (RES, including ASEAN and APEC), Regional Strategic and Political Studies (RSPS), and Regional Social and Cultural Studies (RSCS).

ISEAS Publishing, an established academic press, has issued more than 2,000 books and journals. It is the largest scholarly publisher of research about Southeast Asia from within the region. ISEAS Publishing works with many other academic and trade publishers and distributors to disseminate important research and analyses from and about Southeast Asia to the rest of the world.

Indonesia Update Series

INDONESIA RISING

The Repositioning of Asia's Third Giant

Edited by
Anthony Reid

ISEAS
INSTITUTE OF SOUTHEAST ASIAN STUDIES
SINGAPORE

First published in Singapore in 2012 by
ISEAS Publishing
Institute of Southeast Asian Studies
30 Heng Mui Keng Terrace
Pasir Panjang
Singapore 119614

E-mail: publish@iseas.edu.sg
Website: http://bookshop.iseas.edu.sg

All rights reserved. No part of this publication may be reproduced, translated, stored in a retrieval system, or transmitted in any form or by any means, electronic, mechanical, photocopying, recording or otherwise, without the prior permission of the Institute of Southeast Asian Studies.

© 2012 Institute of Southeast Asian Studies, Singapore
First Reprint 2012
Second Reprint 2012

The responsibility for facts and opinions in this publication rests exclusively with the authors and their interpretations do not necessarily reflect the views or the policy of the Institute or its supporters.

ISEAS Library Cataloguing-in-Publication Data

Indonesia rising : the repositioning of Asia's third giant / edited by Anthony Reid.
(Indonesia update series)
This book emanates from the 29th Indonesia Update Conference organized by the Australian National University Indonesia Project on 30 September and 1 October 2011.
1. Indonesia—Foreign relations—Congresses.
2. Indonesia—Foreign economic conditions—Congresses.
3. Indonesia—Politics and government—1998- —Congresses.
4. Indonesia—Economic conditions—1997- —Congresses.
5. Climatic changes—Indonesia—Congresses.
I. Reid, Anthony, 1939-
II. Australian National University. Indonesia Project.
III. Indonesia Update Conference (29th : 2011 : Canberra, Australia)
DS644.4 I41 2011 2012

ISBN 978-981-4380-39-3 (soft cover)
ISBN 978-981-4380-40-9 (hard cover)
ISBN 978-981-4380-41-6 (e-book, PDF)

Cover photo: Indonesian President Yudhoyono talks to US President Obama during a breakfast meeting at the G20 Summit in Toronto on 27 June 2010.
Source: Jason Reed/Reuters.

Edited and typeset by Beth Thomson, Japan Online, Canberra
Indexed by Angela Grant, Sydney
Printed in Singapore by Mainland Press Pte Ltd

CONTENTS

TABLES

FIGURES

CONTRIBUTORS

Anthony Reid is a Southeast Asian historian in the Department of Political & Social Change at the Australian National University (ANU). He was founding Director both of the Asia Research Institute at the National University of Singapore (2002–2007) and of the Centre for Southeast Asian Studies at the University of California, Los Angeles (1999–2002). Before taking up these positions, he was a longstanding member of the former Department of Pacific & Asian History at the ANU. His books include *The Indonesian National Revolution* (1974); *The Blood of the People: Revolution and the End of Traditional Rule in Northern Sumatra* (1979); *Southeast Asia in the Age of Commerce* (2 volumes, 1988 and 1993); *Charting the Shape of Early Modern Southeast Asia* (1999); *An Indonesian Frontier: Acehnese and Other Histories of Sumatra* (2004); *Imperial Alchemy: Nationalism and Political Identity in Southeast Asia* (2010) and *To Nation by Revolution: Indonesia in the 20th Century* (2011).

M. Chatib Basri is a Senior Lecturer in the Department of Economics, University of Indonesia; Vice Chairman of the National Economic Committee of the President of Indonesia; a co-founder and Senior Partner of the CReco Research Institute; and a member of the Asia–Pacific Regional Advisory Group of the International Monetary Fund. He served as a Special Adviser to the Indonesian Minister of Finance in 2006–2010; as Sherpa to the President of Indonesia for the G20 in November 2008; and as an acting Deputy Minister of Finance for the G20 from 2006 to 2009. His more recent publications include *Ideas, Interests and Oil Prices: The Political Economy of Trade Reform during Soeharto's Indonesia* (2004) (with Hal Hill), *Should Indonesia Say Goodbye to Its Strategy of Facilitating Exports?* (2011) (with Sjamsu Rahardja) and 'Indonesian growth dynamics' (*Asian Economic Policy Review*, June 2011) (with Hal Hill).

Martin van Bruinessen is Emeritus Professor of Comparative Studies of Contemporary Muslim Societies at Utrecht University, and from 1999 to 2008 was one of the chairs at the International Institute for the Study of

Islam in the Modern World. He has carried out extensive anthropological fieldwork in Turkey and Kurdistan as well as Indonesia. His books include *Tarekat Naqsyabandiyah di Indonesia* (1992), *Kitab Kuning, Pesantren dan Tarekat* (1995) and the (co-)edited volumes *Sufism and the 'Modern' in Asia* (2007), *The Madrasa in Asia: Political Activism and Transnational Linkages* (2008) and *Islam and Modernity: Key Issues and Debates* (2009).

R.E. Elson taught at Griffith University's School of Modern Asian Studies (1979–2003), where he served as Dean of the Faculty of Asian and International Studies and Foundation Director of the Griffith Asia Pacific Research Institute (now Griffith Asia Institute). In 2003 he was appointed Professor of Southeast Asian History at the University of Queensland. He is the author of five books and numerous articles and chapters on the modern history of Indonesia and Southeast Asia, including a contribution to the *Cambridge History of Southeast Asia* and a political biography of former president Suharto. His most recent book is *The Idea of Indonesia: A History* (2008).

Donald K. Emmerson heads the Southeast Asia Forum at Stanford University, where he is also affiliated with the Center on Democracy, Development, and the Rule of Law and the Abbasi Program in Islamic Studies. Recent publications include a chapter on the sociology of knowledge of Indonesian politics (forthcoming); an article on Southeast Asian politics in the *Journal of Democracy* (2012); essays on 'Asian regionalism and U.S. policy' and 'The problem and promise of focality in world affairs' (2010); chapters in *Islamism: Contested Perspectives on Political Islam* (2009); and an edited volume, *Hard Choices: Security, Democracy, and Regionalism in Southeast Asia* (2009). Activities in Indonesia in 2011–2012 have included accompanying Stanford students on a study trip, covering the East Asia Summit in Bali for the *Asia Times* and addressing a conference on futurology in Jakarta.

Gareth Evans AO QC is Chancellor of the Australian National University, Professorial Fellow at the University of Melbourne and President Emeritus of the International Crisis Group, which he led from 2000 to 2009. He was a member of the Australian parliament for 21 years, and a cabinet minister in the Hawke and Keating governments for 13, including as foreign minister from 1988 to 1996.

Ross Garnaut AO is a Vice Chancellor's Fellow and Professorial Fellow in Economics at the University of Melbourne and a Distinguished Professor at the Australian National University. He is one of Australia's most distinguished and well-known economists and the author of numerous publications on international trade, public finance and economic development, particularly in relation to East Asia and the Southwest Pacific.

In addition to his distinguished academic career, Professor Garnaut has had longstanding and successful roles as policy adviser, diplomat and businessman. He was the Senior Economic Adviser to Australian Prime Minister R.J.L. Hawke and subsequently served as the Australian Ambassador to China (1985–88).

Scott Guggenheim is a social policy adviser to the AusAID Indonesia program. Before joining AusAID he worked for many years at the World Bank, where he developed and managed large-scale community development projects, such as Indonesia's National Program for Community Empowerment and the National Solidarity Project in Afghanistan. Dr Guggenheim is the co-editor of several publications, including *Power and Protest in the Countryside* (1984), *Anthropological Approaches to Involuntary Resettlement* (1996), *The Search for Empowerment* (2006) and, most recently, *Invisible People: Poverty and Empowerment in Indonesia* (2011).

Frank Jotzo is the Director of the Centre for Climate Economics and Policy at the Australian National University's Crawford School of Economics and Government. He has advised several governments on climate change policy in the context of development and economic reform, including the Indonesian government through its Ministry of Finance. He is a Lead Author of the Fifth Assessment Report by the Intergovernmental Panel on Climate Change.

Rizal Sukma is Executive Director of the Centre for Strategic and International Studies, Jakarta; Chairman of International Relations, Muhammadiyah Central Executive Board; and a member of the Board of Governors of the Institute for Peace and Democracy. Since receiving a PhD in International Relations from the London School of Economics and Political Science in 1997, he has worked extensively on such issues as Southeast Asian security, ASEAN, Indonesia's defence and foreign policy, military reform, Islam and politics, and domestic political changes in Indonesia. Dr Sukma has served as a member of the National Committee on Strategic Defence Review at the Ministry of Defence, and as a member of the National Drafting Committee for the National Defence Bill (2000–2002) and the Armed Forces Bill (2002–2003). He was the first Indonesian to receive the Nakasone Award, in July 2005, and was named one of *Foreign Policy* magazine's 100 Global Thinkers in 2009. His many publications include, most recently, 'The ASEAN Political and Security Community (APSC): opportunities and constraints for the R2P in Southeast Asia' (*Pacific Review*, March 2012) and 'Indonesia finds a new voice' (*Journal of Democracy*, October 2011).

FOREWORD: INDONESIA, AUSTRALIA AND THE WORLD

Gareth Evans

I have always had a strong personal sense of engagement with and commitment to Indonesia. It started with visits long before I entered politics, but was much reinforced by the very warm professional and personal relationship I developed with Ali Alatas after we became the foreign ministers of our respective countries around the same time in 1988, and pledged ourselves to restore ballast to a relationship that seemed to have conspicuously lost it.

My affection did not do me much good with the Australian public, with East Timor the running sore it remained for so long, but it was something of which I have remained proud. Indonesia is a country that has an enormous amount to contribute to wider global and regional governance, and our relationship with it, though still so undervalued, remains incredibly important to us.

So it gives me particular pleasure, wearing my new hat as chancellor of this great university, to introduce this important volume, the outcome of the 29th Indonesia Update conference in the series the Australian National University has been running continuously since 1983. The annual Update conference, convened with great flair by Professor Tony Reid, is a unique event, the only one of its kind for Indonesia (though it has become an exemplar for similar series that the ANU now runs with several other countries). Its longevity and quality, and the strong public interest it generates as an open and inclusive event, are testimony to the continuing strength of Indonesian studies at the ANU – and the continuing strong support given to this event by AusAID, which it is always a pleasure to acknowledge.

The 2011 Update was marked by two milestones, one sad and the other happy. The sad one is that this is the first since 1983 that Jamie Mackie, who passed away peacefully in April aged 86, has not been with us. Together with Herb Feith and Heinz Arndt, he was one of the founders of Indonesian studies in Australia and his legacy will be long remembered.

The happy milestone is that this is the first Update since Budy Resosudarmo assumed the directorship of the Indonesia Project at the ANU's Crawford School. The Project plays an important role in monitoring and analysing economic developments, in particular, and informing government, business and the wider community about them. It is crucial that it continue to play that role and, through this volume, the role of informing the Australian community about a wider range of developments as well.

In this respect it is important to do something to counter the old stereotypical habits of thinking about Indonesia that still remain depressingly familiar: that it is military dominated, authoritarian and undemocratic, and a hotbed of Islamic extremism which makes it a dangerous country for Australians to be in. This last perception has been prolonged rather than alleviated by overcautious Australian government travel advisories.

There is now, once again, an unhappy shortage of that ballast which Ali Alatas and I worked so hard to create. One manifestation of that is the falling away in Australia of commitment to language teaching. Another is the drop in the level of overseas student enrolments at all levels. One would have thought that, as our next-door neighbour, with an increasingly outward-looking population of more than 240 million, Indonesia would rank very high, and be the subject of a huge amount of recruitment activity. But on the last full comparative figures I have seen, for 2009, Indonesian student commencements were just 2.5 per cent of the national total, ranking not only after China and India, but below South Korea, Thailand, Vietnam, Malaysia, Nepal and Brazil as well.

So this book, like the conference that gave birth to it, is a crucial tool in the process of getting to know each other better as mature and important democratic neighbours, both now G20 members as well as key players in Southeast Asia and the Asia–Pacific. Outstanding chapters by Indonesian, Australian and other experts well communicate that understanding and sense of relevance about the relationship. The book's theme is Indonesia's rising place in the world, and the chapters cover, as usual, a very wide terrain, including both good and less good news stories.

On the less good side:

- Indonesia's anti-corruption drive has been looking decidedly shaky since the departure of Sri Mulyani Indrawati.

- Religious freedom has been under stress, with little action taken to stop violent attacks by conservative extremists on religious minorities, and Christian and Muslim communal tensions surfacing again in Ambon.
- There has been continuing concern about general government weakness, with a decent but hypercautious president constantly confronting problems posed by a divided, fractious and not very reform-minded legislature.

But the good news far outweighs the troubling developments.

- Democracy is holding together. Far-reaching institutional changes have been implemented effectively, notably including regional devolution, and the contrasts with the authoritarianism of the military regime under Suharto remain very stark.
- The economy is basically thriving, despite all the infrastructure and corruption problems that inhibit it, and the difficulties posed by the international environment.
- The religious environment remains overwhelmingly moderate, with Indonesia a talismanic example to much of the rest of the Muslim world. The handling of terrorist risk – for all the formidable difficulties so well documented by the International Crisis Group's living national treasure, Sidney Jones – is being done well by any international standard.
- Indonesia is beginning to show signs of punching closer to its weight in international forums, showing a certain amount of impatience with ASEAN's paralysing caution, and – on some United Nations issues very dear to me – playing a real flag-bearing role. In particular I want to emphasize Indonesia's strong support for the concept of 'the responsibility to protect' against genocide and other mass atrocity crimes when the acceptance of this new obligation was delicately poised in 2009 and 2010, and its announcement that it will at last ratify the Comprehensive Nuclear Test Ban Treaty, setting a significant example to the United States, China, India and other hold-out countries.

All these and many more issues are discussed in this volume. There is much here to encourage both optimists and pessimists to rethink their positions. For specialists and non-specialists alike seeking a balanced and timely evaluation both of how far Indonesia has risen and of how far it is likely to go, or simply fascinated by this immensely attractive and important country, this book will be a superb resource.

PREFACE

This book is the latest to appear in a long and distinguished lineage. The Australian National University's Indonesia Update began in 1983, when the late Jamie Mackie and Peter McCawley conceived and implemented the idea of an annual public conference in Canberra to assess conditions in Indonesia. From the beginning it was understood as an alliance between economic and political analysts, with numerous other disciplines playing appropriate roles. As the format congealed the conference was held annually on a weekend in late September, and began with two surveys of the past year – one economic and the other political. The remaining papers were clustered around a theme of particular topical importance.

With Hal Hill playing a lead role through the ANU's Indonesia Project, which he headed for many years, the Update books have been published regularly since 1989. They now constitute a kind of record of an evolving nation. The two survey papers were initially published in the Update books, but since 2005 they have been published quickly in the *Bulletin of Indonesian Economic Studies*, while the papers clustered around the theme of each year's conference became the basis of a substantial book published in the following year. This book is the 23rd publication in the Indonesia Update series, and it emanates from the 29th conference. Greg Fealy (politics) and Chris Manning and Raden Purnagunawan (economics) provided the two overviews, which were published in the *Bulletin of Indonesian Economic Studies* of November 2011.

The theme of the Update, held on 30 September and 1 October 2011, was 'Indonesia's place in the world'. After a series of volumes naturally focusing on Indonesia's difficult transition to a democratic and decentralized format, it was felt to be time to look at the country's international stance and standing. Admission to the G20 group of nations was one factor making this timely; the pressures of globalization on every country were another. The concept of 'Indonesia's rise' emerged at Don Emmerson's suggestion in the planning process as the title for one panel of the conference, very much in quotes. One paper after another, however, grappled in some way with the international perception that this might at last be Indonesia's moment, unlikely as it seemed to oft-disappointed specialists. The book has therefore cohered around this issue. There is much to be said both for and against it, and the book aims to provide a reliable guide to those arguments.

Thanks are due in many quarters. Firstly I acknowledge Michael O'Shannassy, who shared the burden of organizing the Update conference until called to a position in Bangkok. Dewi Fortuna Anwar made a splendid contribution to the conference, though regrettably the intense demands on her time prevented the completion of a paper within the tight deadlines of this book. Budy Resosudarmo, who took over the leadership of the Indonesia Project in 2011, has been a constant source of guidance and support, as was his predecessor Chris Manning. In organizing the Update, the well-practised Indonesia Project team of Cathy Haberle and Nurkemala Muliani made things very easy for the nominal convenors, and coped smoothly with the large flow of people on the day. Liz Drysdale, Allison Ley, Thu Thuy Pham and Daniel Suryadarma were also unfailingly helpful. The funding of the Australian Agency for International Development (AusAID), as well as the support of the ANU, were essential for the realization of both the Update and this book.

I owe a great debt in both constructing the Update conference and preparing this book for publication to my wonderful colleagues at the ANU. The economists and political scientists were generous with their time and patience in guiding a mere historian. I thank in particular Ross McLeod, Hal Hill, Chris Manning, Peter McCawley, Ed Aspinall, Greg Fealy, Marcus Mietzner, and again always Budy, for their help.

Finally, I would like to thank all those who assisted with the production of the book: Rahilah Yusuf and her team at the Institute of Southeast Asian Studies; Angela Grant, who produced the index; and Beth Thomson, who managed the copy editing, formatting and myriad problems of presenting tables and graphs with her usual skill and professionalism.

Anthony Reid
Canberra, March 2012

GLOSSARY

3G	global growth generators (Bangladesh, China, Egypt, India, Indonesia, Iraq, Mongolia, Nigeria, the Philippines, Sri Lanka and Vietnam)
abangan	syncretic or Javanist Muslims
ADB	Asian Development Bank
AKP	Adalet ve Kalkinma Partisi (Justice and Development Party) (Turkey)
Al-Irsyad	Jam'iyah al-Islah wa al-Irsyad (Union for Reformation and Guidance), founded 1913
APEC	Asia–Pacific Economic Cooperation
APRA	Angkatan Perang Ratu Adil (Legion of Ratu Adil)
ASEAN	Association of Southeast Asian Nations
AusAID	Australian Agency for International Development
Balitbang	Badan Penelitian dan Pengembangan (Office for Research and Development)
Bappenas	Badan Perencanaan Pembangunan Nasional (National Development Planning Agency)
BASIC	Brazil, South Africa, India and China
BBVA	Banco Bilbao Vizcaya Argentaria
bebas-aktip	free and active (foreign policy)
BPS	Badan Pusat Statistik (Central Statistics Agency)
BRIC	Brazil, Russia, India and China
BRICS	Brazil, Russia, India, China and South Africa
CIVETS	Colombia, Indonesia, Vietnam, Egypt, Turkey and South Africa
Comintern	Communist International
CSIS	Centre for Strategic and International Studies
Darul Islam	Abode of Islam (rebel movement of the 1950s)
DDII	Dewan Dakwah Islamiyah Indonesia (Indonesian Council for Islamic Propagation), founded 1967

DNPI	Dewan Nasional Perubahan Iklim (National Climate Change Council)
DPR	Dewan Perwakilan Rakyat (People's Representative Council, also known as 'House of Representatives' and as 'parliament')
dwifungsi	dual function (political and military, of the armed forces)
EAGLE	emerging and growth-leading economies (Brazil, China, Egypt, India, Indonesia, Mexico, South Korea, Taiwan and Turkey)
EAS	East Asia Summit
EU	European Union
FDI	foreign direct investment
Fitra	Forum Indonesia untuk Transparansi Anggaran (Indonesian Forum for Budget Transparency)
FPI	foreign portfolio investment
G7	group of seven industrialized countries: France, Germany, Italy, Japan, the United Kingdom, the United States and Canada
G20	group of 20 countries or regions: the G7 plus Argentina, Australia, Brazil, China, European Union, India, Indonesia, Mexico, Russia, Saudi Arabia, South Africa, South Korea and Turkey
GANEFO	Games of the New Emerging Forces
GDP	gross domestic product
Golkar	orig. Golongan Karya (the state political party under Suharto and now one of the parliamentary parties)
HTI	Hizbut Tahrir Indonesia (Indonesian Liberation Party)
IAIN	Institut Agama Islam Negeri (State Islamic Institute)
IBRIC	Indonesia, Brazil, Russia, India and China
IGGI	Intergovernmental Group on Indonesia
IMF	International Monetary Fund
JiKTI	Jaringan Peneliti Kawasan Timur Indonesia (Eastern Indonesia Researcher Network)
Kemitraan	Partnership for Governance Reform
kiai	title of a religious scholar or leader (Java)
KPK	Komisi Pemberantasan Korupsi (Corruption Eradication Commission)
LIPI	Lembaga Ilmu Pengetahuan Indonesia (Indonesian Institute of Sciences)
LIPIA	Lembaga Ilmu Pengetahuan Islam dan Arab (Institute for Arabic and Islamic Studies), founded 1980

LPEM-FEUI	Lembaga Penyelidikan Ekonomi dan Masyarakat, Fakultas Ekonomi, Universitas Indonesia (Institute for Economic and Social Research, Faculty of Economics, University of Indonesia)
madhhab	school of Islamic law
madrasah	Islamic school or college
mandala	'circle' (from Sanskrit), concentric diagram in Indic iconography, and metaphorically a field of influence surrounding a political centre
Masyumi	Majelis Syuro Muslimin Indonesia (Indonesian Muslim Consultative Council), Islamic umbrella organization (1943–45) and a leading political party (1945–60)
MDG	Millennium Development Goals
medrese	*madrasah* (Turkey)
MIST	Mexico, Indonesia, South Korea and Turkey
Muhammadiyah	modernist Islamic organization, founded 1912
N-11	Next Eleven (Bangladesh, Egypt, Indonesia, Iran, Mexico, Nigeria, Pakistan, the Philippines, South Korea, Turkey and Vietnam)
NEFOs	new emerging forces
NEKOLIM	neo-colonialism, colonialism and imperialism
New Order	the Suharto era, 1965–98
NGO	non-government organization
NU	Nahdlatul Ulama, traditionalist Islamic organization, founded 1926
NYU	New York University
OLDEFO	old established forces
OPEC	Organization of the Petroleum Exporting Countries
P4	*Pedoman Penghayatan dan Pengamalan Pancasila* [Guide for Instilling and Experiencing Pancasila]
Pancasila	'five principles' (of the Indonesian state)
PAS	Parti Se-Islam Malaysia (Pan-Malaysian Islamic Party)
PDI-P	Partai Demokrasi Indonesia-Perjuangan (Indonesian Democratic Party of Struggle)
PECC	Pacific Economic Cooperation Council
pembaruan	reform, renewal
Pendidikan Nasional Indonesia	Indonesian National Education (movement, 1930s)
Persis	Persatuan Islam (Islamic Association), reformist Islamic organization, founded 1923
pesantren	traditional Islamic boarding school
PKI	Partai Komunis Indonesia (Indonesian Communist Party)

PKS	Partai Keadilan Sejahtera (Prosperous Justice Party)
PLN	Perusahaan Listrik Negara (State Electricity Company)
PRRI	Pemerintah Revolusioner Republik Indonesia (Revolutionary Government of the Republic of Indonesia)
REDD	reducing emissions from deforestation and forest degradation
reformasi	reform (particularly in politics from 1998)
Salafism	movement emphasizing the *salaf* ('predecessors'), or the Islamic first generation
Sayyid	title of descendants of the Prophet Mohammad
SBY	Susilo Bambang Yudhoyono (Indonesia's president)
Shia	branch of Islam claiming legitimate descent from the Prophet through Ali
SIPRI	Stockholm International Peace Research Institute
SSCI	Social Sciences Citation Index
Sufism	Islamic mysticism
Sunni	majority branch of Islam
Susenas	Survei Sosio-Ekonomi Nasional (National Socio-Economic Survey)
tafsir	exegesis, particularly of the Qur'an
TIMBI	Turkey, India, Mexico, Brazil, Indonesia
UK	United Kingdom
UKP-PPP	Unit Kerja Presiden Bidang Pengawasan dan Pengendalian Pembangunan (Presidential Unit for Development Supervision and Control)
ulama	Islamic scholar/s
ummah	the Islamic community
UN	United Nations
UNESCO	United Nations Educational, Scientific and Cultural Organization
US	United States
USSR	Union of Soviet Socialist Republics
WTO	World Trade Organization

Currencies

$	US dollar
A$	Australian dollar
Rp	Indonesian rupiah

1 INDONESIA'S NEW PROMINENCE IN THE WORLD

Anthony Reid

'GOODBYE CHINA, HELLO INDONESIA'?

Surprising as it sounds to cynical Indonesians and disillusioned Indonesianists, there are reasons for thinking that this is at last Indonesia's moment on the world stage. The world's fourth-biggest country by population has an unenviable reputation for not living up to expectations, epitomized by the subtitle of Anne Booth's economic history of Indonesia: 'A history of missed opportunities' (Booth 1998). She traced over almost two centuries a sequence of hopeful new beginnings followed by disappointments, leaving Indonesia one of the world's poorest and most conflicted countries in the 1960s. As other Asian tiger economies leapt ahead in the latter part of the twentieth century, Indonesia also grew, but failed to close the gap with its neighbours. In 1998 the Asian financial crisis caused a 13 per cent drop in GDP, and an IMF bullying of the Suharto government into taking the kind of stern medicine that helped precipitate its fall.

Yet now we have international pundits declaring that Indonesia is the future. The influential US journal *Foreign Policy* used the heading 'The Indonesian tiger' for a story proclaiming the country the quiet achiever of the moment (Keating 2010). Much quoted NYU Stern School economist Nouriel Roubini, known as 'Dr Doom' for his forecasting of global financial crisis and especially a coming crash in China, went further. In a speech reported under the heading 'Roubini: goodbye China, hello Indonesia', he noted that China's growth rate was falling while Indonesia's was rising (6.1 per cent in 2010, 6.3 per cent in 2011, 6.5 per cent expected in 2012). He argued moreover that Indonesia had the right model to sustain growth, with its low inflation, low debt (about 26 per cent of GDP), young demographics, and the insulation provided by two-thirds of its GDP being derived from domestic consumption. It therefore stood a better chance than China, let alone the developed world, of long-term growth even in the hard times he expected the world to face (Deutsch 2011). Indonesia's admission to the G20 club of influential states seems no more than its due in light of such predictions.

Inside Indonesia all this is hard to believe. The headlines are all about corruption scandals, political stalemate, extremist Islamic rhetoric and natural disaster. Even when a reformist policy survives the vested interests and outrageous corruption of a multi-party legislature, the difficulties of making it effective on the ground appear as remote as ever. The transition from Suharto's hierarchical and centrally driven political economy to a democratic environment of fragmented power appears to have demoralized more than it has galvanized the young reformers who gave birth to the change.

This book is intended to weigh the arguments about Indonesia's present and future standing in the world. It includes the good news and the bad, and avoids the type of glib optimism expressed in the Roubini headline, but on the whole it offers some concrete reasons why the present opportunity is Indonesia's best yet.

STRATEGIC ARCHIPELAGO TO THIRD WORLD EXPERIMENT

The archipelago that constitutes Indonesia today was destined by its geography to be a passageway between oceans and continents, but also in the longer term a major source of threats to our planet. This section of the Pacific 'Ring of Fire', where the India–Australia plate pushes under that of Eurasia, has been the source of the most devastating volcanic eruptions to threaten humanity. The eruption of the volcano that created Lake Toba in Sumatra 74,000 years ago is now thought to have caused six years of global winter and reduced the human species to a small remnant. More recently, the eruptions of Tambora (in Sumbawa) in 1815 and Krakatau (between Sumatra and Java) in 1883 also had global as well as regional effects in changing the world's climate. The layer of ash thrown into the atmosphere by a similar eruption in the twenty-first century would have catastrophic effects on global air traffic. Research since the shock of the world's worst known tsunami in 2004 reveals that Indonesia is also exceptionally exposed to major tectonic earthquakes that can cause terrifying tsunamis around the heavily populated Indian Ocean littoral.

In historical times that archipelago's moments of global prominence owed more to its environment, its tropical produce (Java and Makassar entered the English language to mean coffee and a vegetable oil respectively) and its role as an international meeting place than to the achievements of its people. It was a major centre for the mediation of Buddhism to eastern Asia in the seventh to tenth centuries. In the fifteenth and sixteenth it became the object of desire in the global spice race that incidentally united the world. The Dutch had won that race by the 1650s and had little difficulty, in the Treaty of Breda (1667), surrendering to the British their claims to what would become New York and New England, provided they were unchallenged in their possession of the far more lucrative nutmeg-producing Banda Islands in Maluku. As the Asian capital for the early modern world's most successful trading company, Jakarta (Dutch Batavia) became one of the key ports of Asia in the period 1630–1780. While the Dutch/Indonesian monopoly of cloves and nutmeg was broken in the mid-eighteenth century, modern colonial capitalism again made Indonesia one of the major sources of the world's supplies of coffee, sugar, pepper, copra, indigo, tin and rubber in the century from 1830 to 1930.

The peoples of Indonesia made less impact on the world's capitals, after the brief excitement of Aceh embassies to Turkey (1563) and Holland (1601), and a Banten one to England (1684). They were dismissed as savage when independent (like the Acehnese, Balinese and romanticized 'Malay pirates'); as passive and over-refined when colonized (like the Javanese and post-1910 Balinese). The major Indonesian contributions to global civilization in recent centuries were Javanese music, which famously influenced Claude Debussy and Erik Satie through the Paris Exposition of 1889, and Javanese and Balinese graphic arts and dance, starting with Gauguin at the same Paris Exposition. In the twentieth century Béla Bartók, Francis Poulenc, Olivier Messiaen, Pierre Boulez and Benjamin Britten, and more profoundly the Canadian Colin McPhee and the Australian Peter Sculthorpe, introduced *gamelan* themes or instruments into their work.

That Indonesian achievement did not and does not feature more prominently in the world's sense of its cultural heritage can perhaps be attributed to three factors. First, unlike Japan, China and Siam/Thailand, Indonesia did not force itself on the world's attention in the form of a strong state, since its pre-colonial political genius had been directed rather to smaller communities held together by religion, kinship, culture, commercial exchange and irrigation collectives (Reid 1998; Scott 2009: 98–126). Second, having the Dutch language as the primary portal to European culture made Indonesia far less accessible than India, Burma or China (through English) and Indochina (through French). And finally, the population of pre-colonial Indonesia was small and scattered through an overwhelmingly forested environment, perhaps as a consequence of earlier environmental disasters. Indonesia had only about 12–15 million people in 1800, compared with over 300 million in China, more than 180 million in India and nearly 30 million in Japan. Java began its rapid modern expansion in population in the nineteenth century and the other islands in the twentieth, in tandem with a smothering colonial embrace characterized by Clifford Geertz (1963) as an 'agricultural involution' in which Indonesians grew in numbers but not wealth, as a peasant people without a dynamic middle class. Indonesia's demographic weight as one of the world's most populous countries is of recent origin.

The crisis that overwhelmed the Indonesian export economy during the Great Depression (1929–35) was compounded by Japanese occupation (1941–45) and revolutionary upheaval (1945–49, with continuing rebellions until the 1960s). At least until the 1970s Indonesia appeared the epitome of a Third World country mired in political conflict, populist sloganeering, counterproductive economic nationalism and the flight of capital. Against this background the last half-century is particularly worthy of attention.

THE REASONS FOR OPTIMISM

The chief reasons for optimism derive from Indonesia's recent economic growth performance and favourable economic fundamentals, which are outlined in the next two chapters. Some current projections have Indonesia becoming Asia's third-largest economy (after China and India) by 2050, passing Japan during that period on present trends.

Among the structural advantages that allow for economic optimism is the favourable population structure. In common with other Southeast Asian countries such as Vietnam and Thailand, Indonesia is beginning to enjoy a so-called 'demographic dividend' stemming from the rapid reduction in the birth rate in the late Suharto period. In consequence the current decade will be particularly favourable for Indonesia. The proportion of the population of productive working age is expected to peak in 2020, when the dependency ratio will be just 46 dependants per 100 workers. This will compare with about 53 in India, 54 in the Philippines, 56 in the United States and United Kingdom, and 68 in Japan. The more drastic birth-rate reductions in China and South Korea give them an even greater current demographic dividend, but pressures from the 2030s when there will be fewer workers to support the many aged (UN Population Division 2011).

The most important source of Indonesia's current growth is domestic consumption, deriving in turn from the expansion of a middle class with increasing amounts of disposable income, as explained further in Chapter 3. Not unnaturally, private consumption has grown less rapidly than exports and foreign investment (McLeod 2011), but it is less vulnerable to global crises. M. Chatib Basri points out in Chapter 3 that, despite its political difficulties with corruption and vested interests, democratic Indonesia has succeeded in continuing a more successful pattern of macroeconomic management than most of the rich democracies, with a low ratio of government debt to GDP, predicted to decrease further to 24 per cent in 2014. This dramatic contrast with the dire situation in Europe, the United States and Japan should ensure that Indonesia continues to outperform these rich countries economically for decades to come. This optimism should, however, be read alongside Donald K. Emmerson's scepticism about the economic record in Chapter 4.

The trauma of a democratic transition also appears to be behind Indonesia, unlike in some of the other Asian risers. Three free and fair elections at both the national and local levels have taken place with little violence (contrasting with recent experience in the torch bearers of Asian democracy, India and the Philippines). The frequency with which these elections have changed the leadership and the dominant parties makes democratic change no longer threatening to stability, in contrast to neighbouring Malaysia and Singapore, and potentially China – all under one party's rule since the 1950s. These factors have enabled Indonesia to be ranked as fully democratic alongside only a small number of peers in Asia – India, Japan, South Korea and Taiwan – upstaging even Asia's oldest democracy because of the alarming violence of Philippine elections (Freedom House 2012a). Even the widespread popular disenchantment with President Susilo Bambang Yudhoyono's leadership during his second term has not aroused calls for a return to military or neo-Suharto models.

Of Suharto's Indonesia, as of the China of Mao and Deng, it was often said that without the autocratic strong hand at the centre the country would fall apart. The democratic transition in the 1990s of what had been the Soviet Union and Yugoslavia certainly unleashed a number of political and economic demons that have taken more than two decades to exorcize. By that standard Indonesia's trauma of 1998–2002 was relatively contained, despite the thousands of victims of ethnic and religious fratricide (van Klinken 2007). Devolution of budgetary authority to the regions provided much more to fight about, but once the logic of electoral demography was played out, the winner-takes-all mentality gave way to patterns of electoral alliance. Even though most observers, including the authors in this book, were gloomy about Indonesia's prospects a decade ago, its negotiation of this democratic challenge now appears relatively successful. China has yet to undergo such a transition, but as its citizens grow in education, confidence and assertiveness the problem cannot be indefinitely delayed.

The chapters that follow by Ross Garnaut, M. Chatib Basri, Donald K. Emmerson and Rizal Sukma, themselves experienced actors in regional diplomacy, chronicle the ways in which the new and democratic Indonesia has sought to position itself in the world. In stark contrast to the confrontational stance of Sukarno, but more actively than under Suharto, Indonesia has sought to be a good international citizen, with 'a million friends and zero enemies'. While there is disappointment that it has not been better able to blaze a trail for responsible Islamic democracy and open trade, these chapters suggest that Indonesia is again playing a useful role as a Southeast Asian and Muslim voice at the G20 top table.

A REVOLUTIONARY NATIONALIST DIVIDEND?

Indonesia became the world's fourth most populous country because its rivals for that position disintegrated – first Pakistan and then the Soviet Union. Indonesia is an even more improbable amalgam of disparate peoples than those two other post-war creations. It comprises not only the 17,000 islands mentioned by Chatib Basri, but hundreds of ethnolinguistic groups and a range of economic systems from forest-dwelling hunter-gatherers to urban cosmopolitans. It has no prior tradition of an integrated state except the brief and wholly alien Dutch one. Before Dutch military, legal and economic power united the archipelago in the years after 1900, states were relatively personal and ephemeral concentrations of power, never integrating more than small corners of the archipelago. The Sriwijaya and Majapahit 'empires' beloved of nationalist histories did not unify politically or legally even at their brief apogees, though they did provide important networks of trade. What did tend to create coherence were cultural, economic, environmental and especially religious commonalities, which made the exchange of ideas possible through a kind of ecumene of trade networks operating through a lingua franca of Malay.

Thailand, Burma and many other post-colonial creations could seek to build their modern nation-states around a core that had a common and favourable memory of an ancient kingdom. The lack of such a core (though some Javanese nationalists once sought to create one) appeared to give Indonesia a much more difficult challenge in achieving modern statehood, but after a half-century of crises that weakness has become a strength. The modern Indonesian state is patently created on no basis of historical legitimacy save that of Netherlands India, and therefore is spared the inherent inequality between ethnic or 'real' Chinese, Thais, Vietnamese or Burmans and their respective 'minorities' without a comparable identification with a pre-colonial state. The identity of Indonesians was born in 1945.

Indonesia's revolutionary path to statehood was also important in distinguishing it from most of its neighbours. The romantic, in the end millenarian, rhetoric of President Sukarno (dominating in 1956–65) about burying the past and building a new future was not disavowed by the military who seized control with Suharto in 1966, but rather militarized into a legitimation of *dwifungsi* – a dual political and military role for the armed forces. As in the case of the other two Asian countries that followed a revolutionary path to modern statehood, China and Vietnam, Indonesia based its national identity, as taught in all schools and in the P4 ideology courses of the Suharto era, on the invented tradition of anti-imperial struggle, rather than on the very varied past achievements of Indonesia's many cultures. In Indonesia's case the adoption of a neutral lingua franca, rather than a major mother tongue, as the national language added to the newness of the national experiment.

The cost of this revolutionary path was extremely high. It damaged the economy (particularly during the period 1945–70 when Indonesia fell far behind Malaysia and Thailand), undermined the rule of law, fatally disenfranchised the multiple vibrant written cultures of the archipelago and, above all, demanded a high level of political violence, including the half-million or so whose killing in 1965–66 inaugurated and made possible the authoritarian imposition of the new unitary format.

The eventual dividend from all this pain was the unified Indonesia we see today, populated by two generations educated (badly but uniformly) into the exceptionally centralized system of Suharto. Only the national language could be taught in schools or used on television, and the new nationalist myth of unified struggle against Dutch rule largely obliterated the memory of each region's diverse history. Some of the longer-term consequences of this rough passage were also negative, as suggested in the warnings below. But Indonesian political identity is today one of the most consensual and securely established in Asia, with no further need for imposition by force. It made possible the transition to democracy with the loss only of East Timor, occupied by force in 1975. Aceh was a close call, but the relative success of the Helsinki agreement to end its war of rebellion (2005) can also be put down in part to this revolutionary nationalist dividend (Reid 2007; Aspinall 2009).

That dividend may also have contributed to a relatively modest pattern of inequality in Indonesia, even during its two periods of rapid growth – in 1970–97 and since 2002. Economic inequality as measured by consumption appears to have risen only modestly since 1990, whereas income per capita has doubled. This is in marked contrast to the situation in China and some other Asian risers, where, from a more egalitarian base in 1990, inequality has increased greatly (Roland-Holst, Sugiyarto and Loh 2010: 62–4, Table 1). Despite China's higher total gross national product per capita, by 2006 a smaller proportion of the population in Indonesia was living below the poverty line (Hofman, Zhao and Ishihara 2007: 174–5). Since its revolutionary days, Indonesia has retained a resistance to large commercialized landholdings that is both institutional and cultural. Moreover, barriers of ethnicity, class and gender do not on the whole prevent people of talent and energy from succeeding in Indonesia. Although the revolutionary heritage of both China and Indonesia includes a uniform education system, paradoxically it is Indonesia that appears to have retained more of the egalitarian ethos.

The nature of the revolutionary dividend for both countries becomes clearer by contrast with non-revolutionary India or Malaysia, where multiple cultures and regionalisms with distinct legal rights continue to thrive and to make life difficult for national governments. The homogeneity of language and idiom enforced by Indonesia's often-painful first half-century now has the potential to be a distinct asset for the country. Though not enough of them do so, Indonesians can today engage the world in a democratic, open spirit without fear of compromising their identity. The high price paid to achieve that outcome should make them still more determined to use that identity to build a free, open and world-educated society that can compete and flourish in today's globalized world.

MAJOR OBSTACLES

The 14 years since Suharto's authoritarian regime was overturned have delivered impressive reform in the areas of political democracy and press freedom. In neither area is it unqualified. Indonesia today ranks poorly in the most cited ranking of press freedom, but this is largely because of the violence vested interests have visited on robust journalists, who are freer to expose corruption than most (Reporters Without Borders 2012).[1] *Reformasi* has not made much impact, however, on such endemic problems as a weak education system, a justified lack of confidence in the judicial system, corruption in every sphere, apparently rising intolerance of minority ideas, and the weakness, despite a lively and diverse press, of a critical public space where conventional popular myths can be questioned and the world engaged. Although the education system has produced a shared political culture internally, it has left Indonesians rela-

1 Indonesia fell in the Reporters Without Borders ranking from 57th out of 139 countries in 2002 to 146th out of 179 countries in 2011. In contrast, Freedom House (2012b) continues to rank Indonesia in the top half for press freedom, at 71st out of 150 countries.

tively poorly equipped to understand or deal with the world externally. In Chapter 8, Scott Guggenheim shows how far Indonesia is behind the emerging countries it seeks to join, or even its neighbours, on every measure of intellectual engagement with the world. At the Indonesia Update conference that inspired this volume, Merlyna Lim identified one area in which Indonesia leads: it has enthusiastically embraced the new social media, and ranks among the top three countries in the world in terms of the number of Facebook and Twitter users. Whether this can compensate for the deficiencies in more conventional publications remains to be seen, however.

The revolutionary nationalist dividend described above was achieved in part by forcibly silencing those who did not initially find it congenial or believable. First to be placed outside the national conversation were the significant minorities who had appreciated the entrenched diversities of the old Dutch order, or the access that order gave to European civilization, to the extent of failing to endorse the revolutionary republic in time. Many assorted Eurasians, Chinese, Europeans, Arabs, Jews, Japanese and others among the cosmopolitan elite felt they had to leave in the years after 1945. Others who had backed federalism as the best way to relate to the new independent state, notably Christians, Balinese Hindus and other minorities, had to remain silent once their side lost the struggle. Those internationally oriented Muslims who had justified anti-imperial violence as *jihad* in favour of an Islamic state were eliminated or silenced in the wars against Darul Islam, while many of Indonesia's most ardent democrats were silenced for backing the losing PRRI side in the 1950s. Finally, the whole revolutionary left wing, including many of Indonesia's most inquiring and innovative minds, were killed, imprisoned or suppressed in the massive violence of 1965–66. Throughout the Suharto era many of the minority figures best able to deal confidently with the world outside Indonesia were ignored or chose to opt out of domestic public debate.

In today's highly competitive global world, therefore, the successful creation of Indonesia's national identity has a new downside in the relative absence of cosmopolitan global citizens, and the discomfort or difficulty many Indonesians feel when overseas. Although Indonesians are travelling abroad to study in bigger numbers than ever, those in the social sciences focus almost exclusively on writing about their own country. There are very few scholars left in the country's universities who research and teach on any other country than Indonesia. And yet nearly 90 per cent of the writing on Indonesia itself in international scholarly journals is written by people who are not based in the country (see Chapter 8), making Indonesia one of the least effective countries at explaining itself to the world.

In attracting and regulating investment, and making use of its own human resources, Indonesia remains badly handicapped by poor and in some areas declining infrastructure, a legal regime very little trusted by its citizens to provide equal justice to all, and a corrupt and cumbrous bureaucracy. These problems are discussed more fully in the book, particularly Chapters 3–5, and have been well documented elsewhere (Aspinall and van Klinken 2011). As the authors point out, good intentions have been demonstrated through the establishment of an anti-corruption agency, but the capacity of central government agencies such as this to implement laws on the ground is very weak. A more effective weapon in practice is the vigour of a robust and competitive press to reveal wrongdoing at both the national and local levels. In the absence of decisive action by government, however, this often has the effect of demoralizing the public by publicizing the country's worst features.

In comparative terms, the international perception of Indonesian corruption has somewhat improved under the Yudhoyono government from its dismal reputation in the past, but the country remains well below most of those with which it is seen to compete for position. The widely cited Corruption Perceptions Index has been raising its rating of Indonesia slowly, from 2.6 in 2008 to 3.0 in 2011 (out of a possible 10), where it sits in joint 100th position alongside Mexico and Argentina, out of 182 countries ranked. Malaysia and Thailand are substantially better regarded, and even China (3.6) and India (3.1) slightly so (Transparency International 2011). World Audit also gives Indonesia a below-average result at joint 77th out of 150 countries, though as if to demonstrate the great uncertainties of any such ranking, it had Indonesia's performance declining between 2010 and 2011 (World Audit 2011).

The type of corruption that may be the most harmful to economic policy making – and widespread in democracies – is the inordinate influence of corporate vested interests under the guise of nationalism. As Chatib Basri points out in Chapter 3, the government of President Yudhoyono has shown little resolve in facing down pressure from Aburizal Bakrie – the biggest indigenous corporate figure and the chairman of the Golkar Party – even in his second term when re-election should not be an issue. Consumer and environmental lobbies are puny in comparison with those seeking to defend their corporate interests against competition. Chatib Basri describes the turning away from a liberal reform agenda represented by the loss of two of the region's ablest economic ministers who were not sufficiently defended by the president against these vested interests. Dr Sri Mulyani Indrawati resigned as finance minister in May 2010 to become managing director of the World Bank, while Dr Mari Pangestu was demoted from trade minister to 'tourism and creative economy' minister in November 2011. As Hal Hill and Monica Wihardja

(2011) lament, the government commitment to meaningful reform seems lower than ever: 'the anti-reform pressures are now very powerful, and built in to the nation's *modus operandi*'.

There are some areas in which Indonesia appears well equipped to lead. One such is environmental policy, discussed by Frank Jotzo in Chapter 6. Indonesia still has some of the world's most important tropical forests, and preventing their destruction can be parlayed into significant international support, as the Norway agreement demonstrates. Ross Garnaut argues in Chapter 2 that Indonesia is on the right side of the global climate change debate. Jotzo points out, however, that performance has been far below rhetoric in this as in other areas. Although the promises of governments in the post-1998 democratic era have been impressive, in practice their capacity to protect Indonesian forests appears even less than that of Suharto.

As the world's largest Muslim-majority country, Indonesia is well placed to present an attractive democratic model, alongside Turkey, for reform movements in the Islamic world. But as Martin van Bruinessen points out in Chapter 7, Indonesian Muslims simply do not have a habit of leading. In marked contrast to the other major non-Arab Muslim states, Turkey, Iran and Pakistan, Indonesia has not produced thinkers who are widely read elsewhere in the Muslim world. It tends to see itself as a consumer rather than producer of ideas, and devotes far more attention to translating work into Indonesian than out of it into English or Arabic. Indonesia's admirable openness to outside ideas, whether from Western, Eastern or Islamic sources, appears to emanate in part from an assumption of marginality or even irrelevance. The final chapter by R.E. Elson points to a lack of confidence in the legitimacy of Indonesia's distinct identity, which must be overcome for the country to play a role in the world that is commensurate with its size.

BE CAREFUL WHAT YOU WISH FOR

Let me end with the question of whether Indonesia punches below its weight in international affairs, as raised in Gareth Evans's foreword and taken up in several chapters. Some of the obstacles discussed above do appear to limit Indonesia's capacity to make use of the leadership position implied by membership of the G20, let alone its status as the world's fourth most populous country and the one with the largest Muslim majority. Indonesians have long had relatively little to say for themselves in international forums, a consequence of relatively poor education in international languages and a cultural preference for dignified understatement, but also of the lack of confidence referred to by several authors in this book.

One cannot, however, ignore the arms-purchase factor as a vital ingredient in the perception of a nation punching below its weight in international strategic circles. Indonesia has not wielded a big stick in the region, partly because its military was poorly equipped by most measures throughout the Suharto era. Although General Suharto took power in 1965–66 through the military, he proved better able (or willing) than the civilian President Sukarno to resist its demands for hardware, and (with the disastrous exception of East Timor) deployed his forces to suppress internal opposition rather than enforce external claims. The Association of Southeast Asian Nations (ASEAN) has been as successful as it has partly because its giant, Indonesia, was in no position to bully its smaller neighbours militarily. As discussed further by Emmerson in Chapter 4, Indonesia's military expenditure is estimated by the Stockholm International Peace Research Institute to be the lowest of any large country, at 0.6 per cent of GDP in 2001, rising to no more than 1.3 per cent over the years 2003–2008 (SIPRI 2009), though the CIA gives a different figure.[2] This was a constructive choice for regional stability, providing greater security for Indonesia's smaller immediate neighbours (Malaysia, Singapore, East Timor and Papua New Guinea in particular) and avoiding the kind of regional arms race that would have made development even more difficult. It could be said to represent Asian leadership of a more positive kind than muscular military expenditure.

There are signs that this benign strategy may be ending, and that Indonesia's growing economic strength will be reflected in much greater purchase of arms. Military expenditure doubled between 2001 and 2003 under the nationalist President Megawati Sukarnoputri, and after stabilizing rose again by 28 per cent in 2010, the largest increase in Asia. A further 46 per cent increase is projected by 2015, designed to give a fleet of 274 ships by 2024 (Supriyanto 2012). It is likely that in this respect too Indonesia will punch much closer to its weight in the future than it has in the past, with consequences that may not be stabilizing for the region.

---

2 The CIA (2011) gives a radically higher estimate of 3 per cent of GDP in 2005, probably based on the 70 per cent of military income judged by some observers to come from off-budget sources, including the army's economic fiefdoms and some corruption. Like Emmerson in this volume, I have preferred the SIPRI estimate; it appears to be based on official sources, presumably because the off-budget income is unknowable, thought to be declining under Yudhoyono, and in any case not being used for the sharp end of military effectiveness. The CIA figures appear to minimize US expenditure and maximize that of some other countries with opaque budgeting.

REFERENCES

Aspinall, Edward (2009) *Islam and Nation: Separatist Rebellion in Aceh, Indonesia*, Stanford University Press, Stanford CA.

Aspinall, Edward and Gerry van Klinken (eds) (2011) *The State and Illegality in Indonesia*, KITLV Press, Leiden.

Booth, Anne (1998) *The Indonesian Economy in the Nineteenth and Twentieth Centuries: A History of Missed Opportunities*, Palgrave, Basingstoke.

CIA (Central Intelligence Agency) (2011) 'The world factbook', available at https://www.cia.gov/library/publications/the-world-factbook/index.html.

Deutsch, A. (2011) 'Roubini: goodbye China, hello Indonesia', *Financial Times*, 25 October.

Freedom House (2012a) *Freedom in the World 2012*, available at http://freedomhouse.org.

Freedom House (2012b) 'Press freedom table', available at http://www.worldaudit.org/press.htm.

Geertz, Clifford (1963) *Agricultural Involution: The Processes of Ecological Change in Indonesia*, University of California Press, Berkeley CA.

Hill, Hal and Monica Wihardja (2011) 'Indonesia's reform reversal', *Wall Street Journal*, 30 November.

Hofman, Bert, Min Zhao and Yoichiro Ishihara (2007) 'Asian development strategies: China and Indonesia compared', *Bulletin of Indonesian Economic Studies* 43(2): 171–99.

Keating, Joshua E. (2010) 'The Indonesian tiger', *Foreign Policy*, December.

Klinken, Gerry van (2007) *Communal Violence and Democratization in Indonesia: Small Town Wars*, Routledge, London.

McLeod, Ross (2011) 'Survey of recent developments', *Bulletin of Indonesian Economic Studies* 47(1): 7-34.

Reid, Anthony (1998) 'Political "tradition" in Indonesia: the one and the many', *Asian Studies Review* 22(1): 23–38.

Reid, Anthony (ed.) (2007) *Verandah of Violence: The Background to the Aceh Problem*, second edition, NUS Press, Singapore.

Reporters Without Borders (2012) 'Press Freedom Index', available at http://en.rsf.org/press-freedom-index-2011-2012,1043.html.

Roland-Holst, David, Guntur Sugiyarto and Yinshan Loh (2010) 'Asian regional income, growth and distribution to 2030', *Asian Development Review* 27(2): 57–81.

Scott, James C. (2009) *The Art of Not Being Governed: An Anarchist History of Southeast Asia*, Yale University Press, New Haven CT.

SIPRI (Stockholm International Peace Research Institute) (2009) 'SIPRI Military Expenditure Database', available at http://www.sipri.org/databases/milex, accessed 28 January 2012.

Supriyanto, Ristian Atriandi (2012) 'Indonesia's naval modernisation: a sea change?', RSIS Commentary No. 020/2012, Singapore, 27 January.

Transparency International (2011) 'Corruption Perceptions Index 2011', available at http://cpi.transparency.org/cpi2011/, accessed 28 January 2012.

UN Population Division (2011) *World Population Prospects: The 2010 Revision*, available at http://esa.un.org/wpp/Excel-Data/population.htm, accessed 28 January 2012.

World Audit (2011) 'Corruption perception rankings', available at http://www.worldaudit.org/corruption.htm, accessed 28 January 2012.

2 INDONESIA IN THE NEW WORLD BALANCE

Ross Garnaut

The final quarter of the twentieth century saw modern economic growth firmly established in the populous countries of Asia for the first time: China from the late 1970s, Indonesia from the mid-1980s, India from the early 1990s and other Southeast Asian economies at various times over the period. The acceleration in growth in the large Asian countries was associated with an inexorable shift in the centre of gravity of global economic activity and power.

This shift was briefly disturbed and temporarily obscured by the Asian financial crisis in 1997–98. The crisis had its most severe and profound consequences in Indonesia, where it led into the trauma of democratization, and then the painful reconciliation of the pressures from a democratic polity and modern economic growth. But reconciled they were, and the late twentieth-century tendencies and expectations for continued economic growth were re-established in the first decade of the twenty-first century.

In the first seven years of the new century, the world was moving gradually and slowly out of the brief unipolar moment in which the United States appeared to dominate international affairs, towards a new, multipolar balance. The end point was likely to be a balance within which four entities were much more important than others: the United States, China, the European Union and India. In the emerging multipolar world, no consequential international action would be possible if any one of the four great centres of power was deeply uncomfortable with it. The European Union would sometimes be influential through some of its constituent national parts, but increasingly, and eventually mainly, through integrated action.[1]

In a multipolar world, the role of the next tier of substantial economies would be more influential than in the unipolar system of the late twentieth century, or the bipolar system with the Soviet Union that preceded it. Interaction of the four great powers with other considerable countries would be important in shaping what was possible in international cooperation.

The shift to a multipolar world in the late twentieth and early twenty-first centuries was inexorable, but slow and gradual. The unipolar dominance of the United States after the collapse of the Soviet Union seemed likely to fade gradually and slowly, leaving plenty of time for the international community to learn how to make cooperative relations among states work within new power realities.

The Great Crash of 2008 suddenly shifted economic growth in the established industrial economies of the North Atlantic onto a decisively lower trajectory.[2] In the large developing countries, however, growth was not much affected after a disturbing but brief splutter. Growth momentum was quickly restored to its earlier strengths in China and India, and to near those levels in Indonesia. The stronger economic growth that had been established in much of the remainder of the developing world mostly continued.

The result was a marked acceleration in the rate at which global economic weight shifted from the United States and other North Atlantic developed countries to the large developing countries. The new multipolar world of international relations is emerging much more rapidly than thoughtful analysts had anticipated only a few years ago. There is now much less time to learn how to make productive international relations work within the emerging power realities, and to build the institutions that will be needed.

Indonesia has an important place in this new world. Of the countries outside the big four centres of power it is the most populous. It ranks

---

1 I have said elsewhere on several occasions that European integration is likely to be increasingly important over time (Garnaut 2006, 2011, forthcoming). The Great Crash of 2008, the subsequent recession in the North Atlantic economies and the currency crisis in the Euro region have raised fundamental questions about the future of the European Union. In my view, this leaves Europe with a choice between greater integration and disintegration. While there may be disintegration at the margins, I expect that the pain of greater integration is likely to be more acceptable to European leaders than the pain of disintegration.

2 For an analysis of the Great Crash, see Garnaut with Llewellyn-Smith (2009).

eighth in economic size outside the big four (the European Union, the United States, China and India) (World Bank 2011). Indonesia is growing much faster on a sustained basis than any of the seven countries ranked immediately behind India in current economic size. Its demographic profile, savings and investment rates, and capacity to grow through absorption of international economic institutions and technologies underpin stronger continuing growth prospects than in any of the seven. Indonesia is likely within a decade to surpass in economic size all of the second tier except Japan and Russia.

Some other characteristics add to Indonesia's current and potential geopolitical influence. Indonesia is the world's fourth most populous country and the largest with a Muslim majority. It is by far the most populous country in Southeast Asia and it has the largest economy in this successful and rapidly growing region. It is the accepted political leader of Southeast Asia. This matters the more because Southeast Asia is an increasingly integrated region, and if viewed as a whole the only reasonably cohesive grouping of countries outside Europe that has anything like the economic weight of the least of the four great powers.

Indonesia matters on a global scale for all these reasons. It is influential in world forums - already one of the most influential outside the big four. It is an important member of the G20, the main forum for international responses to the Great Crash since being elevated to heads-of-government level in late 2008. Its leadership of the Association of Southeast Asian Nations (ASEAN) puts it at the centre of intensive security and economic dialogue with the major powers. Its hosting of a UN climate change conference in December 2007 gave it a leading role in climate change policy. And it has a demonstrated record of diplomatic leadership in Southeast Asia - and through that beyond the region - on international economic policy, security and climate change.

We can identify some distinctively Indonesian contributions to the evolution of the Asia–Pacific international system over the past quarter-century. As I will explain below, the ideas and international political culture embodied in these contributions are highly relevant - indeed crucial - to making the international system work in the rapidly emerging multipolar world.

What is distinctive about the ideas and international political culture contributed by Indonesia had its origin in relations within ASEAN. ASEAN was established in 1967 and immediately began to play a role in building shared security perspectives after the upheavals of the Malaysian confrontation, during the strategic reorientation of Indonesia under Suharto and through the uncertainties of the war in Indochina. ASEAN never lost its underlying political rationale - to build trust among countries of immense importance to each other but with a limited history of productive interaction. In 1975, in response to new dimensions of insecurity with the end of the war in Vietnam, regional economic integration became the agenda area that attracted most activity and public attention.

While the members of ASEAN made some formal attempts to establish a traditional preferential trading area, these never came to much. Helpfully, when reductions in protection were agreed, they were mostly implemented on a most favoured nation basis, without discrimination against external trading partners. What turned out to be important in ASEAN economic cooperation was the building of confidence in internationally oriented development, the crafting of mutually supportive positions on global trade and other economic issues that affected more than one economy (and sometimes all economies) in the region, and the sharing of knowledge about the policies and institutions that supported outward-looking economic policies and made them more productive. Indonesian and ASEAN influence was important to the establishment of Asia–Pacific Economic Cooperation (APEC) in 1989 as a major venue for international economic cooperation, and to the building of policies and ways of working during the ensuing decade, until the Asian financial crisis. The role of this 'open regionalism' in Asia–Pacific economic cooperation is discussed in more detail elsewhere (Soesastro 1994; Garnaut 1996).

Indonesian leadership was centrally important to the cohesion and considerable international influence of ASEAN through to the end of the Suharto era. International relations receded for a while in Indonesian priorities during the Asian financial crisis and the early years of democratic government. That made ASEAN temporarily less important in broader regional and global affairs.

The hosting in Bali in December 2007 of the Conference of the Parties to the United Nations Framework Convention on Climate Change marked Indonesia's return to a central place in the international policy arena. This re-emergence of a more prominent global role was reinforced by the country's membership of the G20 and the increasing importance of that forum. In 2011, Indonesia made a distinctive and valuable contribution to G20 deliberations by drawing attention to the role that concerted investment in development infrastructure could play in strengthening global economic growth.

Indonesia both contributed to and led the emergence of an ASEAN political culture that was characterized by the importance of sensitivity to dissent; by frequent communications leading to informal understandings rather than formal negotiations and agreement as a basis for cooperative action; by the avoidance of ambush and duress for representatives of countries whose national positions were initially different from that of the majority; and, as a result, by an emphasis on moving in similar directions through concerted unilateral decisions rather than binding agreements.

The ASEAN approach to collective decision making was sometimes described as requiring 'consensus'. This is not strictly accurate; some decisions were taken despite the reservations of one or a small number of members, but only after extensive consultation.

If my description of ASEAN political culture sounds a bit 'Javanese' – in that it is characterized by accommodation of different points of view and a search for common ground – it may be because it and the Javanese style of leadership emerged for similar reasons. Within the ASEAN political culture, while Indonesian views were highly influential, decisions were not imposed by the leader of the strongest state but emerged from interaction among members. In similar fashion, Anthony Reid has suggested that polities in pre-independence Java – as well as the post-independence Indonesian state – did not have much military, bureaucratic or legal muscle, and were always highly plural, so that consensus building was often the only approach to collective decisions that did not risk fracturing the polity (see, for example, Reid 2011: 198–204).

The first officially supported, systematic discussion of economic cooperation among Asia–Pacific countries took place at the Pacific Economic Community meeting at the Australian National University in Canberra in 1980 (Crawford and Seow 1981).[3] Those present discussed a range of approaches to regional cooperation. If there had been any inclination to build a formal preferential trading block in the Pacific region – and some participants at first thought that this might be a reasonable long-term goal – it did not survive the firm assertion of a contrary view by ASEAN participants. The idea of a preferential trading area – and therefore of 'traditional' (that is, European-style or what was to become North American-style) economic cooperation – having been firmly rejected, the issue became whether there was value in regional cooperation at all. The ASEAN view was that there was value in developing alternative forms of regional economic cooperation.

ASEAN and Indonesian support for continuing discussion of Asia–Pacific economic cooperation ensured that less formal approaches to regional arrangements were explored. The Pacific Economic Cooperation Council (PECC) was established in 1980 to continue these talks. Indonesia – especially through the creative and persuasive executive director of the Centre for Strategic and International Studies, Hadi Soesastro, and its energetic and influential chairman, Jusuf Wanandi – contributed

---

3 Although officially supported, these talks were explicitly unofficial; in the language of a later era, they were 'second-track' discussions.

much of the energy and ideas and lent considerable ASEAN legitimacy to PECC as it defined a new approach to regional cooperation.

In early 1989, Australian prime minister Bob Hawke formed the view that talking about cooperation had proceeded far enough and that there was a basis for productive action. This led to the Australian initiative to call the first APEC meeting in Canberra in November 1989. The Indonesian response was crucial in ensuring that the meeting was not a once-off gathering of economic and foreign ministers, but the first of a series.

When President Clinton, with the support of President Suharto and Prime Minister Keating, elevated the Seattle APEC meeting in 1993 to the heads-of-government level, the Indonesian president underwrote the elevation by offering personally to host the fourth meeting. Indonesia and ASEAN then put their weight behind open regionalism – regional economic cooperation without discrimination against outsiders – as the main organizing idea for the APEC process.

In terms of content, the fourth heads-of-government meeting in Bogor in 1994 was the most substantial and important of the APEC gatherings. The Bogor meeting committed members to free and open trade and investment in the region by 2010 for developed countries and 2020 for developing countries. Fatefully, however, there was no agreement about what 'free and open trade' in the Asia–Pacific really meant. Whatever it might mean, there was no meeting of minds either on the means through which the objective would be reached.

For Indonesia, ASEAN, Australia and the Western Pacific countries, the Bogor Declaration embodied a commitment for the Asia–Pacific to become a region of countries maintaining free and open external trade and investment policies. Within this framework, APEC would provide strong support both for unilateral liberalization in individual countries and for non-discriminatory liberalization within article 1 of the General Agreement on Tariffs and Trade (later incorporated into the World Trade Organization).

For the United States and most APEC members in the Eastern Pacific, however, the Bogor Declaration was a commitment to work towards a formal free trade area in the APEC region, with discrimination against trading partners outside the regional grouping. This conceptualization of 'free and open trade and investment' followed the lines of the soon-to-be-fashionable bilateral preferential trade agreements for which the North American Free Trade Agreement was to become a model.

An old Chinese saying talks of 'one bed, different dreams'. Open regionalism within the APEC framework was such a case of 'one bed, different dreams'. However, the presence of differences was not fundamentally challenging to the ASEAN and Indonesian dreams. The different dreams could live inside the different heads, and practical decisions on moving towards more open trade and investment could still be made case by case as issues arose. Different countries could rationalize those decisions in different ways. The ASEAN countries would interpret the Bogor Declaration consistently with open regionalism.

The dominant Australian view at the time, like the Indonesian, ASEAN, Japanese, Chinese and South Korean views, was also based on the dream of non-discrimination. However, the more pedantic (perhaps 'Western') Australian intellect was troubled more than the Indonesian and ASEAN mind by the dissonance between dreams. We in Australia, especially at the Australian National University, sought to define and to provide a rationale for non-discriminatory, open policies for trade and investment (Garnaut and Drysdale 1989; Elek 1992). Definition and rationalization made it difficult to avoid acknowledging the conflict between open regionalism and the North American dream of formal, binding and discriminatory free trade agreements of a traditional kind. Our Indonesian and ASEAN colleagues enjoyed watching us try to define the dissonance. They were instrumental in my being asked to engage in debate with Fred Bergsten, the director of Washington's Institute of International Economics (now the Peterson Institute), on the meaning of the emerging Bogor Declaration at international conferences in Kuala Lumpur in March 1994 and in Jakarta on the eve of the Bogor APEC leaders' meeting in November 1994 (Garnaut 1996: Chs 3 and 5).

In practice, the Western Pacific dream to which Indonesia had made a large and essential contribution guided APEC through its first decade. From the late 1980s until the Asian financial crisis, a high tide of unilateral liberalization and trade expansion lifted economic growth in all Western Pacific economies except the few whose leaders had kept them outside the main streams of the international economy. The trade liberalization, trade expansion and economic growth were mutually reinforcing. One country's liberalization, economic growth and import expansion enhanced its neighbours' export opportunities. Greater export opportunities increased the reward for unilateral liberalization. At the same time, the recognition that trade liberalization was associated with economic prosperity in the liberalizing country strengthened support for and weakened resistance to trade liberalization everywhere. This was open regionalism working as it was designed to do.

The liberalization was most far-reaching in the ASEAN economies (especially some of those that had imposed the highest levels of trade protection at the beginning, such as Indonesia, the Philippines and Vietnam); Australia and New Zealand; and China. In all of these economies, reductions in trade barriers were non-discriminatory and unilateral. Formal negotiations in a bilateral, regional or multilateral context made hardly any contribution at all during this period. In Japan, South Korea and Taiwan, trade liberalization was also non-discriminatory, but combined unilateral and multilateral initiatives with bilateral agreements that were implemented in a non-discriminatory way through multilateral mechanisms.

The APEC understandings supported unilateral liberalization decisions in quite specific ways in many countries. Indonesia (in 1994) and the Philippines (in 1996) announced major liberalization packages alongside the hosting of heads-of-government meetings. The Australian government placed the APEC commitments prominently among explanations for maintaining the program of liberalization announced in March 1991, in the face of political pressure for a protectionist response to persistently high unemployment as the country slowly recovered from the deep recession of the early 1990s. China used the heads-of-government meeting in Osaka in 1997 to announce a major new liberalization package.

The APEC understandings were inextricably linked to the unprecedented rates of trade liberalization and trade and economic expansion from the late 1980s until the Asian financial crisis.

The 1997–98 Asian financial crisis and the election in 2000 of a US government committed to expansion of preferential trading arrangements ended the era of concerted unilateral liberalization, and of open regionalism.[4] For a time, the political ballast of established economic success had been lightened or removed, and the ideological winds from across the Pacific faced weakened resistance. Resistance was weakened as well by the preoccupation of the Indonesian polity with the democratic transition, and Indonesia's temporary retreat from ASEAN and international political leadership. The shift to preferential trade in Australia was motivated most strongly by an idea from outside the main currents of economic policy: the wish and intention of the conservative Howard government to build close relations with the new Republican leadership of the United States.

The beginnings of discussions in late 2000, and then negotiations between Australia and the United States for what would become the first major bilateral preferential trade agreement involving a Western Pacific economy, marked a turning point for trade policy in the Western Pacific. The proponents of preferential trade agreements held high hopes for a while that bilateral and preferential trading areas would lead to genuine trade liberalization and expansion, and that they would eventually coalesce into wider regional arrangements that would at least avoid discrimination among Asia–Pacific economies. As it turned out, there was no more substantial unilateral trade liberalization in the Western Pacific – or

4 On the Asian financial crisis, see McLeod and Garnaut (1998) and Arndt and Hill (1999).

for that matter in the Eastern Pacific – after 2000. Large-scale and non-discriminatory liberalization in China and Vietnam in the early twenty-first century was achieved through negotiations supported by the World Trade Organization (WTO). The role of the WTO and the absence of discrimination made this new phase of liberalization consistent with the open regionalism ideal. It was not, however, straightforwardly attributable to APEC – although APEC's strong endorsement of China's entry into the WTO at the Shanghai leaders' meeting in October 2001 contributed to the positive WTO decision on China at Doha in the following month.

While there was no liberalization of substance within the proliferating preferential arrangements, neither was there any negation of the trade policy legacy of the era of open regionalism. The huge gains from trade liberalization in the era of open regionalism remained in place in the new era of preferential trade, contributing to the resilience of the Western Pacific developing economies and Australia and New Zealand in the aftermath of the Great Crash.

The new stage of Chinese and Vietnamese liberalization was highly advantageous to the rest of the world, especially those two countries' Western Pacific trading partners. It would eventually be crucial to the maintenance of growth in the Western Pacific (outside Japan) during the Great Crash of 2008 and its recessionary aftermath in the developed countries of the northern hemisphere. For the Asia–Pacific and the world as a whole, this new stage of liberalization was as consequential as the concerted unilateral liberalization that had preceded it.

The Indonesia-influenced culture of collective decision making within ASEAN and APEC in the late twentieth century will be important to successful global cooperation among states in the emerging multipolar world. In the remainder of this chapter, I will develop a couple of examples of how the ideas that underpinned open regionalism may have an important role to play in the future international system. I make the point mainly through reference to international trade and climate change policy.

Let us go back to the observation that the Indonesian approach to international cooperation, which became the guiding theme of ASEAN's international political culture, and then for a while of APEC's political culture, had its origin in limits to the power of the Javanese and then the Indonesian state.

Every state, even the United States, will be limited in the power that it can exercise as a matter of national will in the new international system. This will place a premium on discussion, respect for the perspectives of others and the building of coalitions in which compliance is undertaken because each country comes to see this as being in its own national interest. On many issues, international agreements will be legally unenforceable, or there will be no agreements at all. In the new, multipolar international system, concerted unilateral action is likely to be the normal *modus operandi* of much effective international action, and not an idiosyncratic approach to trade policy favoured by a dozen countries in one region.

On trade policy, we can still hope that the Doha Round launched in November 2001 will reach a conclusion that locks in the gains made available by past negotiations. Such gains will not be bound together in a single undertaking. It is possible that the Australian suggestion to divide agreements into sectoral elements, with countries voluntarily choosing which to join, may unlock these potential gains. Whether or not that is the case, it is now clear that there will be no more formal, comprehensive global trade negotiations after the Doha Round. It is just as clear that the objective of trade liberalization cannot be served by bilateral or regional preferential agreements: they empower protectionist and weaken liberalizing elements of the political economy; and they can accommodate neither the complex patterns of fragmented trade in many components that is a feature of the modern global economy, nor the contemporary reality that domestic standards, institutions and policies to promote open trade and investment are centrally important elements in national economic success. The need is still for multilateral liberalization, alongside the building of globally compatible domestic institutions, standards and policies.

It is difficult to see how this need of the modern global economy can be secured without its being underpinned by some version of concerted unilateral liberalization. The special task of international cooperation in this new world is to spread knowledge of what others are doing, of the practical effects of institutional arrangements that inhibit open international exchange, and of what the accumulated experience of humanity reveals about the benefits of open trade and investment for the liberalizing country itself. Global trade liberalization now depends on the establishment in many countries of the eclectic, somewhat inelegant process of trade liberalization that Indonesian international political culture helped shape, and that was so productive in the Western Pacific region in the decade leading up to the Asian financial crisis.

Concerted unilateral action that is bound not by formal agreement but by broadly shared ideas, and implemented eclectically, is the only way that international cooperation will work in some other major areas in the new multipolar world. This is a lesson of the diplomatic fiasco at the UN climate change conference in Copenhagen in December 2009, and of the productive subsequent conferences in Cancun in December 2010 and in Durban in December 2011. That recognition underpins the international agreement on climate change mitigation that emerged from the UN meetings in Bali in December 2007, Copenhagen in December 2009, Cancun in December 2010 and Durban in December 2011.

The Kyoto agreement of 1997 was a legally binding agreement on emission reductions in all developed countries but two, until Australia signed on in Bali in 2007. The one that held out mattered, as it was the largest. Developing countries were only going to be required to enter binding commitments at some unspecified later time. Kyoto contributed some valuable components to the international agreement that is now current after Cancun and Durban: a good and necessary set of institutions for consolidating global knowledge about climate change, mitigation and adaptation; rules on how to define and measure commitments; processes for measuring and verifying emissions; and mechanisms to transfer resources for mitigation and adaptation from developed to some developing countries.

The Kyoto agreement also had flaws, most importantly the binary distinction between developed and developing countries, with little pressure for the latter to reduce their emissions. The flaws became more obvious over time, as the developing countries became overwhelmingly the main source of emissions growth in the early twenty-first century. Most fundamentally, the Kyoto agreement depended on the willingness of major developing countries to bind themselves to emission reduction targets when there was never a good prospect that the United States would do so.

The Kyoto arrangements became even further separated from the realities of the global power structure as the world moved more quickly to a new, multipolar structure after the Great Crash. They were inconsistent with US constitutional culture and contemporary congressional politics, and they were unacceptable to newly critical large developing countries (China, India, Brazil, South Africa). These weaknesses mattered even more than before within the new international power structure.

It was not at all clear that the Kyoto arrangements would provide the best possible framework for strong mitigation, even if they had been feasible in the new international power structure. The agreement that emerged from the Cancun conference was based instead on the unilateral setting of mitigation targets, voluntary commitments (that is, with no recourse to international legal remedies), serious domestic political commitments, and peer review of targets and performance that might lead to the deepening of effort over time. The unilateral commitments made after Cancun added up to substantially stronger global reductions in emission trajectories than would have been possible with a binding agreement. Moreover, it soon became apparent that major countries – first of all China and the United States – were on paths that held out reasonable prospects that they would meet their announced mitigation targets.

I have observed over the years that formal negotiation of binding agreements on trade liberalization leads to less ambitious commitments to reduce protection than would have been offered in non-binding discussions of the mutual interest in reducing barriers to trade. This would not be interesting if serious non-binding commitments were less likely to be honoured than legally binding agreements. There is some evidence, however, that the most effective trade liberalization decisions are the serious domestic commitments that countries make for themselves (Rattigan and Carmichael 1996).

It is starting to look that way as well with pledges to reduce the rate of growth of greenhouse gas emissions – at least at this early stage of international cooperation. Canada was on a path to breaching its 'legally binding' Kyoto commitment before it repudiated that commitment in late 2011. In the important case of the United States, while the Cancun pledges represent a serious domestic but not internationally binding commitment to reduce 2005 emissions by 17 per cent by 2020, the US president broke new ground in a statement to the Australian parliament in November 2011 that his country would meet its Cancun pledges. China has been taking strong action since 2009 to lower its emission trajectories, in line with the requirements of its pledge at Copenhagen, confirmed at Cancun, to reduce the emissions intensity of production by 40–45 per cent on 2005 levels by 2020.

So on climate policy for the world, as on trade policy in the Western Pacific, the attempt to negotiate legally binding agreements (Kyoto, and the preferential trade agreements) led to more caution in the setting of objectives, and to slower progress towards shared international objectives, than would have been possible under concerted unilateral action. Experience with the Kyoto agreement led the world into a climate change policy version of the Western Pacific's open regionalism.

The agreement that emerged from the UN climate change conferences in Bali, Copenhagen, Cancun and Durban removes the hopeless bifurcation of the global mitigation effort between developed and developing countries. It has brought the United States within the global mitigation framework for the first time. That would not have been possible so early within a system of binding agreements.

There was always a view among proponents of open regionalism that untying the least tractable knots of protectionism – agriculture in some countries, textiles in others – would need to be negotiated formally with the support of the appropriate global organization, the WTO. That is probably the case also with climate change mitigation, with the United Nations Framework Convention on Climate Change providing the forum. However, considerable progress can be made within the framework of open regionalism or the Cancun agreements, and that progress should make it possible later to tackle harder questions within a framework of formal global negotiations.

Indonesia has much to offer the emerging international system. The approach that it brings to international cooperation was important and valuable to Asia–Pacific economic cooperation in the late twentieth century, and will be valuable to international cooperation more generally in the new power structures of the twenty-first century. For Indonesia to play as important a role in the current international system as it did in the late twentieth century will require continued political stability and economic progress at home, and an expansion of administrative capacity in its foreign affairs and economic ministries. Fortunately, Indonesia in 2012 has sound foundations from which to build a productive role as one of the next few great powers outside the big four in the emerging multipolar international system.

REFERENCES

Arndt, H.W and Hal Hill (1999) *Southeast Asia's Economic Crisis: Origins, Lessons and the Way Forward*, Institute of Southeast Asian Studies, Singapore.

Crawford, John and Greg Seow (eds) (1981) *Pacific Economic Cooperation: Suggestions for Action*, Heinemann Asia for the Pacific Community Seminar, Petaling Jaya, Selangor.

Elek, Andrew (1992) 'Trade policy options for the Asia–Pacific region in the 1990s: the potential of open regionalism', *American Economic Review* 82(2): 74–8.

Garnaut, Ross (1996) *Open Regionalism and Trade Liberalization: An Asia–Pacific Contribution to the World Trade System*, Institute of Southeast Asian Studies, Singapore, and Allen & Unwin, Sydney.

Garnaut, Ross (2006) 'Making the international system work for the platinum age', paper presented at the University of Queensland Seminar in Honour of Angus Maddison's 80th Birthday, Brisbane, 5–6 December, available at http://rossgarnaut.com.au/AsiaPacific_Devel.html.

Garnaut, Ross (2011) 'Making the international system work for the platinum age of Asian growth', in S. Armstrong and V.T. Thanh (eds) *International Institutions and Asian Development*, Routledge Publishing, Abingdon and New York.

Garnaut, Ross (forthcoming) 'Making the international system work for the platinum age', in D.S. Prasada Rao and Bart van Ark (eds) *World Economic Performance: Past, Present and Future*, Edward Elgar Publishing, Cheltenham.

Garnaut, Ross and Peter Drysdale (1989) 'A Pacific free trade area?', in J.J. Schott (ed.) *Free Trade Areas and US Trade Policy*, Institute for International Economics, Washington DC.

Garnaut, Ross with David Llewellyn-Smith (2009) *The Great Crash of 2008*, Melbourne University Press, Melbourne.

McLeod, Ross H. and Ross Garnaut (1998) *East Asia in Crisis: From Being a Miracle to Needing One?* Routledge, London and New York.

Rattigan, G.A. and W.B. Carmichael (1996) *Trade Liberalisation: A Domestic Challenge for Industrial Nations*, National Centre for Development Studies, Australian National University, Canberra.

Reid, Anthony (2011) *To Nation by Revolution: Indonesia in the 20th Century*, NUS Press, Singapore.

Soesastro, Hadi (1994) 'Pacific economic cooperation: the history of an idea', in R. Garnaut and P. Drysdale (eds) *Asia Pacific Regionalism: Readings in International Economic Relations*, HarperEducational, Pymble.

World Bank (2011) 'Data on gross national income purchasing power', *World Development Report 2010*, World Bank, Washington DC.

3 INDONESIA'S ROLE IN THE WORLD ECONOMY: SITTING ON THE FENCE

M. Chatib Basri

A friend once told me that Indonesia is a 'disappointing' country: it disappoints optimists because it never reaches its full potential, and it disappoints pessimists because they expect it to collapse at any moment.[1] I think there is some truth in this joke. Indonesia is indeed a country that oscillates between optimism and pessimism.

It is a similar story with trade policy. As an archipelago made up of more than 17,000 islands, Indonesia naturally evolved as a free trader. Indonesian history is a history of trade. Yet the country's politicians, media and even academics are reluctant to openly embrace globalization and free trade. Indonesia also has a contradictory attitude towards international institutions: it deeply distrusts institutions such as the IMF and the World Bank yet is very enthusiastic about and participates actively in the G20 and the Association of Southeast Asian Nations (ASEAN).

Indonesia's active participation in the G20 is seen as one of the successes of Susilo Bambang Yudhoyono's presidency. During a meeting of G20 leaders in Pittsburgh, the president proudly shared Indonesia's experience with far-reaching policy changes in 2005 and 2008 that raised fuel prices and allocated the extra funding to the poor in the form of cash transfers and health and education programs. This policy had three main benefits: it created fiscal space, which was good for macroeconomic policy; it allowed the government to increase spending on the poor, which was good for income distribution and poverty reduction; and it reduced demand for fossil fuels and therefore carbon emissions, which was good for the environment. The Indonesian president's remarks informed a

---

1 I first heard this joke from Indonesia observer James Castle and economist Umar Juoro.

Pittsburgh communiqué that recommended countries 'phase out and rationalize ... inefficient fossil fuel subsidies while providing targeted support for the poorest' (G20 2009: 3). But strangely, Indonesia itself is currently extremely hesitant about implementing another round of cuts in fuel subsidies.

Trade policy has swung from one extreme to another over the past 60 years. Indonesia disengaged from trade with the rest of the world in the early 1960s, then shifted to a very open regime later in the decade. The high-growth period from the 1970s to mid-1980s was accompanied by relatively high levels of protection, giving way to deregulation and other trade reforms in the late 1980s and 1990s. The Asian financial crisis of 1997–98 ushered in a new era of 'extreme' openness under the IMF program. How can we explain these oscillations in trade policy? Why does Indonesia tend to take contradictory positions in its international economic diplomacy, and sit on the fence when it comes to trade policy? This chapter will discuss Indonesia's role in the global economy and explain the factors that have influenced its decision to engage – or not to engage – in international economic agreements.

The chapter is organized as follows. In the next section, I will discuss Indonesia's history of involvement in the regional and global economies, and its potential to play a greater role. I will then provide a brief overview of trade policy developments over the past six decades. Finally, I will analyse the factors that have influenced Indonesia's contradictory positions and its tendency to sit on the fence rather than engage actively with global economics.

INDONESIA'S ROLE IN THE GLOBAL ECONOMY

Many recent studies have concluded that Indonesia has a promising future in the global economy.[2] Nouriel Roubini, known as 'Dr Doom' for his gloomy economic predictions, has even asserted that Indonesia is better positioned than China for long-term economic growth (Deutsch 2011). Admittedly the track record on long-term projections is somewhat patchy. In the early 1990s the World Bank predicted that Indonesia would become one of the Asian tiger economies. Instead, the Asian financial crisis hit and the Indonesian economy tanked, prompting Hill (2000) to write an article on 'the strange and sudden death of a tiger economy'. Nevertheless, I think there are strong reasons to believe that Indonesia has the potential to play an important role in the global, or at least Asia–

2 See, for example, Wilson and Purushotaman (2003), Indonesia Forum (2007) and Buiter and Rahbari (2011).

Pacific, economy. Whether this potential is realized will of course depend on the government's economic policies as well as global economic conditions. But it is also important to understand the other factors that will affect Indonesia's ability to play a greater economic role.

In my view, at least four factors will influence Indonesia's ability to play an important role in the global economy (Basri 2012). They are the demographic bonus provided by a relatively young population; Indonesia's generous endowments of energy and commodities; its stable macroeconomic conditions; and its political stability. I discuss each in turn below.

The demographic bonus and the rise of a new consumer class

Modigliani and Brumberg (1955) formulated a 'lifecycle' hypothesis that theorizes that consumption and saving patterns are influenced by the human lifecycle. An increase in the dependency ratio as a result of an ageing population will negatively affect government savings because government spending on pensions and health care will increase while revenue will decrease. An increase in the dependency ratio also reduces productivity, which in turn affects economic growth.

A study by Kim and Lee (2008) predicts that demographic changes in the G7 countries will result in lower savings, less spending and decreased productivity and economic growth in this group of countries. In contrast, countries with relatively young populations will benefit from a demographic bonus in the coming decades. By 2025, Indonesia will have a lower dependency ratio than most other countries in Asia. This should help it close the gap with more developed countries, catapult it into the rapidly growing group of BRIC economies - Brazil, Russia, India and China - and make it an important player in the world economy (Table 3.1).

Modigliani and Brumberg (1955) noted that countries with young populations tend to have higher levels of consumption than countries with older populations. Young people at the start of their careers buy more cars, houses, furniture and other household goods, whereas older age groups consume less and save more. I predict that levels of consumption will remain strong in Indonesia. Consumer-oriented companies can therefore expect to do well. With consumption currently accounting for 65 per cent of the economy, high demand should continue to stimulate economic growth.

Indonesia's demographic transition is evident in the rise of a new consumer class, as I have observed from my own experience. Only 10 or so years ago, one never had to make a reservation at even the most popular Jakarta restaurants because it was so easy to get a table. People

Table 3.1 *Summary of dependency and economic support ratios, selected Asian countries, 2000, 2025 and 2050*

	Total dependency ratio			Child dependency ratio			Old age dependency ratio			Economic support ratio		
	2000	2025	2050	2000	2025	2050	2000	2025	2050	2000	2025	2050
East Asia	0.462	0.474	0.649	0.349	0.265	0.266	0.113	0.210	0.383	0.761	0.675	0.575
Southeast Asia	0.568	0.460	0.570	0.494	0.336	0.308	0.074	0.124	0.262	0.709	0.705	0.661
South Asia	0.649	0.472	0.522	0.573	0.360	0.306	0.076	0.112	0.216	0.658	0.660	0.623
Japan	0.468	0.673	0.838	0.217	0.226	0.254	0.250	0.447	0.583	0.637	0.582	0.545
South Korea	0.393	0.477	0.678	0.299	0.252	0.270	0.094	0.226	0.417	0.647	0.622	0.564
Indonesia	0.546	0.456	0.573	0.473	0.333	0.313	0.073	0.123	0.260	0.683	0.695	0.652
Philippines	0.676	0.458	0.521	0.615	0.353	0.305	0.061	0.105	0.216	0.677	0.672	0.649
Thailand	0.450	0.453	0.660	0.366	0.274	0.278	0.084	0.178	0.382	0.787	0.728	0.653
Bangladesh	0.622	0.428	0.523	0.569	0.344	0.309	0.052	0.084	0.213	0.753	0.761	0.728
India	0.620	0.459	0.531	0.540	0.336	0.300	0.081	0.123	0.232	0.641	0.638	0.601

Source: Mason, Lee and Russo (2000).

Table 3.2 The rise of Indonesia's middle class

Class	Per capita expenditure per day ($)	Share of population (%)	
		2003	2010
Low	<1.25	21.9	14.0
	1.25–2	40.3	29.3
Total		**62.2**	**43.3**
Middle	2–4	32.1	38.5
	4–6	3.9	11.7
	6–10	1.3	5.0
	10–20	0.3	1.3
Total		**37.7**	**56.5**
High	>20	0.1	0.2

Note: Per capita expenditure per day is in 2005 purchasing power parity terms.

Source: World Bank (2011).

sometimes queued to buy tickets for a soccer match, the Thomas Cup badminton final or a famous international rock band, but such events only rarely came to Indonesia. Otherwise, queues were virtually unknown. The situation is very different today. Reservations are mandatory at popular restaurants. People form long queues to buy the latest 'must-have' gadgets. It is not surprising to see long lines at supermarkets, concert halls and cinemas. Airline tickets are often sold out – and not just during the holidays.

But what do the statistics say? Using consumption data from the National Socio-economic Survey (Susenas), the World Bank (2011) shows that the proportion of the Indonesian population with per capita expenditure of between $2 and $20 per day increased from 37.7 per cent in 2003 to 56.5 per cent in 2010 (Table 3.2). The World Bank defines this group as the middle class.

It is of course debatable whether expenditure of $2 per capita per day is enough to make one a member of the middle class; by international standards it seems very low – too low, in my opinion. Academics also argue about the definition of the middle class – whether it should be defined in terms of income, expenditure, job type, political leanings or something else. Putting this to one side, what is clear is that Indonesia is one of many emerging economies in Asia and elsewhere witnessing the rise of a new consumer class, even when one uses the higher measure of income (of $10–100 per capita per day in purchasing power parity terms)

Figure 3.1 Share of population living in an urban area, selected Asian countries, 1980–2050 (%)

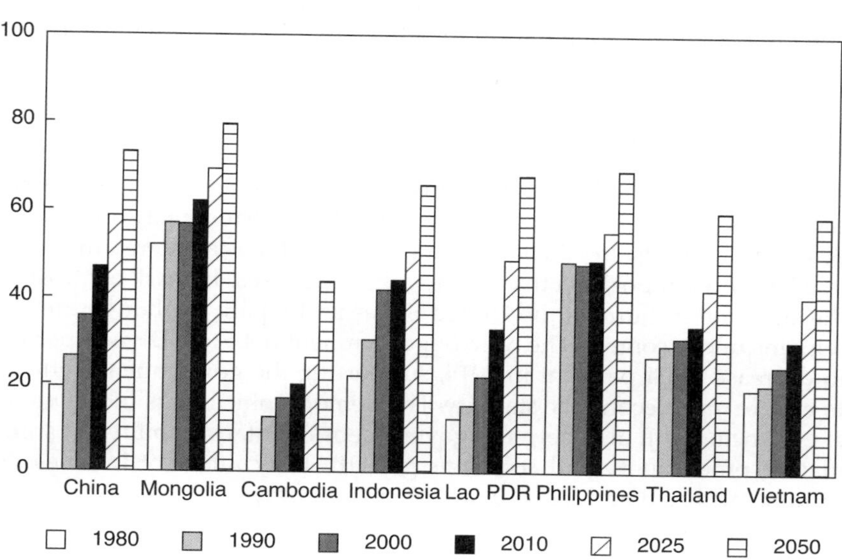

Source: United Nations (2010).

favoured by Kharas (2010). In Indonesia, the emergence of this new consumer class is being supported by the demographic bonus of a young population, which helps to explain the changes in consumption patterns and lifestyles.

What are the implications? First, demand for cars, motorcycles, cell phones, houses and lifestyle goods is likely to increase sharply. Where in the past consumption was dominated by basic goods, in the future consumption patterns will be determined by desire rather than necessity. Second, rates of urbanization will increase. The United Nations (2010) projects that by 2025 approximately 50 per cent of Indonesians will live in an urban area, increasing to nearly 70 per cent by 2050 (Figure 3.1). This rapid increase in urbanization must be anticipated with huge investments in logistical infrastructure such as electricity, telecommunications, trains and roads.

Energy and commodities

Indonesia has large reserves of energy and commodities, putting it in a good position to cater for rising domestic and global demand. As the price of oil climbs, countries are increasingly turning to crops that can be converted into sources of energy. With the era of cheap crops and energy over, countries that can produce both have a good future. Given this potential, there is strong reason to believe that Indonesia will soon join BRIC, transforming it into a larger 'IBRIC' grouping.

Macroeconomic stability

Largely because of its good macroeconomic management, Indonesia came through the global financial crisis of 2007–2009 relatively unscathed. Basri and Rahardja (forthcoming) argue that Indonesia entered the crisis in a better fiscal position than many other countries. In stark contrast to the situation in Europe, the United States and Japan, the budget deficit remains under control. The ratio of government debt to GDP is expected to decrease to 24 per cent in 2014, supporting the government's efforts to ensure macroeconomic stability. The demographic bonus Indonesia is experiencing will also help the government maintain stability, by stimulating productivity and economic growth. The caution of Indonesia's technocrats has paid off in a more robust economy.

Political stability

Despite making the transition from authoritarian to democratic rule in the space of just two years, against a backdrop of deep economic crisis, Indonesia is arguably one of the most politically stable countries in Asia. Fourteen years after the regime change, institutional and political reform has created a vibrant if somewhat unpredictable democracy. Political life has become significantly more democratic, and the establishment of the Corruption Eradication Commission (KPK) has strengthened the country's institutions. Nevertheless, Indonesia still needs to undertake further reforms before it can be considered substantively democratic. Also, despite advances in macroeconomic stabilization, there is growing concern that the pace of implementation of economic reform has slowed.

Indonesia is back on the radar screen of foreign investors. Foreign direct investment (FDI), especially portfolio investment, has increased steadily since 2006, reflecting a renewal of confidence in Indonesia. From being focused primarily on export-oriented industries in the 1980s and 1990s, due to the country's cheap labour costs, the current crop of foreign investors hopes to reap the benefits of a huge and strong domestic market. This helps to explain why the domestic economy is performing better than the export-oriented sector. Of course, the sluggish performance of exports is attributable to other issues as well, including the real appreciation of the rupiah against foreign currencies, rigidity in the labour market, competition from other Asian countries and, most importantly, poor logistical infrastructure.

The positive developments described above show that Indonesia has the potential to play a bigger role in the regional and world economies. However, as I argued earlier, Indonesia continues to be a half-hearted globalist. This contradiction is reflected in the swings in trade policy and the ambivalence towards openness, as discussed in the next section.

TRADE POLICY AND OPENNESS

Indonesia's degree of involvement in the global economy has fluctuated widely over time. In the early 1960s, Indonesia allied itself with Beijing, Hanoi and Pyongyang and began to isolate itself from global economic diplomacy, particularly in relation to Western countries. The political lexicon of the early 1960s reflected this diplomatic preference, with Sukarno using terms such as NEKOLIM (neo-colonialism, colonialism and imperialism) and OLDEFO (old established forces) to describe the West, and even establishing games for emerging countries to counter the Olympics – the Games of the New Emerging Forces (GANEFO), first held in Jakarta in November 1963 (Hill 1996). By the mid-1960s, Indonesia had almost completely disengaged from the world economy. In 1965, Sukarno severed Indonesia's ties with the United Nations, the IMF and the World Bank and declared his intention to develop Indonesia independently. Although he claimed to seek a middle road between the West and the Russian bloc during the Cold War, the president's political lexicon reveals the strength of suspicions of 'the West', which was viewed as representing the forces of colonialism and feudalism.

The situation changed markedly after Suharto wrested control from Sukarno. Under his New Order regime the economy became extremely open, especially to foreign capital. Indonesia's capital investment laws and capital account regulations made it one of the most liberal countries in the world. Indonesia rejoined the United Nations, the IMF and the World Bank and again began to become involved in global economic diplomacy (Hill 1996; Basri and Hill 2010).

The changes in Indonesian trade policy since 1966 have fluctuated with global economic conditions, oil prices and domestic political interests (Basri and Hill 2004). Broadly speaking, it is possible to identify six main periods, each characterized by unique policies and macroeconomic conditions. These are examined in turn below.[3]

---

3 This part draws heavily on Basri (2001) and Soesastro and Basri (2005).

1966–72

Sweeping changes in the regulation and organization of the foreign trade sector took place between 1966 and 1972 (Pitt 1991). The period saw a dramatic shift from direct control of almost all aspects of the economy towards heavy dependence on market signals. In 1967, the government enacted a new foreign investment law that constituted the basis for its open-door foreign investment policy, introduced an open capital account with no foreign exchange controls and launched an export bonus scheme to encourage exports. In 1970, it removed the multiple exchange rate system and introduced a market-consistent rate (Hill 1996). The rupiah was devalued in August 1971. Foreign trade was relatively liberal during this period.

1973–82

Late 1973 marked the start of a decade-long oil bonanza during which the economy grew on average by 7.5 per cent per annum. The influx of oil revenues allowed the government to finance a number of highly subsidized projects in strategic industries such as aircraft and steel. The open-door policy towards foreign investment that had characterized the previous period met a nationalist backlash, most famously in the Malari affair of January 1974,[4] forcing the government to take a more protectionist and interventionist stance. Regulations on foreign investment became more restrictive: all new foreign investment was to be in the form of joint ventures; the share of Indonesian equity was to be increased within a specified period of time; and the list of sectors closed to foreign investment was extended (Pangestu 1996). During this period, trade and industrial policy was directed at influencing the pattern of industrialization by protecting domestic industries. Like other developing countries, Indonesia adopted an import substitution strategy, starting with consumer goods and extended later to intermediate and capital goods. The trade regime was characterized by increasing protection through tariff and non-tariff barriers.

1983–85

This period witnessed a fall in oil prices and the beginning of economic reform, although the trend towards trade protection also continued.

4 On 15 January 1974, during the visit of Japanese prime minister Kakuei Tanaka, there was widespread rioting in Jakarta against the perceived domination of Japanese capital and products.

Pangestu (1991) and Hill (1994) therefore identify this period as one of contradictions. In March 1983, the government devalued the currency to Rp 970 to the dollar, primarily in reaction to the falling oil price, and deregulated the banking sector by removing the interest rate ceiling, abolishing the credit ceiling and reducing liquidity credits. Several capital and import-intensive projects were postponed, and income and sales taxes were rationalized. In the trade sector, in contrast, quantitative restrictions on imports were increased under a system of approved imports. Hill (1994) has observed that during this period trade policy became a much more explicit instrument for industrial policy.

Despite the increase in protection, by the end of the oil boom in 1985 the government had introduced some substantive reforms with respect to tariffs and customs procedures. In 1985, in an extensive rationalization of the tariff system, it implemented an across-the-board reduction in the range and levels of nominal tariffs. In the same year, it tackled the country's dysfunctional customs system by contracting out the inspection, valuing and classifying of imports to a private Swiss surveying company, Société Générale de Surveillance (SGS) (Pangestu 1991; Fane 1996; Hill 1996).

1986–90

The oil price fell sharply in 1986, and with it government revenue. This decline in revenue was the catalyst for significant deregulation and a change in policy to promote exports. The government introduced a set of trade policies to stabilize the economy and to shift it from a protected, inward-looking stance to an outward-looking and internationally competitive one. These policy changes occurred in two steps. The first step was to stabilize the economy by devaluing the rupiah (in 1986) and bringing inflation under control. The second step was to reduce the country's dependence on oil and gas revenues, increase efficiency and maintain the momentum for development through economic liberalization.

1991–96

Trade reform continued in the 1990s. The government boosted its economic liberalization and trade reforms through the May 1994 deregulation package, which permitted 100 per cent foreign ownership in most sectors, and the May 1995 package, which resulted in significant reductions in average tariffs. But important new regulations were also introduced, including the creation of a private monopoly in cloves in 1991, the introduction of minimum wage regulations in 1993–94 and the transfer of customs inspection duties from SGS back to an Indonesian company in 1995 (Fane 1996). In addition, in 1995–96, the government introduced a potentially interventionist industrial policy that included giving special tariff protection to a giant petrochemical company, Chandra Asri, and introducing a national car policy. Despite these trends, trade policy generally remained liberal during the period.

1997 – present

Under the structural programs imposed by the IMF in the aftermath of the Asian financial crisis of 1997–98, Indonesia's trade regime became increasingly open and 'extremely' liberal. Although Thailand and some other countries were also obliged to accept help from the IMF, the packages for Indonesia were the only ones to stipulate trade reform as a condition of assistance, even though this was actually outside the IMF's mandate.

The structural adjustment program encouraged a gradual reduction in import tariffs and stipulated the full deregulation of domestic trade in agricultural products, including rice (Soesastro and Basri 1998: 18–19). The clove marketing board, which was owned by Suharto's son, was abolished. In February 1998, all other restrictive marketing arrangements were terminated, specifically those for cement, paper and plywood, and the formal and informal barriers to investment in oil palm plantations were removed. This was followed by the removal of all investment restrictions in wholesale and retail trade. The IMF packages captured most of the World Bank agenda for trade deregulation (Soesastro and Basri 1998: 25). Clearly the trade reform program was very significant, leading to a broad reduction in tariffs and the removal of most non-tariff barriers.

Resistance to market reform from protectionist groups continues and it would be unwise to assume that pressure for trade protection will subside any time soon. Representatives of such groups remain influential in the government and the business sector, as indicated by the rise in protection between 2001 and 2004, particularly for agricultural products such as rice – the country's most politicized commodity (Patunru and Basri 2011). In 2011 the government imposed further trade restrictions on products such as salt and fruit, and approved a request to ban exports of rattan. Nevertheless the Indonesian economy has remained broadly open since 1997, due to various international trade agreements that prevent backtracking. Basri and Hill (2010: 24) point out that average tariffs are moderate at about 6 per cent; total exports and imports are equivalent to about 55 per cent of GDP, the lowest in ASEAN with the probable exception of Myanmar; and the stock of realized FDI is equivalent to about 14 per cent of GDP, the lowest in ASEAN alongside the Philippines. They argue that this mixed picture shows that Indonesia is 'precariously' open, that is, that it continues to be exposed to contradictory forces as it attempts to engage with the world economy.

One factor in this contradictory attitude could be Indonesia's experience during the Asian financial crisis, when the country was subjected to a structural adjustment program that is now generally regarded as faulty. This led to deep distrust of international institutions, particularly the IMF. Even today the government continues to accumulate foreign reserves as insurance against future economic crises, so that Indonesia will never again have to ask the IMF for assistance. Relations with the World Bank have also cooled; in 2007 President Yudhoyono disbanded the Consultative Group on Indonesia, established by the World Bank and the Indonesian government in 1992 to channel aid from a consortium of countries and institutions.

But interestingly, despite its deep distrust of international institutions, Indonesia has become increasingly active in international diplomacy through organizations such as the G20 and ASEAN, and has been active in negotiating trade agreements such as the Indonesia–Japan Comprehensive Partnership and the ASEAN–China Free Trade Area. Basri and Hill (2010: 26) predict that the degree of regional and global engagement will continue to rise under the current Yudhoyono administration (2009–2014).

Indonesia's contradictory position leads us to ask two important questions. Why does Indonesia exhibit such contradictory attitudes towards globalization? And why does it tend to sit on the fence rather than engage actively with globalization? I will try to answer these questions in the following section.

WHY DOES INDONESIA TEND TO SIT ON THE FENCE?

I have argued that Indonesia has the potential to play an important role in the global, or at least regional, economy because of its young population, large energy and commodity reserves, and macroeconomic and political stability. Yet despite this, its leaders remain reluctant to exploit the country's potential and participate actively in globalization. Why is this so?

Supply-side constraints

Soesatro and Basri (2005: 4) point out that the increase in Indonesia's non-oil exports between 1995 and 2001 was driven mainly by rising international commodity prices and increases in demand from foreign markets rather than by improvements in the competitiveness of Indonesian producers and their ability to increase market share. That is, external demand has not been a constraining factor for Indonesia's exports, and growth has been dictated more by supply than by demand.

These supply constraints have created uncertainty about whether Indonesia would be able to benefit from further trade liberalization. Although liberalization gives Indonesian producers greater access to overseas markets, they cannot take advantage of this if they are unable to provide goods in sufficient quantity to the standard required. The benefits of lower tariffs would be enjoyed, rather, by the country's trade partners, while Indonesia itself would continue to struggle to address quality, infrastructure and innovation bottlenecks. Consistent with this argument, Bhagwati, Sutherland et al. (2011: 17) examine the important role 'aid for trade' can play as an incentive for developing countries such as Indonesia to develop an interest in trade liberalization:

> 'Aid for trade' programs where these countries are offered funds and technical assistance for developing the missing or inadequate institutional and physical infrastructure necessary to undertake increased trade are best seen as a way of giving these countries that traction. There is growing realization of this 'supply side' constraint on effective trade performance rather than the 'demand side' constraint resulting from lack of market access.

As discussed below, the main supply-side constraints to Indonesia playing an important role in the global economy are inadequate infrastructure, poor human resources, and a lack of product diversification and innovation.

During the Asian economic crisis, the overall quality of infrastructure declined as public spending fell in real terms and private providers suspended or cancelled many infrastructure projects. This in turn led to a deterioration in supply and reduced potential growth rates to below pre-crisis levels.

Solikin (2004) finds that the impact of the output gap on inflation increased from a relatively moderate 0.2–0.3 during the pre-crisis period (when the Phillips curve tended to be flat) to 0.4–0.6 after the economic crisis (when the Phillips curve became steeper).[5] His findings reinforce the argument that Indonesia faces supply constraints, because aggregate supply became less responsive to changes in aggregate demand after the

---

5 The output gap is the difference between the actual and potential growth rates of an economy. The Phillips curve traces the inverse relationship between unemployment and inflation. Put simply, the lower (higher) the rate of unemployment, the higher (lower) the rate of inflation.

crisis. This is evident, for example, in the manufacturing sector, where low levels of investment have made the supply side less responsive, leading to sluggish performance in labour-intensive exports in particular.

To some extent, supply constraints also reflect exchange rate appreciation (Basri and Patunru 2006) and a 'high-cost' economy. Indonesia's investment climate problems include poor-quality infrastructure, corruption and high logistical costs (Soesastro and Basri 2005). In addition, there has been a shift in the pattern of investment from tradable to non-tradable goods owing to relatively high wages in the modern sector (including garments and footwear) (Bird 2004).

High logistical costs, related particularly to customs clearance for imports and exports, have reduced profitability in the tradable sectors, especially manufacturing. In a joint study with the Japan Bank for International Cooperation, the Institute for Economic and Social Research at the University of Indonesia has shown that logistical costs, including transport costs and weigh-station charges, account for 14 per cent of exporters' total production costs (LPEM–FEUI 2005). Manufacturers cannot pass these costs on to consumers because the tradable price is given; that is, they are price takers in the world market. Producers competing with imports are similarly hurt by widespread corruption and high logistical costs, which reduce their profitability. Figure 3.2 indicates the extent of the problem: Indonesia performs worse than its neighbours, as well as China and India, on the World Bank's Logistics Performance Index, an average of six key dimensions of logistical performance.

One consequence of Indonesia's poor logistical and distribution system is huge disparities across the country in the prices of basic goods (Table 3.3). The price of a bag of cement, for example, ranges from Rp 30,500 in South Sulawesi to Rp 38,000 in East Java, and is particularly high in Papua, where it ranges from Rp 60,000 (in Paniai) to Rp 230,000 (in Nabire). It is more expensive still in Wamena, which has extremely poor infrastructure.

A second constraint is the poor quality of human resources. To take advantage of the demographic transition that is occurring, Indonesia must improve the quality of its human resources, notably in health and education. Like Guggenheim in Chapter 8 of this volume, Woo and Hong (2010) argue that Indonesia must place greater emphasis on developing a science-based economy. This does not mean reverting to the failed policies of the past when Indonesia tried to leapfrog the intermediate stage of development by pursuing a high-technology agenda. Rather, what is needed are advances in agriculture such as new crop varieties, better approaches to water and environmental management, greater mechanization, and improvements in animal husbandry and infrastructure to support agriculture.

Figure 3.2 Logistics Performance Index, selected countries, 2010

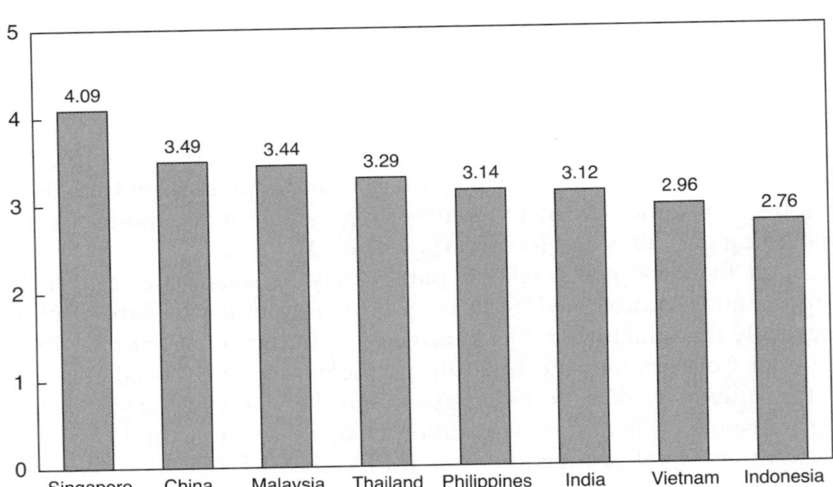

Note: The scores are from 1 to 5, with 1 representing the worst performance. The index is an average of six key dimensions of performance: customs, infrastructure, international shipments, logistics competence, tracking and tracing, and timeliness.

Source: World Bank (2010) 'Logistics Performance Index', available at http://info.worldbank.org/etools/tradesurvey/mode1b.asp#moreinfo.

Table 3.3 Retail prices of basic goods by region (Rp)

Region	Rice	Wheat flour	Sugar	Cooking oil	Salt	Cement
East Java	4,250	3,800	6,000	4,450	1,600	38,000
West Kalimantan	4,400	4,000	5,800	4,500	2,400	37,500
East Kalimantan	4,500	4,000	6,500	4,500	2,000	37,000
South Sulawesi	4,400	3,500	6,500	4,500	2,000	30,500
East Nusa Tenggara	4,200	4,500	5,800	6,300	2,000	31,000
Papua						
Merauke	5,000	7,000	7,000	6,670	3,000	62,000
Nabire	6,000	10,000	11,000	11,000	4,000	230,000
Paniai	10,000	7,500	8,000	7,000	8,000	60,000

Source: Ministry of Transport.

Figure 3.3 Contribution of intensive and extensive margins to export growth, 1990–2008 (%)

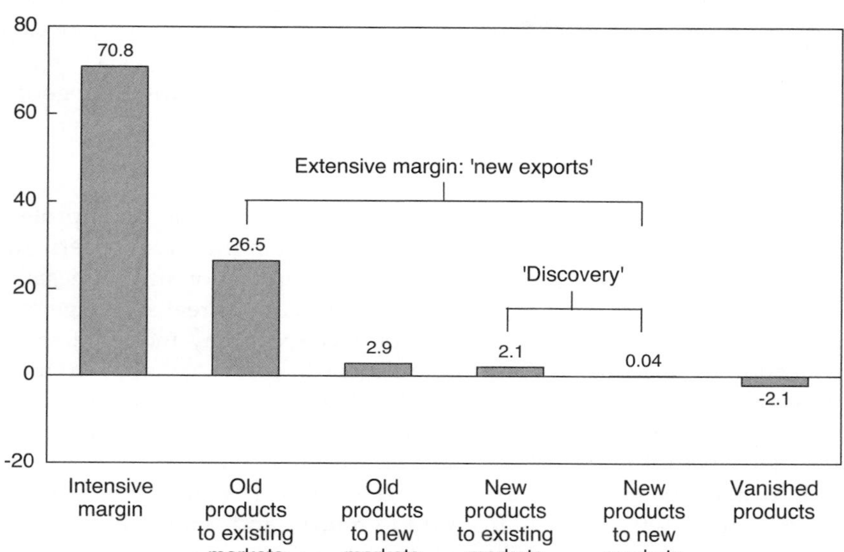

Note: The intensive margin is defined as exports of the same set of products to existing markets. The extensive margin is defined as: exports of old products to existing markets (where those products have not been sold before); exports of old products to new markets; exports of new products (never produced before) to existing markets; and exports of new products to new markets.

Source: Basri and Rahardja (2011: 227).

Also holding Indonesia back are a lack of export product diversity and a failure to innovate. Basri and Rahardja (2011: 225) find that the export concentration index (Herfindahl Index) for Indonesia has been flat since 2003 because exports are increasingly concentrated in primary products. The decline in manufacturing exports and increase in commodity exports have coincided with an appreciation in the real exchange rate, suggesting that, to support export diversification, Indonesia should do what it can to ensure a competitive exchange rate. On the innovation front, Basri and Rahardja (2011: 226–7) find that Indonesia's exports are still focused on existing rather than emerging products and markets. They show that growth in the same set of products sold to the same markets accounted for the vast majority of the increase in exports between 1990 and 2008, with new discoveries accounting for less than 5 per cent. The contribution of new products to new markets was so small as to be virtually nonexistent (Figure 3.3).

Supply-side constraints mean that Indonesia cannot take full advantage of globalization. This makes it reluctant to engage in trade agreements that would open its markets to global competition, because the benefits appear to be one-sided. According to this view – popular among the media, policy makers and even some academics – Indonesia is a victim of globalization and trade liberalization does more harm than good.

Domestic political interests

Understanding who benefits from and who is harmed by trade protection is vital to help explain trade policy changes in Indonesia. Basri and Hill (1996, 2004) have shown that the level of protection in Indonesia is determined by several factors, including oil prices, the real exchange rate and political pressure. The standard political-economy model of trade protection usually focuses on simple short-run profit-seeking activities. However, the reality is far more complex than this model would suggest. It is therefore important to examine how reform affects different groups in society, including its distributional effects on income.

Rodrik (1998) has stated that support for trade liberalization is highly dependent on who benefits from trade reform and who is harmed by it. The problem is that it is difficult to determine in advance who wins and who loses; due to the dynamic nature of trade reform, a group that appears to lose in the short term may gain in the long term. The reform dilemma is that the cost of reform is immediate whereas the benefit appears only in the medium term. Despite these limitations, it is possible to establish a taxonomy of actors in trade reform in Indonesia, and to identify their likely policy stances (Table 3.4).

In Indonesia's political system, the president and members of parliament are directly elected by the people. President Yudhoyono's party does not enjoy a majority in the country's multi-party parliament, making it difficult for him to set a firm policy agenda. In forming his cabinet, the president is obliged to make sure that a 'rainbow coalition' of political parties is represented, leaving little room for appointments based solely on merit (Basri and Hill 2010: 19). With policy making such a contested area, trade liberalization is not easy. Against this background, it is difficult to expect technocratic decision making, as policy must be balanced against political considerations. Even so, it is surprising that the Yudhoyono–Boediono government has been as cautious as it has in eschewing reform in order to maintain political support. Since Yudhoyono cannot stand for re-election in 2014, he could afford to push for a much more assertive reform agenda.

The best hopes for reform hang on the country's technocrats and professionals (Table 3.4). The problem is that there are very few technocrats

Table 3.4 A taxonomy of actors in the economic reform process

Actor	Policy stance
Technocrats/professionals	Pro-reform but number of actors is limited
Politicians	Will push for reform as long as it does not jeopardize their own or their parties' political interests
Bureaucracy	In favour of the status quo
Media	Swayed by political interests and views of owners
Civil society/academia	Pro-reform but divided over the issue of globalization
International community (through trade agreements)	Will prevent major backtracking

Source: Author.

in cabinet. The highly respected trade minister, Mari Pangestu, lost her post in the 2011 cabinet reshuffle and was put in charge of tourism. Some speculate that this was because she fought too hard for trade liberalization. In May 2010, Sri Mulyani Indrawati resigned as finance minister to become managing director of the World Bank. Many analysts have connected Indrawati's resignation with her decision to provide a bail-out for Bank Century in 2008. But the political backlash from this decision is difficult to separate from the tensions between Indrawati and Aburizal Bakrie – the chair of the Golkar Party, a former cabinet minister and one of the country's most powerful businesspeople. In an article published in the *Asian Wall Street Journal* in December 2009, Indrawati is reported as saying that the tensions between the two arose when she opposed an extension to the closure of the Jakarta Stock Exchange, ordered by Bakrie in the last quarter of 2008 amidst a run on his companies (Wright 2009). These examples demonstrate how hard it is to implement economic reform, including trade reform. Politicians will only support trade reform if it benefits them or their parties.

What about the bureaucracy? Its position on trade reform tends to favour the status quo. Despite the enthusiasm for reform among individual civil servants, as a group the bureaucracy is harmed by reform, which tends to lessen its power and reduce opportunities to earn 'extra income'. Pressure for reform is therefore unlikely to come from the bureaucracy. The media and academics, meanwhile, are divided over the merits of globalization. Given such a taxonomy, it is not difficult to understand why it is so difficult to undertake trade reform in Indonesia.

CONCLUSION

In view of the supply-side constraints facing producers as well as the taxonomy of domestic interests, I believe that the trade reform process is likely to move extremely slowly in Indonesia. There is even a risk of creeping protectionism, especially if developed countries do not demonstrate leadership by, for example, implementing the Doha Development Agenda (Bhagwati, Sutherland et al. 2011).

It is true that Indonesia has the potential to play an important role in the regional and global economies, but only if it can overcome supply-side constraints. If it were able to overcome the constraints discussed above, then the government would have more confidence to engage in international agreements. But paradoxically, overcoming these constraints requires economic reform. Economic reform, including trade reform, is also very much dependent on the taxonomy of actors charged with making decisions about Indonesia's political economy, in which the role of technocrats is limited. Under such conditions, it is difficult to expect bold reform or a clear commitment from Indonesia to engage in globalization. But it would also be a mistake to assume that the country will become overly protectionist.

Basri and Hill (2010) argue that there are at least two factors preventing Indonesia from backtracking in the current trade reform process. First, Indonesia already participates in international trade agreements, making it hard for it to backtrack and become more protectionist. Second, competitive liberalization happening across Asia will force Indonesia to sign more trade agreements. If it does not, trade will be diverted to other countries and it will be left behind. Thus, I would not be surprised if Indonesia continues to be a land of contradictions. Indonesia was born a free trader yet is consistently reluctant to accept globalization. Unwilling and unable to turn decisively in that direction, it will continue to sit – rather uncomfortably – on the fence.

REFERENCES

Basri, M. Chatib (2001) 'The political economy of manufacturing protection in Indonesia: 1975–1995', unpublished PhD thesis, Australian National University, Canberra.

Basri, M. Chatib (2012) 'Why we must be optimistic and sceptical abut Indonesia', *Strategic Review* 2(1): 49–57.

Basri, M. Chatib and H. Hill (1996) 'The political economy of manufacturing protection in LCDs: an Indonesian case study', *Oxford Development Studies* 24(3): 241–59.

Basri, M. Chatib and H. Hill (2004) 'Ideas, interests and oil price: the political economy of trade reform during Soeharto's Indonesia', *World Economy* 27(5): 633–55.

Basri, M. Chatib and H. Hill (2010) 'Indonesian growth dynamics', Working Paper No. 2010/10, Working Papers in Trade and Development, Arndt-Corden Department of Economics, Australian National University, Canberra, October.

Basri, M. Chatib and A.A. Patunru (2006) 'Survey of recent developments', *Bulletin of Indonesian Economic Studies* 42(3): 295–319.

Basri, M. Chatib and S. Rahardja (2011) 'Should Indonesia say goodbye to its strategy of managing facilitating exports?', in M. Haddad and B. Shepherd (eds) *Managing Openness: Trade and Outward-oriented Growth after the Crisis*, World Bank, Washington DC.

Basri, M. Chatib and S. Rahardja (forthcoming) 'Mild crisis, half-hearted fiscal stimulus: Indonesia during the GFC', in Takatoshi Ito (ed.) *Fiscal Stimulus in Asia*, ERIA, Jakarta.

Bhagwati, J., P. Sutherland et al. (2011) 'Last chance for the Doha Round', Final Report of the High Level Trade Experts Group, May, available at http://www.voxeu.org/sites/default/files/file/__HTLEG%20FINAL%20REPORT%20 24%20May%202011.pdf.

Bird, K. (2004) 'Recent trends in foreign direct investment', in M. Chatib Basri and P. van der Eng (eds) *Business in Indonesia: New Challenges, Old Problems*, Institute of Southeast Asian Studies, Singapore.

Buiter, W. and E. Rahbari (2011) *Global Economics View*, Citigroup Global Markets, London, 21 February.

Deutsch, A. (2011) 'Roubini: goodbye China, hello Indonesia', *Financial Times*, 25 October.

Fane, G. (1996) 'The trade policy review of Indonesia', *World Economy* 19(supplement): 101–17.

G20 (2009) 'Leaders' statement, the Pittsburgh Summit, September 24–25 2009', Pittsburgh, available at http://www.g20.org/pub_communiques.aspx.

Hill, H. (1994) 'The economy', in H. Hill (ed.) *Indonesia's New Order: The Dynamics of Socio-economic Transformation*, Allen & Unwin, Sydney.

Hill, H. (1996) *The Indonesian Economy since 1966: Southeast Asia's Emerging Giant*, Cambridge University Press, Cambridge and New York.

Hill, H. (2000) 'Indonesia: the sudden and strange death of a tiger economy', *Oxford Development Studies* 28(2): 117–39.

Indonesia Forum (2007) *Indonesia 2030*, Yayasan Indonesia Forum, Jakarta.

Kharas, H. (2010) 'The emerging middle class in developing countries', Working Paper No. 285, OECD Development Centre, Paris, January.

Kim, S. and J.-W. Lee (2008) 'Demographic changes, saving, and current account: an analysis based on a panel VAR model', *Japan and the World Economy* 20(2): 236–56.

LPEM–FEUI (Lembaga Penyelidikan Ekonomi dan Masyarakat, Fakultas Ekonomi, Universitas Indonesia) (2005) 'Inefficiency in the logistics of export industries: the case of Indonesia', LPEM–FEUI in collaboration with the Japan Bank for International Cooperation (JBIC), Jakarta.

Mason, A., S.-H. Lee and G. Russo (2000) 'Population momentum and population aging in Asia and Near-East Countries', East-West Center Working Papers, Population Series, No. 107, East-West Center, Honolulu HI, February.

Modigliani, F. and R. Brumberg (1955) 'Utility analysis and the consumption function: an interpretation of cross-section data', in K.K. Kurihara (ed.) *Post-Keynesian Economics*, George Allen & Unwin, London.

Pangestu, M. (1991) 'Managing economic policy reforms in Indonesia', in S. Ostry (ed.) *Authority and Academic Scribblers: The Role of Policy Research in East Asian Policy Reform*, International Centre for Economic Growth, San Francisco CA.

Pangestu, M. (1996) *Economic Reform, Deregulation and Privatisation: The Indonesian Experience*, Centre for Strategic and International Studies, Jakarta.

Patunru, A.A. and M. Chatib Basri (2011) 'The political economy of rice and fuel pricing in Indonesia', in A. Ananta and R. Barichello (eds) *Poverty, Food, and Global Recession in Southeast Asia: Is the Crisis Over for the Poor?*, Institute of Southeast Asian Studies, Singapore.

Pitt, M.M. (1991) 'Indonesia', in D. Papageorgiou, M. Michaely and A.M. Choksi (eds) *Liberalizing Foreign Trade. Volume 5: The Experience of Indonesia, Pakistan and Sri Lanka*, Basil Blackwell, Cambridge MA.

Rodrik, D. (1998) 'The rush of free trade in the developing world: Why so late? Why now? Will it last?', in F. Sturzenegger and M. Tomassi (eds) *The Political Economy of Reform*, MIT Press, Cambridge MA.

Soesastro, H. and M. Chatib Basri (1998) 'Survey of recent developments', *Bulletin of Indonesian Economic Studies* 34(1): 3–54.

Soesastro, H. and M. Chatib Basri (2005) 'The political economy of trade policy in Indonesia', CSIS Working Paper No. WPE 092, Centre for Strategic and International Studies, Jakarta, March.

Solikin (2004) 'Kurva Phillips dan perubahan struktural di Indonesia: keberadaan, linearitas, dan pembentukan ekspektasi' [The Phillips curve and structural change in Indonesia: evidence, linearity and expectation formation], *Buletin Ekonomi Moneter dan Perbankan*, Bank Indonesia, March.

United Nations (2010) 'World urbanization prospects: the 2009 revision', Department of Social and Economic Affairs, United Nations, New York NY, available at http://esa.un.org/unpd/wup/index.htm.

Wilson, D. and R. Purushotaman (2003) 'Dreaming with BRICs: the path to 2050', Global Economics Paper No. 99, Goldman Sachs, 1 October.

Woo, W.T. and C. Hong (2010) 'Indonesia's economic performance in comparative perspective and a new policy framework for 2049', *Bulletin of Indonesian Economic Studies* 46(1): 33–64.

World Bank (2011) *Indonesia Economic Quarterly*, World Bank, Jakarta.

Wright, T. (2009) 'Jakarta official defends bailout', *Asian Wall Street Journal*, 10 December.

4 IS INDONESIA RISING? IT DEPENDS

Donald K. Emmerson

Increasingly since the mid to late 2000s, Indonesia has been chosen for inclusion in creative acronyms that shortlist countries with unusually bright prospects for material growth. In this upbeat genre, Indonesia has been seen both as a cat (a 'tiger', or one of the CIVETS) and as a bird (an EAGLE).[1] 'And it's not just an economic story', enthused Joshua Keating in *Foreign Policy* in December 2010. 'Indonesia stands a good chance of becoming the world's first Muslim and democratic superpower' (Keating 2010).

Will Indonesia's political economy fulfil these high expectations? As a Muslim Indonesian might say, *Wallahu'alam* – only God knows. This chapter aims merely to explore and characterize the recent 'rise of Indonesia' to the extent that it is already taking place.

The domestic roots and repercussions of foreign policy are important in this context but they are not my focus here. Indonesia's perceived ascent is largely a product of its interaction with, and its portrayal by, the outside world. The stronger the political economy of Indonesia, other things being equal, the more likely its leaders will be to engage proactively, on Indonesian terms, with that wider world. But because other things are not equal, the argument in this chapter is contingent and possibilistic. One cannot infer a benign or a malign 'rise of Indonesia' from economic growth and political stability alone. The country's large size, young population and stable democracy have contributed to that perception, but they are not a sufficient condition for its existence. Structure

---

1 These and other such acronyms are explained later in this chapter. See also Jeremy Grant's posting on 'the global game of acronyms' (Grant 2010).

without agency is mere potential. Actual outcomes will depend on what both local and foreign decision makers see, say and do – and do not see, say or do – to augment, diminish or reorient Indonesia's position in foreign affairs.

Is Indonesia rising? This chapter examines the question from different angles. Objectively, how steeply upward are Indonesia's rates of economic growth and military spending compared with the trends in other countries? Subjectively, in global discourse, is Indonesia seen to be rising, again compared with the profiles of other states? On balance, is the acronymic optimism cited above a recognition of Indonesia's past success – or a prediction of future achievement that is causing what it foretells? To what extent have domestic problems and priorities pre-empted attention to foreign affairs? Has that balance of concern changed over the course of Susilo Bambang Yudhoyono's tenure as president, and if so, in which direction? What is his vision of Indonesia's position in the world, and is there an alternative on offer? Are the catchphrases of Indonesian foreign policy first voiced in the late 1940s and early 1950s being repeated – or replaced? Finally, what are some of the qualities – the styles – of Indonesian foreign policy whose illustration might usefully complicate the quantitative notion of a raised or lowered profile?

OBJECTIVE INDICATORS

Is Indonesia rising? The question cannot be answered without prior specification: 'rising' in what sense, by what measure and compared to what?[2] To illustrate, consider an obvious possible answer: that Indonesia's economy has been expanding – or 'rising' – faster than the economies of other countries.

---

2 The case for specification applies as well to the idea that Indonesia is declining, as the following two very different examples suggest. First, according to the annual Press Freedom Index produced by Reporters Without Borders, Indonesia suffered back-to-back declines in media freedom in 2010 and 2011: its position among the world's countries and territories fell from the 43rd percentile in 2009 to the 34th in 2010 and then to the 18th in 2011 (based on data at http://en.rsf.org/). Second, according to the World Bank's Logistics Performance Index, which measures the capacity 'to efficiently move goods and connect manufacturers and consumers with international markets', Indonesia's position worsened from the 71st to the 52nd percentile between 2007 and 2010 (based on data at http://siteresources.worldbank.org/INTTLF/Resources/index-chart.jpg [for 2007] and http://www1.worldbank.org/PREM/LPI/tradesurvey/mode1b.asp#ranking [for 2010]). The percentiles identify the proportions of countries or territories that ranked below Indonesia on a given dimension.

At the end of 2011, *The Economist* believed that Indonesia had achieved the sixth-highest rate of growth in GDP for that year – 6.5 per cent – among the 43 major economies around the world tracked weekly by that magazine. Sixth place is a respectable performance, but the estimates on which it is based are preliminary and will undergo correction. It should also be noted that the GDPs of most countries expanded in 2011; among *The Economist*'s 43, only the Japanese and Greek economies shrank.[3] Indonesia was hardly unique in enjoying positive growth.

If 2011 is too recent a year, *The Economist*'s estimates too preliminary and its roster of 43 economies too short, consider where Indonesia stood on the Central Intelligence Agency's list of 215 jurisdictions ranked by their rates of change in real GDP in 2010: in 51st place at 6.1 per cent (CIA 2010). Indonesia placed at the bottom of the top quarter of economies in this larger set, and seven of Indonesia's 10 Southeast Asian neighbours grew faster than Indonesia in 2010.[4] Two years of data are better than one, but a decade is better still. Was Indonesia's economy rising fast enough for it to be among the 20 countries with the highest average rates of GDP growth between 2000 and 2010? No, it was not.[5]

A rise may be perceived at a given time in relation to other, presumably less buoyant economies, or it can be seen as the acceleration of a single economy over time. Evidence of the latter depends greatly on one's choice of starting and ending years. For Indonesia, the best way to find and feature an upward trend, without going all the way back to the disastrous mid-1960s for one's point of departure, is to start the clock ticking in the uniquely negative year 1998, when the Asian financial crisis shrank Indonesian GDP by a devastating 13.1 per cent. By selectively contrasting that nadir with the positive 6.1 per cent growth rate registered in 2010, one can say that the economy upped its annual performance by a massive 19.2 points over the intervening period – a stunning rise indeed.

However, by 2000, just two years after its double-digit contraction, Indonesia's GDP had already recovered to a positive 5.4 per cent. The

---

3 'Economic and financial indicators', *The Economist*, 31 December 2011, p. 72. The five countries ahead of Indonesia on the list for 2011 were China with 9.2 per cent; Argentina, 8.5 per cent; India, 7.6 per cent; Turkey, 7.5 per cent; and Saudi Arabia, 6.7 per cent. At the bottom of the list were Japan with –0.3 per cent and Greece with –5.2 per cent.

4 Listed in order from fastest to slowest, Indonesia's rate of 6.1 per cent was outpaced by Singapore, Thailand, Laos, the Philippines, Malaysia, Vietnam and Timor-Leste, and lagged by Cambodia, Burma and Brunei.

5 This answer reflects the IMF data conveyed by Aridas (2010). Nor did Indonesia appear on an updated list of the 20 highest-growth economies in 2002–2012 provided by Ventura and Aridas (2012), in which the data for 2011 are estimates and the data for 2012 are forecasts.

rate plateaued after that, fluctuating between 4 and 6 per cent. Apart from a slowdown from 6.0 per cent in 2008 to 4.6 per cent in 2009 – fall-out from the American financial crisis – the growth rate since 2006 has remained essentially unchanged (Index Mundi 2011, reporting IMF data). Indonesia's recovery immediately following the *annus horribilis* of 1999 was impressive, but more recent evidence shows a sustained rather than a rising pace of economic growth.

The rates achieved under Suharto's New Order regime were consistently higher than they are now. In 1980–81, 1984 and each of the eight years from 1989 through 1996, Indonesian GDP grew more rapidly than it has in any year since, and it never fell below 6 per cent (Index Mundi 2011). Back then a 6 per cent rate was considered the minimum needed to accommodate yearly additions to the labour force. The 5–6 per cent annual growth over most of the latest decade suffers by comparison. Then again, if a slowing global economy has lowered the 'new normal', a sustainable national rate within that range doesn't look too bad. In this respect, Indonesia's perceived economic 'rise' is partly a function of reduced expectations.

Among the non-economic ways of measuring a country's rise, its military profile comes readily to mind. If the economic-growth-rate case for Indonesia's recent ascent seems not to justify the acronymic hype, can the country's 'rise' be discerned instead in accelerated spending on defence as a proportion of GDP?

No, it cannot. The Stockholm International Peace Research Institute (SIPRI) has defined a high-spending profile as a level of military expenditure equivalent to at least 4 per cent of GDP in any of the years 2004–2009. Indonesia is not among the 24 countries that met this criterion. In 2009, the latest year for which SIPRI data are available, Indonesia is estimated to have spent a mere 0.9 per cent of GDP on its military. Of the 16 East Asian countries covered, only the Philippines and Laos spent less by this measure – respectively 0.8 per cent and 0.3 per cent (SIPRI 2009a).

Across the full span of SIPRI data from 1988 through 2009, Indonesia's military spending as a proportion of GDP has fluctuated far more narrowly than its GDP growth rate. Military expenditure reached an estimated 1.3 per cent of GDP in 1988, a level that was never exceeded during the entire 22-year period. Flat at around 1.1 per cent in 1991–97, the figure fell to 0.6 per cent in 2001 before rising to 1.3 per cent in 2003 and 2004, but then receded to 0.9 per cent in 2009 (SIPRI 2009b).

In these GDP-proportional terms, the top military spender among all East Asian countries was Singapore. From 1998 through 2009 its annual spending went below SIPRI's high-outlay threshold of 4.0 per cent only twice, before quickly recovering – from 3.7 per cent in 2007 to 3.9 per cent in 2008 to 4.3 per cent in 2009. Given Singapore's location on the vulnerable edge of the Indonesian archipelago, one might have thought that the authorities in Jakarta would have responded to their neighbour's robust military allocations by proportionally enlarging their own. The reverse occurred. While Singapore boosted defence outlays between 2007 and 2009, comparable estimates of Indonesian spending slipped, albeit in minor gradations, from 1.2 per cent in 2007 to 1.0 per cent in 2008 and then to 0.9 per cent in 2009 (SIPRI 2009b).[6]

GDP growth is the outcome of complex and multivariate interactions. Military spending as a share of GDP is more directly volitional insofar as its absolute level may be raised or lowered by official choice. By neither of these different measures, however, can Indonesia be said, unambiguously, to have 'risen'.

VIRTUAL DISCOURSE

If the ostensibly objective, economic-cum-military evidence for Indonesia's rise is ambiguous, perhaps the question should be recast in more subjective terms: is Indonesia *seen to be* rising? The answer to this query must be yes.

Consider the evidence in Table 4.1, which is based on a Google search to see how frequently the name of each one of five countries is juxtaposed with either of two descriptive words – 'rising' or 'declining'. Surprisingly, among the five countries shown, it is the subjective image of Indonesia, not of China or of India, that is proportionally most associated with ascent rather than descent.

Caveats are in order. The phrases featured in the table are necessarily taken out of context. The notion that Indonesia or any of the other countries is 'rising' or 'declining' could involve any of a wide range of phenomena other than the seven dimensions of interest here: a country's political, military, economic, social, cultural, demographic or environmental profile. The 'rise' or 'decline' of a particular country in a particular document could be meant in comparison with other countries, or in comparison with the way that the country used to be. A country's perceived movement in either direction could be mentioned simply to deny or qualify its occurrence. A document could, for instance, ask 'Is Indonesia rising?' only to answer 'No', although the decision to raise the question in the first place implies that enough people are saying 'Yes' to warrant the objection.

---

6 I am not complacent about the exactness of the SIPRI data. If GDP is hard to measure in ways that are comparable across countries and years, military spending as a percentage of GDP is even more subject to cautionary reservations, especially when it comes to narrow differences such as those cited here.

Table 4.1 Estimated number of online documents describing Indonesia, China, India, Australia and America as 'rising' or 'declining'

Country	Number of documents containing the name of the country and:		Ratio of 'rising' to 'declining'
	'rising'	'declining'	
Indonesia	143,996	1,766	81.5 to 1
China	1,589,603	23,103	68.8 to 1
India	438,916	21,516	20.4 to 1
Australia	92,985	9,285	10.0 to 1
America	250,953	101,953	2.5 to 1

Note: The data in the first two columns were generated on 16 January 2011 by Googling the phrases shown. A document is a web page in which the indicated phrase (or an equivalent variation, as determined by Google) appears at least once. Although in principle both phrases (or variations) could appear in the same document, this was the case in only a trivial number of instances: four for Indonesia, 397 for China, 84 for India, 15 for Australia and 47 for America. These were subtracted from the gross data to minimize overlap between the columns. The equivalent-variation problem arises because Google tries to catch as many documents as possible for the words being searched, even if the searcher tries to limit the scope of the scan by putting quotation marks around the phrase being sought.

Are these qualifications fatal? How safely can the results in the table be generalized? Can one infer from them a corresponding empirical hierarchy of subjective perceptions in cyberspace regarding the rise or decline of each country along one or more of the seven dimensions identified above? This question of validity was addressed in a preliminary way by inspecting the actual content of the first 10 items yielded by each of the searches for 'rising' or 'declining' – a hundred documents in all.

By this method, the data for Indonesia and China appeared to have the greatest validity. Of the 10 documents linked to 'Indonesia rising', only two were substantively invalid; both focused on rising religious intolerance. The remainder concerned the country's overall profile, including its growing economy, its developing democracy and the 'stature in the world' it had regained since recovering from the social, economic and political turbulence associated with the transition from Suharto's authoritarian rule. In one such document, for example, Amazon.com offered a book entitled *Indonesia Rising: Islam, Democracy and the Rise of Indonesia as a Major Power* (Tamara 2009). In another, *Foreign Policy* touted Indonesia as an economic 'tiger' – 'a rising Asian power' whose ascent the magazine featured as the first of 10 trends or events that had been overlooked in 2010 but could be 'leading the headlines in 2011' (Keating 2010).

The data for 'China rising' and 'China declining' proved to be just as valid by this method as those for Indonesia. The figures linked to 'India rising' were also highly valid, the sole exception being a document that viewed macroeconomic gains in the light of massive and 'shocking' rural poverty. But of the 10 results for 'India declining', six were invalid, including one questioning the quality of Indian cricket. The reverse pattern appeared to mark the results for Australia and America. Of the 10 'rising' results for each of these two countries, all 10 were invalid for Australia, and nine out of 10 for America, whereas only three of the 10 'declining' documents were invalid in these cases.[7]

In summary, one may tentatively conclude that the top rankings of Indonesia and China in Table 4.1 are likely to be valid; that the ratio of 'rising' to 'declining' for India may underestimate the optimism about that country on the internet; and conversely, that the ratios for Australia and America may understate the pessimism – the declinist sentiments – associated with those two cases as they are portrayed in virtual discourse. Although these adjustments could move India's position closer to China's and Indonesia's, and would substantially downgrade the positions of Australia and America, the general ranking of the five countries in the table is probably about right. The plausibility of each ratio lies in its ordinal location, not its numerical precision.[8]

Google also distinguishes the 'reading level' of each document. 'Advanced' items tend to be complex and are likely to have been prepared by experts. 'Intermediate' documents are simpler and may be aimed at the general public. 'Basic' items are pitched at a still more accessible reading level that might be suitable for, say, students in junior high school.

For every one of the countries in the table, items perceiving decline were more likely to be pitched at the advanced level than were items perceiving rise. Of the items oriented towards a 'declining' Indonesia, for example, 48 per cent were prepared at the expert level, compared with only 16 per cent for items in which Indonesia was seen as 'rising' – a threefold difference. In contrast, at each of the two simpler reading levels, items referencing rise outnumbered those citing decline for all five

7 Inflation, obesity and sports were among the topics featured in the nine invalid documents about 'Australia rising'. In nearly all of the nine invalid results for 'America rising', Republicans were pictured as 'rising up' against the Democratic administration of President Barack Obama.

8 Ten first-screen documents per country is a risibly small and non-random sample. Yet the sheer preponderance of 'rising' over 'declining' for Indonesia and China argues against the likelihood that the order is reversed in these cases. The data do, however, compress chronology, leaving open the question of change in the balance of a perceived rise or decline over time.

countries. But the declinist bias of advanced items – the apparent pessimism of experts – was higher for Indonesia than for any other country except America. This finding is at least consonant with the proposition that foreign and indigenous observers with greater knowledge of Indonesia are especially likely to acknowledge its shortcomings, such as poverty, violence, corruption, intolerance, inequality, degraded infrastructure and damaged resources.

That said, however, if professional investment advisers and credit rating agencies can be considered unusually knowledgeable about the economies that they promote or demote, their marked optimism about Indonesia must qualify the idea that the professional analysts are relatively downbeat. Is optimism more typical in business than in academe? Arguably so. Whatever the explanation, favourable reviews among 'street economists' in the private sector have lifted Indonesia into the company of other emerging markets in invented groupings of economies that are thought to be worth putting one's money into.

ACRONYMIC ENTHUSIASM

Cleverly named, and listed here from most to least exclusive, these imagined 'clubs' of up-and-coming countries include MIST (Mexico, Indonesia, South Korea and Turkey); TIMBIs (Turkey, India, Mexico, Brazil and Indonesia); CIVETS (Colombia, Indonesia, Vietnam, Egypt, Turkey and South Africa); the EAGLE group of 'emerging and growth-leading economies' (Brazil, China, Egypt, India, Indonesia, Mexico, South Korea, Taiwan and Turkey); the Next Eleven, or N-11 (Bangladesh, Egypt, Indonesia, Iran, Mexico, Nigeria, Pakistan, the Philippines, South Korea, Turkey and Vietnam); and the 3G 'global growth generators' (Bangladesh, China, Egypt, India, Indonesia, Iraq, Mongolia, Nigeria, the Philippines, Sri Lanka and Vietnam).

In 2001 Jim O'Neill, an economist with the multinational investment banking and securities firm Goldman Sachs, chose a novel way of promoting Brazil, Russia, India and China as investment choices for his clients. As if these emerging economies would make a solidly profitable 'brick' in the building of one's portfolio, he fused them into a single felicitous BRIC. To that bloc he later added South Africa, making BRICS.[9] O'Neill also coined the term MIST to represent a slightly cloudier – less promising – set of investment destinations (Gupta 2011). Unlike BRICS, MIST includes Indonesia.

9 In this instance life has followed art. In 2011 China hosted the third summit of the heads of the five BRICS (Cooper 2011).

A professor of public policy offered the TIMBIs in 2011 (Goldstone 2011). By then MIST had become a subset of the N-11 (Wilson and Stupnytska 2007). The Economist Intelligence Unit thought up CIVETS – Indonesia and five other dynamic economies with growing populations – in 2009 (Knowledge@Wharton 2011). In 2010 a Spanish bank – Banco Bilbao Vizcaya Argentaria (BBVA) – spotted Indonesia among what it called the EAGLEs – economies presumed likely to soar.[10] In 2011 an analyst with the financial services giant Citigroup used six variables to select what he dubbed the '3G' countries with unusually high investment potential.[11]

These are projective accolades. Their purpose is not to acknowledge past performance but to identify future potential. Portfolio investors are looking to ride a rising curve with upside room, not a risen one that could decline. Direct investors and export manufacturers seek untapped markets, not ones that are already saturated. Indonesia's acronymic success is thus more of a leading indicator than a trailing one.

An upbeat review that triggers inflows of capital into the favoured economy – foreign portfolio investment (FPI) in local securities or foreign direct investment (FDI) in durable facilities – often becomes a self-fulfilling prophecy. Indonesia's acronymic fame thus boosted investor confidence: FDI into Indonesia rose an estimated 18.4 per cent in 2011 compared with the year before. Admittedly, after stunning gains of 87 per cent in 2009 and 46 per cent in 2010, FPI slowed to a mere 3.2 per cent in 2011 (Yulisman 2012). But that slim gain looked fatter in a year when the MSCI index of global stock markets registered negative 8.5 per cent. Worldwide, Indonesia was one of only four countries whose markets were higher at the end of 2011 than at the beginning.[12]

In December 2011 Fitch Ratings ratcheted up Indonesia's credit standing from junk to investment grade. Moody's Investors Service followed suit in mid-January 2012. In the same month, Indonesia obtained a record-low yield on the biggest issue of long-dated bonds ever sold in Asia, namely 5.375 per cent over the 30 years to 2042 (Bellman and

---

10 An EAGLE was defined as a country that could be expected to add more to global GDP in the ensuing decade than the likely average contribution over that period attributable to the members of the Group of Seven (G7), excluding the United States. BBVA also named an additional 'EAGLE's nest' of 11 fledgling economies, including four in Southeast Asia, that could soon take flight: Argentina, Bangladesh, Colombia, Malaysia, Nigeria, Peru, the Philippines, Poland, South Africa, Thailand and Vietnam (BBVA Research n.d.).

11 'BRICS is passé, time now for "3G": Citi', *Business Standard*, 23 February 2011, http://www.business-standard.com/india/news/brics-is-passe-time-now-for-%5C3g%5C-citi/126725/on.

12 'Focus: stockmarkets', *The Economist*, 2 January 2012, http://www.economist.com/blogs/graphicdetail/2012/01/focus. The other countries were Malaysia, Venezuela and (surprisingly) America.

Brereton-Fukui 2012). These events further illustrate the effects of a positive assessment on performance.

Several conclusions follow from this analysis. The strongest case for an ascendant Indonesia lies in the reciprocal relationship between economic expansion and international esteem. Typically the observers who most avidly laud the 'rise of Indonesia' are not passively acknowledging the country's prior developmental success. Rather, they are encouraging investment in Indonesia because they believe it has a promising future. To the extent that these enthusiasts' advice is acted upon, they help to ensure the very rise that they anticipate. In this virtuous-circular sense, the rise of Indonesia is a prophecy that aims to do what it says.

POLICY HORIZONS

The prominence of a country lies in the eyes of its beholders, and Indonesia is no exception to this rule. But the sanguine assessments of Indonesia's future tendered by some investment advisers and rating agencies are not purely wishful thoughts. Their optimism takes into account real assets that the country already has, including natural resources, opportune demography[13] and a burgeoning middle class.

A capacity for good economic policy also matters. In 2012 *The Economist* compared 27 emerging economies on six empirical indicators of their ability to withstand fallout from a worsening of the euro zone debt crisis. The indicators were joined in a 'wiggle-room index' of a country's capacity to loosen its monetary and fiscal policies in order to stimulate its own economic growth in the face of fall-offs in overseas demand and incoming investment. Among the 27, Indonesia tied with Saudi Arabia as best able to afford such an expansionary defence.[14]

The performance of an economy and the performance of a government are not the same thing, of course; having wiggle room is not the same as using it. A fuller understanding of Indonesia's ascent must consider

---

13 Indonesia's demography is opportune insofar as its population, being young but not too young, is in principle more productive than one with proportionally higher proportions of the very old and the very young. The 'sweet spot' in the middle of this range is projected to expand relative to the elderly peak and the pre-teen base, turning the gently sloping age pyramid that Indonesia had in 1990 into a fat diamond by 2050. See http://www.nationmaster.com/country/id-indonesia/Age-_distribution.

14 'Shake it all about: which economies have the most monetary and fiscal wiggle-room?', *The Economist*, 28 January 2012, http://www.economist.com/node/21543468. The indicators were inflation, excess credit, the real interest rate, the current account balance, and a combined measure of government debt and the structural budget deficit expressed as a percentage of GDP.

much more than the prominence attributable to good economic reviews by outsiders. The analysis must be extended to include non-economic sectors of activity and should be refocused on Indonesian intentions and decisions. The question then becomes: to what extent should Indonesia's perceived rise be attributed to the conscious desire and actions of the Yudhoyono government to lift the country's profile in the world?

A plausible answer would acknowledge that Yudhoyono's foreign policy priorities have evolved in two complementary directions over the years of his presidency. Cognitively, although domestic concerns remain paramount, foreign affairs have loomed modestly larger on the government's policy horizons. Conceptually, although the over-riding justification for what the government says and does abroad remains the national interest, serving that interest has come to be rationalized in terms that include greater attention to bolstering Indonesia's image and role in the larger world.

These are contingent trends. The president's second and final term will end in 2014 with the election and inauguration of a new government. Between now and then, the reduced dominance of domestic over foreign policy in public discourse could be reversed in favour of internal concerns, unless foreign policy becomes an issue during the campaign. But even if an inward shift in official attention does occur, it will not undo the record of interest in foreign affairs already compiled by Yudhoyono.

That interest should *not* be construed as having reoriented Indonesia from a nationalist towards an internationalist foreign policy, as if those two things were opposed. Insofar as the president and his collaborators have promoted their country's rise and role on larger stages, they have done so on grounds that privilege official conceptions of the *national* interest – and the same could be said of previous Indonesian regimes.

Compared with what those regimes said and did in foreign affairs, however, Yudhoyono's foreign policy has been distinctive. Most obviously, he has shunned the confrontational anti-imperialism that Sukarno's presidency exemplified in the 1960s. Less evidently, compared with the priority that Suharto placed on economic development and on foreign policies designed to serve that end – the invasion of East Timor glaringly excepted – Yudhoyono has broadened the rationale for Indonesian involvement in foreign affairs. A non-economic case in point has been his desire to leverage his country's stature as the world's third-largest democracy – a priority that Suharto's authoritarian regime, despite calling itself a 'Pancasila democracy',[15] could not plausibly entertain.

---

15 Pancasila's five abstractions – monotheistic belief, humanitarian civility, national unity, consultative democracy and social justice – are as close as Indonesia comes to having an ideology authorized by the state.

Evidence of this broadening over time can be culled from Yudhoyono's speeches, starting with his first presidential address in October 2004 when domestic concerns were especially salient. After initially bouncing back from the trauma of the 1997–98 Asian financial crisis, economic growth had slowed to speeds still well below what the country had known in the mid-1990s (Index Mundi 2011). A peace accord between the government and a rebel movement in Aceh had broken down in 2003. In September 2004 in Jakarta, a month before the president spoke, a terrorist bombing had killed nine people and injured many more. That attack had followed bombings in Bali (2002) and Jakarta (2003) that had left more than 200 dead and many more injured.

Given these domestic preoccupations with poverty and insecurity, not to mention corruption, it is understandable that the president should have focused his first inaugural address almost wholly on the internal challenges facing his country.[16] In December 2004, not long after he spoke, the scale and severity of Indonesia's domestic troubles were brutally intensified when an earthquake-triggered tsunami struck Sumatra, killing an estimated 170,000 Indonesians and rendering homeless more than half a million more.

By the time of the president's second inaugural address in October 2009, Indonesia's internal conditions and external standing had improved. For four years, Aceh had enjoyed a stable peace, based on an agreement that the rebels and the central government had signed and implemented in 2005. By way of acknowledging that achievement, Yudhoyono had been nominated for (though he did not receive) the Nobel Peace Prize.[17] In April 2009 *TIME Magazine* had chosen him as one of seven heads of state or government who, in its judgment, 'most affect our world'.[18]

Meanwhile the economy's annual growth rate had recovered from its earlier doldrums, rising to 5 per cent or higher in 2004–2006 and 6 per cent or more in 2007–2008. Having won by a landslide in the second round of the 2004 presidential election, Yudhoyono bettered that performance in July 2009 by winning in the first round by the same wide margin. These achievements yielded political 'wiggle room' to pay more

---

16 'Now is the time for action: Susilo', *Jakarta Post*, 21 October 2004, http://www.thejakartapost.com/resources/president_speeches.

17 'All eyes on Nobel Peace Prize possibles', *BBC News*, 12 October 2006, http://news.bbc.co.uk/2/hi/europe/5398780.stm. The 2006 prize went instead to Muhammad Yunus of the Grameen Bank.

18 'The 2009 TIME 100', *TIME Magazine*, 30 April 2009, http://www.time.com/time/specials/packages/completelist/0,29569,1894410,00.html.

attention to foreign affairs – room that the president's distinctly international résumé already suited him to use.[19]

TWO VISIONS

Yudhoyono's second inaugural address in 2009 did not privilege foreign over domestic policy. His ambitions were to reduce poverty, strengthen democracy, assure justice, uphold good governance, end corruption and preserve national unity – all within a national frame. But compared with his first inaugural speech five years before, this one was more explicitly and confidently outward-looking.

> There is an identity and a personality that make Indonesia special, superior and not easily torn apart. ... Indonesia is facing a new strategic environment, in which there is no country that considers Indonesia an enemy, and there is no country that Indonesia considers its enemy. Thus Indonesia can now freely implement an *all directions foreign policy* and have *a million friends and zero enemies*. Indonesia will cooperate with whoever shares our intentions and goals, above all to build a world order that is peaceful, just, democratic and prosperous.
>
> Indonesia will continue to stand in the vanguard of endeavour to create a better world order. We will continue to be a pioneer in the effort to rescue the world from climate change; in reforming the world economy, especially through the G20; in struggling for the Millennium Development Goals; in advancing multilateralism through the United Nations; and in supporting the achievement of inter-civilizational harmony – *harmony among civilizations*.
>
> At the regional level, Indonesia will continue to endeavour, together with the other ASEAN states, to establish the ASEAN Community, and to render

---

19 Although the influence of background on behaviour is hard to pin down, it is safe to suggest that the amicable relations enjoyed by Indonesia and the United States on Yudhoyono's watch are not unrelated to his positive and career-advancing experiences training with and learning from Americans. He acquired a good command of English early in life; took airborne and ranger courses at Fort Benning, Georgia, in the mid-1970s; returned to Fort Benning for further training in an advanced infantry course and with the 82nd Airborne Division in the early 1980s, including time in the US jungle warfare school in Panama; and attended the US Army Command and General Staff College at Fort Leavenworth, Kansas, at the turn of the 1990s, while earning his 1991 master's degree in business management from Webster University in St Louis, also in Kansas. (For more information, see Yudhoyono's biography at http://wn.com/yudhoyono.) No previous Indonesian president had spent as much time in the United States before achieving that office, and none had been more exposed to American education. (Yudhoyono also took military training courses in Belgium and West Germany in the 1980s and served as an observer with the UN peacekeeping mission to Bosnia in the mid-1990s.)

Southeast Asia a peaceful, prosperous and dynamic region (Yudhoyono 2009).[20]

The scope of this passage was global. The world upstaged the region, and ASEAN was mentioned last and least. This allocation of priority seemed to revise the conventional idea that Southeast Asia was the first, nearest and thus arguably the most important of the concentric circles in which Indonesia might exercise influence.

That revision had already been discussed privately in Jakarta, and had just surfaced in public discourse. In October 2009, two weeks before Yudhoyono spoke, a co-author of this volume, Rizal Sukma (2009), proposed that Indonesia adopt a 'post-ASEAN foreign policy': without quitting ASEAN, or ignoring it, Indonesia should treat it as 'no more important than other venues such as the G20' – the Group of 20 major economies, including Indonesia, that Yudhoyono would soon reference in his own remarks.

The G20 had begun as an informal meeting of finance ministers and central bank governors. It was first convened in 1999 in response to the Asian financial crisis. In 2008 the US president, George W. Bush, asked Yudhoyono and the leaders of the other G20 states to meet in Washington DC in November to coordinate responses to the American financial crisis and its global repercussions – an upgrade from ministerial to summit level that was quickly institutionalized at the urging notably of London and Paris. Jakarta gained prestige in this instance less at its own initiative than by external invitation. Once accredited at that elite global level, however, Indonesia could more readily project itself as something more than a large fish in a small Southeast Asian – ASEAN – pond.

Sukma wanted Indonesia to be more proactive in foreign affairs, as befitted a large, economically dynamic and politically democratic Muslim-majority nation, and thus to 'stop punching below its weight'. 'Countries such as Singapore, Malaysia, Japan, Australia, China, India and the United States' were in his view 'far more important to Indonesia than any other countries'. Indonesia had paid too much heed to multilateralism on a Southeast Asian scale and not enough to bilateral relations with 'major powers, especially the United States, Japan, Australia, India, South Korea and China'. In pursuing a 'free and active' foreign policy, Indonesia should 'free itself from any undeserving obligation to follow the wishes of any state or a grouping of states, including ASEAN, if by doing so we sacrifice our own national interests' (Sukma 2009).

---

20 In translating this text I have italicized the words that were spoken in English and changed 'zero enemy' to 'zero enemies'. ASEAN is the Association of Southeast Asian Nations.

Although seven of Indonesia's nine ASEAN partners were pointedly missing from Sukma's list of 'far more important' countries, he did urge a deepening of Indonesia's relations not only 'with Malaysia and Singapore (for strategic necessity)' but also 'with the Philippines and Thailand (for shared values of democracy)' (Sukma 2009). The selectively bilateral focus of that advice, however, only reinforced the impression of impatience with ASEAN's limitations. He was diplomatic enough not to specify them, but one can readily guess that his disappointments included the success of ASEAN's more authoritarian members in watering down Indonesian efforts to get the organization to pay more than lip service to the need to protect human rights and encourage democracy in Southeast Asia (Emmerson 2009: 35–6).

In addition to heading Indonesia's Centre for Strategic and International Studies in Jakarta, Sukma sits on the executive board of a leading Muslim organization, Muhammadiyah, and is well known for his scholarship on Islam and Indonesian foreign policy.[21] One might suppose on that basis that Islam and Muslim countries would loom large in his sketch of a 'post-ASEAN foreign policy' for Indonesia. He did note that 'our identity as a moderate Muslim-majority nation also obliges us to play a more active role in the Muslim world' (Sukma 2009). But that duty was an add-on, not the heart of what he had in mind.

This is not to minimize Indonesia's role in the Organisation of Islamic Cooperation (formerly the Organisation of the Islamic Conference), or the role of Muslim sensibilities in sustaining Indonesia's support for Palestine, its criticism of Israel and its reluctance to side with the United States against Iran.[22] There was even a possibility during the 'Arab Spring' that Yudhoyono, as the head of a large and mostly Muslim democracy, might travel to the Maghreb to express solidarity with the rise of pluralist politics there. But these linkages are too specialized, and Indonesians are too diverse, to sustain an utterly or indelibly 'Muslim' outlook on the world.

Sukma's critique of Indonesian foreign policy reflected his own 'free and active' status as an independent analyst of his country's affairs. One could not expect that Indonesia's president would, in his second inaugural address two weeks later, risk further ruffling diplomatic feathers inside ASEAN by turning Sukma's proposals into policy.

---

21 See, for example, Sukma (2003). See also Tamara (2009) and Anwar (2010: 37–54).

22 In November 2011, for example, the International Atomic Energy Agency's governing board adopted a resolution expressing concern about the opacity of Iran's nuclear program. The resolution urged Tehran to return to talks on the matter and to restrain its nuclear effort in line with previous UN Security Council decisions. In the 32–2–1 vote, Cuba and Ecuador opposed the statement while Indonesia abstained (Landle and Cowell 2011).

Nor indeed did that occur. Like Sukma, Yudhoyono endorsed a 'free and active' foreign policy for his country. Unlike the analyst, however, the president interpreted that phrase in far more inclusive, less discriminating and more idealistic terms. Where Sukma had urged the pursuit of Indonesia's own national interest in bilateral contexts where its negotiators would be less pressured to defer to a consensus among multiple states, the president envisioned a tactful, eclectic and multilateralist foreign policy that offered all things - good things - to all people.

In his speech Yudhoyono assured his audience, which included foreign diplomats and the heads of four Southeast Asian governments, that Indonesia would (somewhat incongruously) 'fire up a cool and moderate kind of nationalism full of friendship, while at the same time upholding dynamic internationalism'. Lacking adversaries, Indonesia could practise an 'all directions foreign policy' of attracting 'a million friends and zero enemies'. Whether such a policy could be anything but merely inoffensive, or whether international relations should be more than a contest for popularity, was not explained. Although the president implied that Indonesia would not cooperate with anyone who did not share its 'intentions and goals', it was not clear how anyone could reasonably oppose his government's desire for a 'peaceful, just, democratic and prosperous' world order. Finally, in contrast to Sukma's case for serving Indonesia's national interest bilaterally with selected partners of real consequence, Yudhoyono promised in effect to serve global and regional interests in multilateral venues - the United Nations, the G20 and ASEAN (Yudhoyono 2009).

It is unfair to compare a scholar's op-ed with a head of state's speech as if other things were equal, which of course they were not. But the contrast shows just how different are the performances that a 'rising' profile can imply. Note also the feedback effects of performance on profile. A Sukma-style foreign policy would in part be enabled by Indonesia's underlying or structural 'weight', to use his language. Indonesia's great physical, demographic and economic size would make other states more inclined to attend to whatever it said or did. But in 'punching' above that 'weight' - behaving proactively and even, if necessary, at the expense of good-neighbourly consensus - Indonesia would heighten its fixed profile by contingent and changeable means.

A virtuous spiral could result if Indonesia's actions served not only its own interests but regional and global ones as well. But what if nationalism trumped altruism? What if Indonesia became an 'irresponsible stakeholder' in world affairs? In such an event, 'punching' could become an all-too-literal metaphor.

Acclaim and notoriety both presuppose prominence, but for morally opposite reasons. Neither the president nor the analyst proposed notoriety, but the difference between their presentations framed a key issue that Indonesia will face if its upward trajectory continues: whether, as the balance of productive internationalist acquiescence versus narrowly nationalist insistence in Indonesian foreign policy tilts in the former or the latter direction, the country's 'free and active' stance will induce cooperation or backlash in the foreign policies of others.

TWO REEFS?

The notion of a 'free and active' foreign policy seems general and desirable to the point of banality. What government would want to play a 'shackled and passive' role in foreign affairs? Nor is the appeal of an 'all directions foreign policy' unique to Indonesia.[23] But omni-directional engagement, or making 'a million friends and zero enemies', in Yudhoyono's words, is not the same as 'rowing between two reefs' – a precept of necessity that has recurred in the history of Indonesian diplomacy in counterpoint to being 'free and active' as a matter of choice.

The navigational metaphor dates to the beginning of the Cold War, when it was used to express Indonesia's need to maintain impartiality between the United States and the Soviet Union – the 'two reefs'. Indonesia's then vice-president Mohammad Hatta (1902–80) gave voice to that suitably archipelagic image in a speech he delivered in 1948, two years before his country acquired full sovereignty as a unitary republic (Leifer 1983: 20, citing Hatta 1953a).

In 1948 the People's Republic of China did not yet exist, but the Cold War was already under way. In that context, Hatta objected to having 'to choose between being pro Russian or pro American' (Leifer 1983: 20). By implication, charting a course towards either reef in search of protection against the other could risk major underwater damage to the ship of state – the danger of being 'torn apart' that Yudhoyono would dismiss so assuredly in his second inaugural address more than 60 years later.

Diplomatic promiscuity was far from Hatta's mind in 1948. Nor did non-alignment in the Cold War imply passivity. On the contrary, he wanted Indonesia to be 'an active agent entitled to determine its own goal', namely freedom from colonial rule (Leifer 1983: 20). It was, he later wrote, precisely its 'active and independent foreign policy' – a variation

23 In Asia, Japan's 'omni-directional diplomacy' is a case in point; see, for example, Miyashita and Sato (2001: 83, 114). Other Asian countries whose foreign policies in certain periods and contexts have been termed 'omni-directional' include China, India, South Korea, Thailand and Vietnam.

on the 'free and active' mantra – that prohibited Indonesia 'from drawing close to one bloc at the expense of the other' (Hatta 1958).

These principles – an independent and active foreign policy free of big-power alignment or constraint – would come to constitute the leitmotif of Indonesia's self-assigned position in the world, themes that a succession of its leaders would invoke in speeches delivered down to the present day. But these three commitments – independence, activity and impartiality – were and remain potentially in conflict. Maintaining a course exactly equidistant between two large reefs would make Indonesia reflexively *dependent* on the antagonism between those outside powers. An active and autonomous foreign policy might successfully be reserved for Indonesia's relations with lesser states, but only to the extent that such states were not already aligned with either superpower – a partly counterfactual condition in a Cold War world substantially divided between more or less pro-Soviet and pro-American blocs.

One way of retaining an active role in this bipolarized setting, of course, was to champion a Third World based on neutrality between the First and the Second. But Hatta ruled that out. Indonesia, he wrote in 1953, 'cannot adopt an attitude of neutrality' and 'is not prepared to participate in any third bloc designed to act as a counterpoise to the two giant blocs' already in existence (Hatta 1953b). Yet that disavowal did not stop Sukarno from hosting, two years later, the Bandung Conference that would inspire the Non-Aligned Movement.

While scholars struggle to clarify ambiguities, politicians employ them to advantage. Hatta himself enlarged this repertoire of competing rationales by adding to them the pragmatism of national interest: while 'safeguarding' Indonesia's aversion to alignment in principle, 'the nature of her relationship' with any given country 'in practice will be determined in each case by what is at that time the reigning national interest' (Hatta 1958). Considering the plasticity of the 'national interest' and the licence of unprincipled 'practice', this could almost be taken as saying: anything goes.

This slippage between rhetoric and reality – a disjuncture more or less common to the foreign policies of all states – was evident in what Indonesian leaders said, thought and did from the very inception of the republic. In 1948, despite seeming to locate Jakarta midway between Moscow and Washington, Hatta feared the communist danger far more than the Western one. He was making a domestic argument: against radical-left politics, revolutionary war and alignment with the USSR, and for continuing diplomatic negotiations with the Dutch as the better way for Indonesia to achieve sovereignty as a nation-state.

The Soviet Union no longer exists, but China has the potential to replace that defunct reef as America's big-power adversary in Asia. Sino-

American rivalry does not amount to Cold War II. Not yet. But tensions could build, and if they do, Indonesia could again see itself cross-pressured to navigate between hostile shores.

An optimist in Jakarta today, on the other hand, might construe the perceived rise of Indonesia as opening a vista beyond past, present and even future reefs. The more seriously one takes the country's heightened profile as evidence not only of Indonesia's subjective international popularity, but of its objective national prowess as well, the more plausible is the inference that the country is growing strong enough to abandon equidistance and do pretty much whatever it wishes. That room to do much more than wiggle could include ignoring the polarity that China and America represent, or going around them, or tacking back and forth between them for maximum advantage, or even braving the enmity of the one by sailing definitively into a safe harbour offered by the other.

Futurology of this extreme sort is more playful than prescient, however. Equidistance is mathematical; actual policy is not. Hatta's image of a trajectory of midpoints between Moscow and Washington did not match the actual course of Indonesian foreign policy then or later. Western criticism of Suharto over the violation of human rights and the occupation of East Timor did not lessen his anti-communist preference for security cooperation with the United States. Nor do Beijing and Washington today weigh equally on the scales of Indonesian judgment as to which of the two is the worthier partner in strategic terms. Indonesian opinions on this score vary – with the issue, its context, the identity of the Indonesian source and whether the conversation is public or private. Nevertheless, at the risk of oversimplifying a diverse, complex and nuanced range of views, one can say that many if not most knowledgeable Indonesians disagree with American policies more than they fear American power, and fear China's power more than they disagree with its policies.

In any event, Indonesia's self-ascribed purpose in world affairs cannot be caricatured as the mere avoidance of complicity in rivalry between big powers. More than half a century ago, Hatta himself looked beyond anxious equidistance and nationalist pragmatism to a world in which his country would have become strong enough – risen enough – to be able proactively to serve the *global* interest. 'At present', he wrote in 1953, 'when the task of national construction is just beginning to be tackled, we are receiving more from the international world than we can give to it. But the time will come when we shall make a real contribution to world progress and to the strengthening of international organizations' (Hatta 1953b).

Has that time come? The question is unfair because it implies that Indonesia has not already made such a contribution. A full historical account of Indonesian foreign policy would belie that inference – notwithstanding Sukarno's quixotic decisions to confront and destabilize Malaysia, withdraw Indonesia from the United Nations and link Jakarta to Beijing in an anti-imperialist axis meant to outflank the United Nations. But detailing Indonesian history is not my purpose here. I wish instead to distinguish, however briefly and anecdotally, some of the ways or styles in which Indonesia could express or employ its higher profile in the world.

FIVE STYLES

If Indonesia is rising, how is it rising? The question is too broad to answer in the space remaining, but there is room to lay out a spectrum of categories with corresponding illustrations. The categories are general enough to apply to the foreign policy style of any country; the illustrations are uniquely Indonesian; and both are volitional - that is, they refer not to a country's natural or systemic endowments, such as spatial location, demographic size, mineral resources or accumulated wealth, but to what its officials say or do on its behalf in foreign affairs. The categories - ideal types - are distinctive, but they can co-describe the same policy, and they hardly exhaust how it could be described. The illustrations are not meant to typify the stances or actions they are used to represent; they were chosen mainly because they are relatively recent and came readily to mind.

At one end of this proposed spectrum, the lowest volitional profile would be associated with a distinctly *passive* foreign policy. The remaining profiles and policies would be active to varying degrees and in different ways. A state with a *reactive* policy profile would respond to the initiatives of other countries rather than generating ideas or actions of its own. A *projective* policy profile would disseminate positive images or aspects of a country in the hope of making it more attractive and reputable in foreign eyes. State behaviour that is intended to induce other states to change their behaviour, but does so in an indirect or clearly non-coercive way, may be called *suggestive*. Finally, a *coercive* policy would involve strong pressure - intimidation - but not to the point of physical aggression.[24]

The first style, passivity, informs the following vignette. One day some time ago, I found myself in conversation with the Indonesian

24 An instance of aggression would of course be the Indonesian invasion of East Timor. My timeframe here, however, is more recent than historical, and because I see no convincing evidence of physical aggression by Indonesia beyond its borders since it withdrew from East Timor, that category is ignored in the illustrations that follow.

ambassador in his Washington office. I was thinking of a conventional American wisdom about Indonesian foreign policy at that time: that, in world affairs, the country was 'punching below its weight'. With that notion in mind, I ventured to ask the ambassador if, considering how many different American actors were involved in making and debating US foreign policy, he had made a point of venturing beyond officials in the executive branch to meet with relevant members of Congress and their staffs. 'Why should I?' he replied, gesturing towards the phone on his desk. 'If they want to talk, they can always call me.' To this day, when I think of the least proactive option in the repertoire of styles available to Indonesia – a *passive* foreign policy – I picture the ambassador sitting by his phone, patiently waiting for it to ring.

The second or *reactive* style deserves more detail. On 16 November 2011 US president Barack Obama was in Australia en route to Indonesia. In Canberra he announced plans to raise the American military profile in Australia. Initially 250 and eventually 2,500 US marines, supplied with equipment including combat helicopters, would spend six months in Darwin to train with their Australian counterparts and be available for humanitarian and disaster relief. US military aircraft would also increase their visits to Australia's Tindal air force base southeast of Darwin. The plans would eventually also involve US ships and submarines operating out of an Australian naval base south of Perth (Coorey 2011).

Three days after making this announcement, Obama took part in the sixth East Asia Summit, hosted in Bali by Yudhoyono. Indonesia's foreign minister and its military commander expressed concern that, in the minister's terms, an expanded American military presence in Darwin could engender a 'vicious circle of tension and mistrust' (Saragih 2011). Indonesian journalists and academics reacted more strongly; two of the latter urged the government to reaffirm its 'free and active' policy in order to avoid the pro-American tilt that silence in the face of Obama's decision might imply (Quayle 2011).

These and more vehement comments were motivated variously by worries that an escalated military presence on Indonesia's edge might provoke a Sino-American cold war in which Jakarta could be pressured to side with Washington against Beijing; that it might involve the United States in disputes over the South China Sea; and that it might even some day facilitate American intervention in the Indonesian half of New Guinea. No one spoke of dusting off the oars needed to row between Chinese and American reefs, but as I listened, Hatta's image did come to mind.[25]

25 For more on this theme, see Emmerson (2011b).

A third example will illustrate how Indonesia has been *projective*. On 9 July 2011, on the mall between the Washington Monument and the Capitol building where the US Congress convenes, the largest *angklung* ensemble ever to perform on that indigenous Indonesian instrument – 5,182 individuals in all – played 'We Are the World'. Guinness World Records certified the event.[26] The impresario behind this feat was Indonesia's ambassador to the United States and Yudhoyono's long-time adviser on foreign affairs, Dino Patti Djalal.

Indonesia's distinctive approach to encouraging democracy in other countries frames an instance of the fourth or *suggestive* style of foreign policy. On 8 December 2011, Yudhoyono convened the fourth annual meeting of a uniquely Indonesian experiment, the Bali Democracy Forum. Individuals from a record 82 countries attended, including eight heads of state (Yudhoyono 2011). The forum, which always meets in Bali and is run by the Indonesian foreign ministry, brings together official representatives to share their experiences and understandings of 'democracy'. Invitations are purposely not limited to the leaders of democratic countries. Since the first forum in 2008, China, Myanmar and other authoritarian regimes have taken part.

The Bali Democracy Forum has been criticized as giving legitimacy to dictators. Its supporters respond that including autocrats in international meetings about democracy exposes them to democratic ideas that they may then be more inclined to consider and conceivably adopt. To my knowledge, no systematic evaluation of the effectiveness of the forum has yet been made.[27]

Fifth and finally, a *coercive* foreign policy involving major pressure short of outright physical coercion, to the extent that diplomats engage in it, tends to occur behind closed doors. Sometimes, however, word gets out, as in the following instance, when Indonesia was on the receiving end of the behaviour.

China claims most of the South China Sea. To varying degrees and for varying reasons, several ASEAN countries, including Indonesia, contest that claim. China has refused to negotiate its position multilaterally with the ASEAN states, insisting instead on dealing separately with each counterclaimant. In keeping with that hub-and-spokes approach, Beijing has tried – unsuccessfully – to intimidate the ASEAN states by

26 The ensemble consisted almost entirely of Americans and Indonesians, who rehearsed before performing. Each was given an *angklung* – a bamboo instrument that produces one of several notes. For ease of recognition by the performers, and to publicize the archipelago, each note was given the name of an Indonesian island. See Bayuni (2011) and http://www.guinnessworldrecords.com/records-9000/largest-angklung-ensemble/.

27 An excellent analytic overview, meanwhile, is Currie (2010: 19–25).

telling them they should not meet as a group to discuss the South China Sea, and warning them in strong terms not to broach the subject at international meetings.[28]

I cannot point with comparable assurance to instances of *Indonesian* foreign policy on Yudhoyono's watch that have been as clearly coercive. Certainly Indonesian officials have not been immune to expressing anger or pique in international contexts. One would think, however, that word of premeditated acts of outright intimidation to achieve a goal, performed as a matter of official foreign policy, would have circulated beyond closed rooms, either in public discourse or in private conversation. One might fruitfully seek such evidence in the intramural and *in camera* dynamics of ASEAN, but that is speculation on my part.

Although the styles of Indonesian foreign policy today are of course diverse, they tend to cluster in the middle of this five-part spectrum. Indonesia reacts to the statements and actions of others, normally in a low-key way that is less likely to trigger tit-for-tat polemics. As a matter of public relations – Yudhoyono's omnidirectional hope for 'a million friends and zero enemies' – Indonesia tries to project a generally favourable image of itself in terms that are not designed to induce any specific actor or set of actors to stop doing something and do something else instead. As for focusing on a particular foreign behaviour in order to improve or correct it from an Indonesian standpoint, policies meant to serve that end have tended, on this president's watch, to be more suggestive than coercive. Knowledge of what happens in off-the-record settings could tilt my estimation of Indonesia's approach more towards coercion. But outright bullying would probably still not emerge as the dominant style of Indonesian foreign policy, if only because the alienation of many of those being so vigorously and persistently hectored would already have become more widely known.

Do these passive, reactive, projective, suggestive and coercive qualities of a foreign policy amount to a natural progression from indifference to intransigence? They do not. If Indonesia is rising, will its foreign policy become coercive? That is not foreordained. It will depend on future conditions and contingencies, not least among them the personality and preferences of whoever is elected to replace Yudhoyono as president in 2014. For now, Indonesia's foreign policy entails far less unilateralist table-pounding than multilateralist nesting, in contexts that are more conducive to persuasion than extortion – ASEAN, the East Asia Summit, the Bali Democracy Forum and the G20, among many others.

---

28 My sources are informed Southeast Asians of different nationalities speaking privately and from experience in different venues around the region.

SUMMARY AND CONCLUSION

To answer this chapter's opening question: Indonesia *is* rising. But prominence and performance, though related, are not mutually entailing. The rise of Indonesia is led by the country's prominence and lagged by its performance.

The quantitative evidence of Indonesia's economic and military performance cited at the outset of this essay yielded a mixed picture. The indicators raised relativistic questions. A rise compared to what? The achievements of other countries? Indonesia's own prior record? The evidence suggested that the economy's rates of growth were respectable. But they were not so clearly stellar as to warrant the elite-club coinages of investment advisers, who were in any case more interested in future potential than past performance. Actual declines in defence spending, already meager as a proportion of GDP, made sense in the absence of serious threats from other states. But such modest outlays precluded concluding that Indonesia was an ascendant military power.

In contrast, the evidence for Indonesia's prominence in cyberspace was nothing short of remarkable. Whatever its actual performance, and keeping in mind the caveats regarding Table 4.1, in virtual discourse Indonesia appeared more likely to be considered ascendant even than China. It has garnered further notice as a rare example of a stable and relatively liberal Muslim-majority democracy. That political performance has been marred, however, by President Yudhoyono's flagging campaign against corruption and his toleration of leniency almost to the point of impunity for thugs and hyper-Islamist vigilantes who violate human rights.

If performance has lagged prominence in Indonesia's rise, a more active foreign policy, wider in scope, has begun to narrow that gap. Decisive electoral mandates in 2004 and 2009 enabled Yudhoyono to allocate more time to foreign affairs – a priority already matched by his own prior exposure to the larger world, including familiarity with the United States unmatched by any president before him.

Without neglecting bilateral relations with other countries, Yudhoyono and his foreign policy colleagues have been keen to cultivate multilateral diplomacy, especially inside Southeast Asia. Sukma has acknowledged the importance of ASEAN for Indonesia. But he urges more attention to extra-regional spheres and actors, less faith in abstract norms that boil down to what the least democratic members of ASEAN are willing to accept, and more pragmatic bilateral engagements with key countries whose actions significantly serve or disserve Indonesia's own national interest.

The contrast between the president's vision and the analyst's should not be overdrawn. In his second inaugural address in 2009, Yudhoyono himself mentioned ASEAN last and least. The divergence does nevertheless illustrate the flexible horizons of Indonesian foreign policy. Contrary to the unilinear image of Indonesia 'rising', its actual role in world affairs will zig or zag in tandem with ideas as they are expressed, contingencies as they occur and choices as they are made. The 'free and active' mantra will not be abandoned, but it will keep being reinterpreted. As a matter of rhetoric, Yudhoyono has already updated Hatta's classic 'two reefs' metaphor to fit a more multipolar world, by relocating the Indonesian boat from a narrow Cold War strait to a 'turbulent ocean' of global uncertainty and instability (Tan 2007).

Were a new cold war to develop between Beijing and Washington, one can imagine Jakarta refurbishing Hatta's metaphor in public while privately hedging more against China than against the United States. But the future character of Indonesia's rise will depend on much else as well: the Indonesian economy; the prospects for democracy in China and for its survival in Indonesia; the strength and centrality of ASEAN; the perceived rise or decline of China and the United States; the level of American interest in Southeast Asia; and the actions of future leaders in these and other countries – not to mention all the consequential but unforeseen exigencies that will further complicate the deceptive linearity of Indonesia's 'rise'. Not even an EAGLE can fly beyond the reach of a 'black swan' in the sense of an unpredicted yet momentous event.[29]

These synergies will affect as well the complexion of Indonesian foreign policies – whether they grow more or less passive, reactive, projective, suggestive or coercive in nature. The Yudhoyono administration to date has mixed and matched the middle three of these *modi operandi* in what has for the most part been a doubly moderate foreign policy – mainstream in outlook and low in key. But that too could change, depending on circumstances that include the conceivable election of a corrupt and illiberal populist to replace Yudhyono in 2014.

Understanding Indonesia's recent and possible future role in this dynamic and relativistic way is more useful than trying to determine whether it is 'punching' above or below its 'weight'. Why should a country's geographic, demographic or economic size be the standard for judging its performance? There is something implausibly deterministic in the idea that the extent of a country's physical 'givens' should correspond to how much it actually gives – for good or ill – to the larger world. 'Punching' elides the differences in style illustrated here. If Indonesia had not 'punched' *under* its 'weight' inside ASEAN – lowering its voice in foreign affairs, forsaking Sukarno's high-decibel rhetoric against Malaysia, accepting the need to cooperate with its 'underweight' neighbours – the

29 For more on this subject, compare Taleb (2010) with Emmerson (2008, 2011a).

organization would not have survived and the region might well be less stable today. Weight-to-punch proportionality is being made even more problematic by globalization, which has favoured agility over bulk in foreign affairs.

Unlike the EAGLE it has been hyped as resembling, Indonesia has not taken flight from the multilateral nests where it is necessarily outnumbered. Like Sukma one can debate the priority that Indonesia should attach to a particular venue – ASEAN, say, compared with the G20 – or whether Indonesian foreign policy should be more selectively bilateral in character. But the Indonesian president has not used his country's prominence to justify rebalancing its 'free and active' role away from the constraint of consensus in multi-state meetings and towards the freedom and the activity – the 'punching' – that going solo would allow.

In November 2011 Yudhoyono attended four multilateral summits in a row. He flew from a G20 meeting in Cannes to an Asia–Pacific Economic Cooperation (APEC) Economic Leaders Meeting in Honolulu, and from there to Nusa Dua in Bali to chair an ASEAN summit and the East Asia Summit. Indonesia will host the APEC Economic Leaders Meeting in 2014. These are just a few of the better known among Indonesia's many multilateral engagements, which include hundreds of lesser gatherings convened annually in ASEAN's name.

One can dismiss much of this diplomacy as a waste of time – a category error that mistakes talking for doing. Sukma's critique is at least consonant with the case for talking less, or talking with people who matter more, and thereby accomplishing more. Yet neither he nor his president has construed Indonesia's rise in unilateralist terms. And it is possible that multilateral diplomacy is not a waste of time at all – that it is precisely the modality of discourse and action best suited, in the long run, to calming the turbulent ocean that our twenty-first-century world is turning out to be.

REFERENCES

Anwar, Dewi Fortuna (2010) 'Foreign policy, Islam and democracy in Indonesia', *Journal of Indonesian Social Sciences and Humanities* 3: 37–54.

Aridas, Tina (2010) 'Countries with the highest GDP growth 2000–2010', *Global Finance*, available at http://www.gfmag.com/tools/global-database/economic-data/10304-countries-with-the-highest-gdp-growth-2000-2010.html#axzz1ijQtPMyX, accessed January 2012.

Bayuni, Endy M. (2011) 'Washington DC shakes to angklung world record', *Jakarta Post*, 10 July 2011, available at http://www.thejakartapost.com/news/2011/07/10/washington-dc-shakes-angklung-world-record.html.

BBVA Research (n.d.) 'BBVA EAGLEs: key emerging markets for investors to focus on', Banco Bilbao Vizcaya Argentaria (BBVA), available at http://www.bbvaresearch.com/KETD/ketd/ing/nav/eagles.jsp.

Bellman, Eric and Natasha Brereton-Fukui (2012) 'Indonesia gets ratings boost', *Wall Street Journal Online*, 19 January, available at http://online.wsj.com/article/SB10001424052970203735304577168563581121548.html.

CIA (Central Intelligence Agency) (2010) 'Country comparison: GDP – real growth rate', *The World Factbook*, available at https://www.cia.gov/library/publications/the-world-factbook/rankorder/2003rank.html?countryName=Indonesia&countryCode=id®ionCode=eas&rank=51#id.

Cooper, Ben (2011) 'BRICS summit on Hainan Island: China leading the way?', *China Direct*, 13 April, available at http://cbi.typepad.com/china_direct/2011/04/brics-summit-on-hainan-island-china-leading-the-way.html.

Coorey, Phillip (2011) 'Obama to send marines to Darwin', *Sydney Morning Herald*, 17 November, available at http://www.smh.com.au/national/obama-to-send-marines-to-darwin-20111116-1njd7.html.

Currie, Kelley (2010) 'Bali Democracy Forum (BDF): Indonesia's open invitation', in K. Currie, *Mirage or Reality? Asia's Emerging Human Rights and Democracy Architecture*, Project 2049 Institute, Arlington VA, December, available at http://project2049.net/publications.html.

Emmerson, Donald K. (2008) 'ASEAN's black swans', *Journal of Democracy* 19(3): 70–84.

Emmerson, Donald K. (2009) 'Critical terms: security, democracy, and regionalism in Southeast Asia', in D.K. Emmerson (ed.) *Hard Choices: Security, Democracy, and Regionalism in Southeast Asia*, Institute of Southeast Asian Studies, Singapore.

Emmerson, Donald K. (2011a) 'Crisis, uncertainty, and democracy: black swans, fat tails, and the futures of political science', keynote address, annual convention, Australian Political Studies Association, Canberra, 26–28 September.

Emmerson, Donald K. (2011b) 'US, China role play for ASEAN', *Asia Times Online*, 18 November, available at http://www.atimes.com/atimes/Southeast_Asia/MK19Ae01.html.

Goldstone, Jack A. (2011) 'Rise of TIMBIs', *Foreign Policy*, 2 December, available at http://www.foreignpolicy.com/articles/2011/12/02/rise_of_the_timbis.

Grant, Jeremy (2010) 'What emerging animal are you?' MacroScope, *Reuters*, 15 November, available at http://blogs.reuters.com/macroscope/2010/11/15/what-emerging-animal-are-you/.

Gupta, Udayan (2011) 'MIST: the next tier of large emerging economies', *Institutional Investor*, 7 February, available at http://www.institutionalinvestor.com/Article/2762464/MIST-The-Next-Tier-of-Large-Emerging-Economies.html?ArticleId=2762464.

Hatta, Mohammad (1953a) *Mendajung antara Dua Karang* [Rowing between Two Reefs], Department of Information, Jakarta.

Hatta, Mohammad (1953b) 'Indonesia's foreign policy', *Foreign Affairs*, April, available at http://www.foreignaffairs.com/articles/71032/mohammad-hatta/indonesias-foreign-policy.

Hatta, Mohammad (1958) 'Indonesia between the power blocs', *Foreign Affairs*, April, available at http://www.foreignaffairs.com/articles/71409/mohammad-hatta/indonesia-between-the-power-blocs#.

Index Mundi (2011) 'Indonesia GDP – real growth rate', available at http://www.indexmundi.com/indonesia/gdp_real_growth_rate.html.

Keating, Joshua E. (2010) 'The stories you missed in 2010', *Foreign Policy*, December, available at http://www.foreignpolicy.com/articles/2010/11/29/the_stories_you_missed_in_2010?page=0,1.

Knowledge@Wharton (2011) 'The new BRICS on the block: which emerging markets are up and coming?', Wharton School at the University of Pennsylvania, 19 January, available at http://knowledge.wharton.upenn.edu/article.cfm?articleid=2679.

Landle, Mark and Alan Cowell (2011) 'U.S. plans new sanctions against Iran's oil industry', *New York Times*, 18 November, available at http://www.nytimes.com/2011/11/19/world/middleeast/nuclear-watchdog-seeks-consensus-on-iran.html?_r=2&nl=todaysheadlines&emc=globaleua22.

Leifer, Michael (1983) *Indonesia's Foreign Policy*, George Allen & Unwin, London.

Miyashita, Akitoshi and Yoichiro Sato (2001) *Japanese Foreign Policy in Asia and the Pacific: Domestic Interests, American Pressure, and Regional Integration*, Palgrave, New York NY.

Quayle, Linda (2011) 'Darwin and TPP continue to make waves, *SEAview*, 29 December, available at http://southeastasiaview.blogspot.com/2011/12/darwin-and-tpp-continue-to-make-waves.html.

Saragih, Bagus BT (2011) 'RI "vigilant" on Darwin plan', *Jakarta Post*, 18 November, available at http://www.thejakartapost.com/news/2011/11/18/ri-vigilant-darwin-plan.html.

SIPRI (Stockholm International Peace Research Institute) (2009a) 'Military expenditure as a share of GDP, 2004–2009 (table)', available at http://www.sipri.org/research/armaments/milex/resultoutput/milex_gdp.

SIPRI (Stockholm International Peace Research Institute) (2009b) 'The SIPRI Military Expenditure Database', available at http://milexdata.sipri.org/result.php4.

Sukma, Rizal (2003) *Islam in Indonesia's Foreign Policy*, Routledge, London.

Sukma, Rizal (2009) 'A post-ASEAN foreign policy for a post-G8 World', *Jakarta Post*, 5 October, available at http://www.thejakartapost.com/news/2009/10/05/a-postasean-foreign-policy-a-postg8-world.html.

Taleb, Nassim Nicholas (2010) *The Black Swan: The Impact of the Highly Improbable*, second edition, Random House, New York.

Tamara, Nasir (2009) *Indonesia Rising: Islam, Democracy and the Rise of Indonesia as a Major Power*, Select Books, Singapore.

Tan, Paige Johnson (2007) 'Navigating a turbulent ocean: Indonesia's worldview and foreign policy', *Asian Perspective* 31(3): 147–81, available at http://www.asianperspective.org/articles/v31n3-f.pdf.

Ventura, Luca and Tina Aridas (2012) 'Countries with the highest GDP growth 2002–2012', *Global Finance*, available at http://www.gfmag.com/tools/global-database/economic-data/10304-countries-with-the-highest-gdp-growth-2000-2010.html#axzz1oBOIGdLF, accessed March 2012.

Wilson, Dominic and Anna Stupnytska (2007) 'The N-11: more than an acronym', Global Economics Paper No. 153, Goldman Sachs Economic Research Group, 28 March.

Yudhoyono, Susilo Bambang (2009) 'Pidato Awal Jabatan Presiden RI 2009–2014' ['Inaugural address of the President of the Republic of Indonesia 2009–2014'], Jakarta, 20 October, available at http://www.presidenri.go.id/index.php/pidato/2009/10/20/1237.html.

Yudhoyono, Susilo Bambang (2011) 'Opening statement at the Bali Democracy Forum IV', Nusa Dua, 8 December, available at http://www.presidenri.go.id/index.php/eng/pidato/2011/12/08/1762.html.

Yulisman, Linda (2012) 'FDI rises to $19b amid global woes', *Jakarta Post*, 20 January.

5 DOMESTIC POLITICS AND INTERNATIONAL POSTURE: CONSTRAINTS AND POSSIBILITIES

Rizal Sukma

There are few countries whose international image has undergone as radical a transformation as Indonesia's within such a short period of time. In the mid-1990s, Indonesia was widely viewed as a major contributor to regional stability in Southeast Asia. Following the political turmoil of 1998–99, however, the country quickly became a source of regional and international concern. Its international image was severely dented by a host of domestic challenges: economic adversity, communal violence, the threat of secession and the growing problem of religious radicalism and terrorism. There were even doubts as to whether Indonesia could survive a democratic transition amidst mounting internal political crises and economic difficulties. By 2004, however, a sense of stability and normalcy had gradually returned, and within a decade of the reintroduction of democracy in 1998, it had become fashionable both within and outside Indonesia to describe the country as a democratic 'bright spot' in the developing world.

The changes in Indonesia's international image since Suharto's ascendancy in 1967 – from provider of regional stability to producer of insecurity to consolidating new democracy – have been reflected in differing approaches to foreign policy. As a stable Southeast Asian state for the first three decades, Indonesia was a confident regional player, working to ensure that the maintenance of regional stability would continue to generate prosperity for the region. When domestic order was shattered by dramatic political change in 1998, and national priorities were dictated by the imperative to manage internal political challenges, Indonesia's attention turned inward and it lost its voice in regional, let alone global, affairs. By 2003, however, Indonesia was once again ready to play a more active foreign policy role. It began to take a number of foreign policy initiatives that not only marked the return of a leadership role within the Association of Southeast Asian Nations (ASEAN), but also reflected its desire to invoke a new international image as the world's third-largest democracy and largest moderate Muslim-majority country, and as a 'bridge builder' and 'problem solver' in the wider global community.

This chapter examines the extent to which Indonesia's international posture has been subject to both the facilitating and restraining effects of domestic political realities. It argues that while recent gains in democratic consolidation have given Indonesia the confidence to exert greater influence in the regional arena, its desire to play a bigger global role - as a functioning democracy, as a moderate Muslim country and as a 'bridge builder' and 'problem solver' - remains subject to the limits imposed by persistent domestic weaknesses.

The discussion is divided into three sections. The first briefly discusses the elements of the new activism in Indonesia's foreign policy agenda. The second section examines how key aspects of domestic politics have affected the pursuit of regional and global activism. The third section focuses on Indonesia's strategic repositioning within East Asia. It suggests that this is a more realistic option for the country to address the growing disparity between its global aspirations and its status as a regional middle power.

THE NEW ACTIVISM IN FOREIGN POLICY

When the New Order government came to power in 1966, it immediately signalled its intention to change the course of foreign policy as a matter of national urgency. Suharto quickly abandoned the revolutionary expression of foreign policy pursued by Sukarno, while continuing to maintain 'an aspiration to a pre-eminent role in regional affairs', qualified by the recognition that Indonesia 'shall only be able to play an effective role [in international politics] if we ourselves are possessed of a great national vitality'.[1] The first two decades of foreign policy were therefore shaped primarily by the need to create a peaceful external environment that would allow the government to concentrate on the imperative of national development at home. The desire to play a bigger international role re-emerged only in the late 1980s, when Suharto believed that Indonesia had at last acquired the 'national vitality' to do so, primarily due

1 Speech by President Suharto, 16 August 1969, quoted in Leifer (1983: 112).

to the economic success at home (Heath 1987; Vatikiotis 1993; Sukma 1995). Accordingly, foreign policy in the 1990s was characterized by an attempt to raise the country's international profile within Southeast Asia and beyond.

As Indonesia plunged into severe economic and political turmoil in the wake of Suharto's downfall in 1998, foreign affairs took a back seat and the country's international image took a battering. According to Dewi Fortuna Anwar, an influential academic and an adviser to former president Habibie, 'Indonesia's regional and international standing reached an all-time low as the country seemed to be coming apart at the seams with the rise of religious and communal strife and the loss of East Timor in 1999' (Anwar 2009: 18). This time, however, Indonesia did not wait until it had fully recovered its 'national vitality' before setting in motion a new foreign policy activism. As signs of economic and political normalcy began to emerge, Indonesia quickly expressed its desire to play a more active foreign policy role and to regain an appropriate place in the regional and global arenas. If the foreign policy activism of Suharto's Indonesia had been driven primarily by domestic economic success (Vatikiotis 1993: 218), the renewed confidence of post-Suharto Indonesia was located in the ability of the nation to withstand adverse economic and political challenges amidst a difficult democratic transition. Of course other factors, such as the changing external environment, also played a role in the drive towards a more active foreign policy. However, the extent to which Indonesia's leaders have taken pride in the country's democratic gains, and used them to invoke a new international posture, has been striking.

In less than a decade, Indonesia managed to secure a number of significant democratic gains. It held two relatively peaceful democratic elections (in 1999 and 2004); achieved the peaceful resolution of several violent communal or secessionist conflicts (especially in Aceh); secured the military's withdrawal from politics; engineered a gradual economic recovery; introduced a genuine multi-party system; devolved power from the central government to the regions; fostered the existence of vibrant civil society groups; and accorded greater respect to freedom of speech and free media. In other words, after a brief period of difficult and painful democratic transition, Indonesia soon regained its 'normal country' status, albeit facing a host of problems, like many other democratizing societies (MacIntyre and Ramage 2008). The new activism in Indonesia's foreign policy was another sign of the return to normalcy.

The immediate priority was to restore the country's tattered international image. This was regarded as a serious matter requiring an urgent response for two obvious reasons: it affected Indonesia's confidence and pride as a nation, and it hindered the government's ability to restore economic stability, ensure territorial integrity and overcome other severe domestic problems. Successive post-*reformasi* governments have all regarded the restoration of Indonesia's international image as an important national priority. Former president Abdurrahman Wahid, for example, vowed that his government 'would do its best to … preserve Indonesia's dignity in a world marked by fierce competition between nations' (*Kompas*, 21 October 1999). His successor, Megawati Sukarnoputri, also promised 'to restore the dignity of the Indonesian state and nation, and regain the trust of the international community, including international donors and investors' (Sukarnoputri 2001). In seeking ways to address the country's image problem, policy makers recognized the need to create an international image that reflected important new dimensions of national identity resulting from political changes at home, in particular the transition to democracy and the rise of political Islam. Especially since 9/11, projecting an Indonesian identity as a democracy and as a moderate Muslim-majority country, both at home and abroad, has become a matter of priority in the conduct of foreign policy.[2]

The clearest indications of Indonesia's renewed confidence to once again play an active role in international affairs were naturally expressed within the immediate region. Since 2003, when Indonesia took its turn as the rotating chair of ASEAN, it has become increasingly assertive within the regional body, establishing itself as a voice for democracy in the region. It proposed the creation of an ASEAN Security Community, insisted on the inclusion of democracy and respect for human rights in the ASEAN Charter, and pushed for the establishment of an ASEAN Intergovernmental Commission on Human Rights as a vehicle for cooperation among member states to promote and protect human rights. When the initial draft terms of reference for the human rights commission reflected the preference of some ASEAN members for a body with limited power, Indonesia's then foreign minister, Nur Hassan Wirajuda, criticized the proposal as being 'far below international standards' and demanded that the body have the power not only to promote, but to protect, human rights.[3] After more than 18 months of intense negotiations, in 2009 Indonesia finally agreed to compromise when other ASEAN members accepted its demand for a mandatory five-year review, paving the way for the issue to be revisited in the future. That is, it accepted a less powerful body, but only as a starting point.

2 For a comprehensive discussion of how these two elements of national identity are reflected in Indonesia's foreign policy, see Sukma (2011a).

3 'Badan ham ASEAN jauh dibawah standar' [ASEAN human rights body is far below standard], *Kompas.com*, 9 August 2009.

Indonesia has also taken a stronger stance towards the problematic Burmese case, demanding that the Myanmar government move towards democracy and pay more respect to human rights. In its capacity as the 2011 chair of ASEAN, Indonesia offered to mediate to end the border conflict between Thailand and Cambodia – the first such initiative ever taken by an ASEAN member state. Although Indonesia still abides by the association's cardinal principles of non-interference and consensus, one cannot fail to conclude from these major initiatives that its policy towards ASEAN has begun to change significantly.

The new activism in foreign policy has extended well beyond Southeast Asia into the wider Asia–Pacific region. Indonesia has become more active in promoting cooperation within East Asia, in shaping the emerging regional architecture and in forging a number of strategic partnerships with key regional and global powers. It has been working closely with other ASEAN countries to sustain the centrality of the organization as a pillar of the emerging regional architecture in East Asia, by strengthening ASEAN-driven multilateral processes in the region. These include the ASEAN Plus One and ASEAN Plus Three meetings with China, Japan and South Korea, the ASEAN Regional Forum and the East Asia Summit. Together with a few other countries in the region, Indonesia played an instrumental role in creating, in 2005, an inclusive East Asia Summit that included Australia, India and New Zealand; later, it proposed the expansion of the grouping by inviting the United States and Russia to join, a move formally endorsed at the 17th ASEAN Summit in Hanoi in November 2010. Indonesia has also begun to balance its emphasis on multilateralism by expanding and deepening bilateral relationships with major powers such as Japan, China, India and the United States, and with regional middle powers such as Australia and South Korea. These developments suggest that whereas New Order Indonesia only reluctantly supported initiatives that would allow deeper involvement of extra-regional powers in regional affairs, the new Indonesia is actively encouraging those powers to deepen their engagement with the region.[4]

On the broader global stage, Indonesia has made it clear that it wants a bigger say in world affairs. To play that role, President Susilo Bambang Yudhoyono has stated that the country must use its 'independence and activism to be a peace-maker, confidence-builder, problem-solver, bridge-builder' (Yudhoyono 2005). That aspiration has been expressed in several ways. Indonesia is projecting itself as a moderating voice in the

4 For example, Indonesia rejected Singapore's proposal in 1992 that ASEAN invite the major powers to accede to the Treaty of Amity and Cooperation, arguing that this would increase the threat of intervention by the big powers (Vatikiotis 1995: 226).

Muslim world, and as a bridge between the Muslim world and the West. The country has been an active promoter of regional and global interfaith dialogue. Over the last few years, Indonesia has also taken its membership of the G20 more seriously in order to register its voice on global issues such as climate change, energy, food security and global financial architecture. As the foreign minister, Marty Natalegawa, has put it, 'we see our membership of the G20 as offering a valuable opportunity for Indonesia to project its role onto the world stage as a responsible power' (Natalegawa 2009). Such aspirations and initiatives reflect Indonesia's intention to seek a higher international profile. In Ann-Marie Murphy's words, 'after a decade of focusing on domestic issues, Indonesia has returned to the global stage' (Murphy 2009: 65).

THE FACILITATING AND CONSTRAINING EFFECTS OF DOMESTIC POLITICS

The initiatives pursued by the Indonesian government reflect a number of changes in foreign policy that are too important to be ignored. A regained sense of normalcy and the achievement of democratic gains have instilled new confidence in Indonesia's leaders, convincing them that the time has come for the country to once again play an active and assertive international role. Translating that aspiration into the actual conduct of foreign relations, however, remains subject to both the facilitating and constraining effects of domestic political factors. The following discussion assesses the effects of domestic politics on Indonesia's attempts to raise its international profile on the regional and global stages within the context of four factors: the state of Indonesia's democracy, the role of Islam, the assertion of nationalism and the presence of persistent domestic weaknesses.

Democracy and foreign policy[5]

The introduction of democracy has transformed Indonesia from an authoritarian state into the only free country in Southeast Asia, as assessed by Freedom House (2012). As a significant element of domestic political change since 1998, democracy inevitably serves as an important context for the making and conduct of Indonesia's foreign policy. The most evident effect on foreign policy has been to increase public support – especially among academics, NGO activists and parliamen-

---

5 For a more detailed discussion of the role of democracy in Indonesia's foreign policy, see Sukma (2011b).

tarians – for the inclusion of democratic values and a democracy projection agenda in foreign policy. These domestic constituencies generally agree that the country's foreign policy should reflect democracy as a new national value. Dewi Fortuna Anwar, for example, has argued that 'Indonesia's identity as the third-largest democracy in the world needs to be constructed as the primary image of the country', adding that 'in order for foreign policy to reflect national identity and priorities, democracy and respect for human rights, which have become central to domestic politics, should become the values that serve as the basis for Indonesia's foreign policy' (Anwar 2000: 30).

Support and encouragement for a democracy projection agenda is most strongly expressed in views on the ASEAN Charter, the promotion and protection of human rights in ASEAN, and Myanmar. For example, an editorial in the *Jakarta Post* reviewing Indonesia's role in ASEAN asserts that 'we have constitutional obligations to convince our neighbors that adopting democracy is not an option but mandatory'.[6] On Myanmar, NGO activists are constantly urging the government to take a stronger line. The Asia Forum's Yuyun Wahyuningrum, for example, has been quoted as saying: 'Indonesia has to take the lead in pushing for reform in Myanmar We should not spoil the chance to bring about change in Myanmar' (Budianto 2010a). Parliamentarians such as Eva Sundari of the Indonesian Democratic Party of Struggle (PDI-P) have argued that the government should support the US proposal for a UN commission to investigate alleged crimes against humanity in Myanmar, claiming that 'all other options have been exhausted' (Budianto 2010b). Another parliamentarian, Budiman Sudjatmiko, went further, saying that 'Indonesia needs to encourage ASEAN to evaluate Myanmar's membership in ASEAN'.[7] These sentiments echo the view of former foreign minister Wirajuda that 'since a democracy works best in a democratic environment, we should also like to see the further growth of democratic values in our own neighbourhood' (Wirajuda 2005: 24).

However, democratization has also affected foreign policy in a number of more complicated ways. First, the internal context of policy making has changed. The highly centralized, authoritarian structure of foreign policy making has broken down, forcing it to operate within a new, more pluralistic and more competitive milieu. After four decades of authoritarian rule under both Sukarno and Suharto, Indonesia's post-authoritarian governments can no longer ignore the aspirations and views of the people when formulating and executing foreign policy. Within a democratic

---

6 'Editorial: conducting ASEAN', *Jakarta Post*, 27 October 2010.

7 'Suu Kyi siap temui junta' [Suu Kyi is ready to meet the junta], *Kompas*, 16 November 2010.

order, policy is no longer the exclusive domain of a few members of the policy-making elite. Rather, it has to be formulated within complex power structures where the government is no longer the dominant actor and the role of public opinion and non-government actors has become increasingly important. The large number of stakeholders in turn results in varying and sometimes competing aspirations, agendas and interests, making it difficult for the government to manage diverse expectations and cultivate broad-based public support. Consequently, policy often becomes subject to political compromises, while some form of opposition – especially from those whose policy aspirations have been thwarted – remains inevitable.

Second, the foreign policy agenda has at times been hindered by the volatile nature of Indonesian democracy. To succeed in its intention to project a democratic identity and promote democratic values within Southeast Asia, Indonesia must first persuade a domestic and international audience of its own democratic credentials. It is in this area that the policy of supporting democracy abroad has encountered its most serious challenge. Indeed, Indonesia's democratic credentials are constantly undermined by persistent problems of corruption, terrorism, communal tension, weak law enforcement and religious intolerance. Faced with these challenges, Indonesia's ability to support democracy abroad suffers from the lack of a demonstration effect, making it hard for it to influence the political course of neighbouring countries (Thannhauser 2006: 4).

This constraint is illustrated by the difficulty that Indonesia has encountered in persuading its regional partners of the need for a credible human rights body for ASEAN. Despite Indonesia's attempts to persuade other members that the body should have an explicit mandate to protect human rights, a frustrated Indonesian NGO activist concluded that in the end 'it was a case of one against nine' (Suryodiningrat 2009). Some ASEAN countries have repeatedly criticized the nature of Indonesian democracy, deriding the 'messy' situation the country has gotten itself into since it embraced democracy more than a decade ago. For the less democratic ASEAN states, Indonesia's brand of democracy is not an attractive alternative to their existing political systems. Malaysia's former prime minister Mahathir Mohamad, for example, has maintained that Indonesia's democracy is detrimental to the people's interests because it is 'too free'.[8] The lack of appeal of Indonesian-style democracy, stemming from a host of domestic problems, clearly poses a major challenge

8 'Mahathir: demokrasi Indonesia merugikan karena terlalu bebas' [Mahathir: Indonesia's democracy is detrimental because it is too free], *Voice of al-Islam*, 15 January 2010.

for foreign policy. As long as Indonesia is unable to resolve its domestic problems, the inclusion of democratic values in foreign policy will remain an exercise in the projection rather than promotion of democracy.

Third, the advent of democracy has not necessarily made it easier for Indonesia to forge closer relationships with other democracies. The country's open political system allows many different voices to affect the conduct of diplomacy and foreign relations, with the result that, for example, 'democratization has provided new opportunities for U.S. opponents to influence Indonesian foreign policy, making it costly for Indonesian leaders to cooperate with the United States' (Murphy 2009: 66). In a highly competitive political system, foreign policy is also occasionally used to advance competing political agendas. Illustrative is the case of Indonesia's vote in March 2007 in favour of sanctions against Iran under UN Security Council Resolution No. 1747. Outraged by what they viewed as a betrayal of another Islamic country, politicians summoned the president to appear before parliament to explain the vote – a constitutional right it had never exercised before. Many in the media interpreted this action as simply a jostling for positions in the lead-up to a cabinet reshuffle in the following month.[9] But as this incident shows, there is always a risk that a foreign policy decision can quickly develop into a divisive issue for domestic politics.

The inclusion of democratic values in foreign policy nevertheless serves an important domestic political purpose. In undertaking democracy projection initiatives abroad, the government expects to bolster its democratic credentials at home, as Indonesians see that their country is increasingly recognized by the international community as a 'regional role model'.[10] Equally important, the projection of democratic values beyond the country's borders functions as a reminder to the domestic audience that, as a promoter of democracy abroad, Indonesia needs to consolidate its own democratic credentials. In that context, some within the foreign ministry expect that the inclusion of democratic values in foreign policy may serve as a political deterrent, making it more difficult for anti-democracy forces to reverse the process of democratization.

The Islamic dimension

Before 1998 Islam was never a determining factor in Indonesia's foreign policy, because neither Sukarno nor Suharto would allow foreign policy

---

9 Editorial, *Media Indonesia*, 29 March 2007. In the event the president sent his foreign minister to explain the vote to parliament.

10 'Democracy in South-East Asia: the Indonesian surprise', *Economist*, 2 April 2009.

to be dictated by Islamic considerations.[11] Islam became a part of the national identity only after *reformasi*, when the rise of several Islamic-based political parties placed political Islam at the centre of national politics. The effect on foreign policy has been most evident in the attempts to shape Indonesia's image as a moderate Muslim country. Former foreign minister Wirajuda, for example, remarked that:

> ... the vast majority of Muslims in Indonesia are moderate. The fact that we have been living in the existing arrangements – where Islam is not a state religion – is proof in itself. The two biggest Muslim organizations, the Nahdlatul Ulama and the Muhammadiyah, reflect the face of true Islamic traditions of peace, tolerance and harmony. The few 'extremist' organizations – which have received much media coverage recently – have only a small number of followers and do not have the support of the majority of the population (Wirajuda 2002: 20).

By defining Islam as a force for peace, tolerance and harmony, the government has sought to articulate an image of Indonesia's brand of Islam as a moderating voice between the Muslim and non-Muslim worlds, and within the Muslim world itself.

In projecting such an image, the Ministry of Foreign Affairs has embarked on a series of initiatives to incorporate Islam into foreign policy. In April 2007, for example, Indonesia played a mediating role in conflict between the two factions of Islam in Iraq by hosting the Sunni–Shiite Conference in Bogor. Indonesia also offered to provide a venue for talks between Hamas and Fatah, hoping that dialogue between the two rival factions would lead to a more united Palestine. Over the last five years, Indonesia has been an active promoter of regional and global interfaith dialogue. It also participated in the UN peacekeeping mission in Lebanon, contributing a large contingent.

Nevertheless, when Islamic considerations enter into foreign policy, the government is forced to engage in a delicate balancing act: it is obliged by constiutional considerations not to base its foreign policy on religious considerations, but it also faces increasing demands from segments of the Muslim community that Indonesia identify itself more closely with the Arab Muslim world. Indonesian Muslims often view foreign policy through the prism of co-religionist sympathies, overlooking the broader aspects of policy making. They are therefore generally satisfied with the country's policy of supporting Palestine, interpreting it as a display of solidarity with fellow Muslims, even though the government itself says that the policy is based on opposition to all forms of colonialism. Equally,

---

11 For a discussion of the place of Islam in Indonesia's foreign policy, see Sukma (2003).

many were opposed to the government's support for Security Council Resolution No. 1747, viewing it as a betrayal of another Muslim country rather than – like the government – a means to address the problem of nuclear non-proliferation. Such sensitivities often force the government to find a course of action that balances the realities of international relations on the one hand against the emotional reactions of the domestic constituency on the other.

Moreover, the activities of radical Islamists pose a problem for the moderate Muslim identity and image Indonesia hopes to project across its boundaries. As Dewi Fortuna Anwar has remarked:

> Indonesia's efforts to promote a new face for Indonesia which is moderate, democratic and progressive will be meaningless and futile if the international news on Indonesia is dominated by stories about the burning of churches, attacks against groups accused of deviating from Islam, such as Ahmadiyyah, women being forced to wear the *jilbab* [headscarf] and other non-democratic and non-progressive acts. In such circumstances, Indonesia's public diplomacy would be received with a degree of cynicism by the international community, which would see those efforts as propaganda and disinformation by the Indonesian government (Anwar 2008: 11).

The influence of Islam on foreign policy should not be exaggerated, however. Despite the growing importance of Islam in Indonesian politics, it is important to note that foreign policy is not based exclusively on Islamic considerations and has never been expressed in terms of co-religionist solidarity. The problems of Philippine Muslims in Mindanao, Rohingyas in Burma, Patani Muslims in Thailand and Muslim Uighurs in Xinjiang, China, remain on the margins of Indonesia's foreign policy priorities, with policy on these issues continuing to be dictated by the principle of non-interference in the domestic affairs of other states. Local Muslim groups also pay scant attention to such problems. Moreover, it is not immediately clear how attractive Indonesia's brand of Islam is to its co-religionist partners in the Arab Muslim world. Williamson (2008) points out, for example, that 'Arab countries tend to see [Indonesia] as distant, different and lacking in religious authority' (see also van Bruinessen, this volume), while Suryodiningrat (2007) has observed that 'Indonesia has almost no influence to project in the Middle East'. In other words, the impact of political Islam on foreign policy, and the scope for Indonesia to exercise influence through its moderate brand of Islam, remains limited.

Nationalism in foreign policy

Since independence, nationalism has always been at the heart of Indonesian politics and foreign policy. In foreign policy, it is evident in the longstanding principle of a 'free and active' (*bebas–aktif*) approach to the conduct of foreign relations, which continues to guide foreign policy today. Unlike in the Sukarno and Suharto eras, however, when the expression of nationalism was controlled by the government in a way that suited the regime's interests, in the post-*reformasi* era the display of nationalist sentiment is no longer monopolized by the government. Nationalism is now injected into foreign policy by many actors, in many forms and for different purposes. In democratic Indonesia, the expression and populist appeal of nationalism have become increasingly attractive to competing political forces and politicians. This serves to limit the range of foreign policy choices and courses of action available to the government, making the process of policy making and the conduct of diplomacy more complex.

The sources of nationalism in foreign policy, however, remain unchanged. Policy making continues to reflect the confluence of internal insecurity, suspicion of the external environment, confidence in the domestic situation and a sense of regional entitlement. The most striking expression of nationalism in foreign policy is found in Indonesia's acute sensitivity to the question of territorial integrity and the preservation of the country's political and economic autonomy in the international arena. Segments of the elite and general public still harbour the view that the major powers – especially the United States – want to subjugate Indonesia by keeping the country economically weak and politically divided. This mentality of besiegement manifests in a degree of suspicion towards the agendas of external powers. For example, Indonesians were initially suspicious of the presence of American and other foreign troops in the tsunami-hit province of Aceh in December 2004, despite the obvious humanitarian intention. Indonesia also remains suspicious of Australia's policy towards Papua, although bilateral relations have improved significantly. Closer to home, the recurring emotional upsurge of nationalism over the issue of overlapping territorial claims with Malaysia continues to puzzle many of Indonesia's regional partners.

The expression of nationalist sentiment at times seems indicative of a growing anti-foreign attitude, especially among politicians. For instance, it has become increasingly difficult for the government to provide favourable terms for foreign investors without being accused of selling the country to foreigners (Adriansyah 2010). Similarly, Indonesia's parliamentary leaders recently backed a government plan to evaluate and 'discipline' foreign and foreign-funded NGOs operating in Indonesia, on the grounds that foreign assistance compromised the integrity and independence of NGOs and provided 'an opportunity for foreign parties to intervene [in Indonesia's internal affairs] and advance their own interests in Indonesia' (Sutrisno 2011). In April 2011 the speaker ordered a 'foreign NGO', the United Nations Development Programme, to vacate the office it had occupied for several years in the parliamentary building, despite the fact that the agency was there to support the House of Representatives (DPR). It has also become fashionable for politicians of all parties to say that the government's economic policies serve the interests of foreign capitalists rather than those of the Indonesian people.

While such overt expressions of nationalism may look like growing anti-foreign sentiment, they in fact reflect Indonesia's aspiration for national self-reliance, and the desire to deny any foreign country the opportunity to reap an unfair advantage at Indonesia's expense. That is, the manifestation of nationalism in foreign policy reflects Indonesia's broader desire to preserve national autonomy and defend itself against any form of external interference.

Nationalist feeling is also evident in the DPR's determination to ensure that the conduct of foreign policy should serve, first and foremost, the national interest. While there is nothing wrong with this, it has complicated the task of the government in conducting foreign relations. The clearest example is found in the DPR's refusal to ratify the Defence Cooperation Agreement signed by Indonesia and Singapore in April 2007. Widespread protests against the implementation of the ASEAN–China Free Trade Agreement in 2010 were also driven by the belief that Indonesia should not enter into any agreement that might undermine its own interests. While these cases certainly became a source of diplomatic embarrassment, they also suggest that the government can no longer assume that foreign relations is the business of a few at the Ministry of Foreign Affairs. The role of other actors and public opinion in foreign policy has become too important to ignore.

Domestic weaknesses

Indonesia's aspiration to become a global player is clearly expressed in its desire to play a role as a 'bridge builder' and 'problem solver' on the international stage. In concrete terms, according to Foreign Minister Marty Natalegawa, this requires Indonesia to be 'part of the solution to global problems' and 'a country keen to accentuate the overlapping of interests and concerns rather than competing interests' (Natalegawa 2010). Indonesia has taken a number of initiatives to articulate its global aspirations. Within the G20, for example, it has sought to bridge the differences between the developing and advanced economies, and has been keen to use its membership to contribute to the search for solutions to global problems. Over the last few years, Indonesia has positioned itself to play an active role globally in addressing the problem of climate change. By invoking its status as the largest moderate Muslim-majority country, it has also signalled its desire to serve as a bridge between the Muslim world and the West.

Indonesia's ability to translate its global aspirations into the actual conduct of foreign policy and effect changes on the global stage, however, has been constrained by persistent domestic weaknesses. Indonesia itself is aware that it is not yet in a position to play a global role in a conventional sense. For one thing, it does not have the economic, political or diplomatic clout to contribute to the global public good in a comprehensive manner. Domestically the country still faces a host of challenges, especially on the economic front. Despite recent improvements, the pace of economic recovery and growth remains precarious. Democracy continues to be a work in progress, with the challenges including defective democratic institutions, terrorism, communal violence, religious intolerance, corruption and weak law enforcement. Indonesia also has one of the weakest military capabilities in the region.

Unless it can resolve its domestic problems, Indonesia's efforts to raise its international profile will soon lose their appeal, both at home and abroad. At present, the record suggests that the country's influence in the global arena remains marginal. Indonesia still has a long way to go before it can realize its full potential to matter significantly in the global arena.

A STRATEGIC REPOSITIONING WITHIN EAST ASIA?

Domestic politics has been both a facilitating and constraining factor in Indonesian foreign policy. While providing new opportunities for the country to once again assert a leadership role in ASEAN, it has also complicated Indonesia's efforts to raise its international profile. While there are obvious reasons for Indonesia to continue to play an active role in ASEAN, the government believes it should not limit its foreign policy ambitions to ASEAN. However, the desire to become a true global player beyond the association is constrained by the lack of domestic capacity for such a role, exacerbated by a host of domestic problems. The most realistic foreign policy option in this situation is to craft a middle way and find a new foreign policy locus that can link Indonesia's unwavering attachment and commitment to ASEAN on the one hand with its desire to play a greater global role on the other. Consolidating its place in the wider East Asian region naturally provides Indonesia with such a locus.

Understanding that the growing interconnectedness of Southeast and Northeast Asia required it to make East Asia the new theatre (*mandala*) for its foreign policy, the government has begun to pay more attention to the region over the last few years. This strategic repositioning has been evident in four main areas. First, Indonesia has played an active role in shaping the emerging regional architecture, working to ensure ASEAN's centrality while encouraging greater participation by other major and regional powers in regional processes. For instance, as discussed above, it supported the inclusion of India, Australia and New Zealand in the initial East Asia Summit, and later suggested inviting the United States and Russia to join. Second, Indonesia has made a conscious effort to balance its emphasis on multilateralism by expanding and deepening its strategic bilateral relationships with major powers such as the United States, China, Japan and India, and regional middle powers such as Australia and South Korea. Third, Indonesia has promised to strengthen ASEAN's links with the G20 by articulating the organization's interests at the forum and by securing a permanent invitation for the rotating ASEAN chair to be present at G20 meetings. Finally, as the chair of ASEAN in 2011, Indonesia has taken steps to lay the foundation for the grouping to play a bigger role in the global community of nations.

Indonesia's strategic repositioning in East Asia should allow it to maintain its commitment to ASEAN while increasing its selective participation in the global arena. The new foreign policy activism, and the desire to play a meaningful and effective role on the global stage, will have a greater chance of success if it is pursued by making East Asia the *mandala* of the country's foreign policy aspirations. Any ambition beyond that will have to wait until Indonesia manages to eradicate the constraining factors in its domestic politics.

REFERENCES

Adriansyah, Yasmi (2010) 'Economic nationalism and policy', *Jakarta Post*, 12 November.

Anwar, Dewi Fortuna (2000) *Menggagas Politik Luar Negeri Indonesia Baru* [A Proposal on the Foreign Policy of a New Indonesia], LIPI, Jakarta.

Anwar, Dewi Fortuna (2008) 'Peran diplomasi publik dalam kebijakan luar Negeri Republik Indonesia' [The role of public diplomacy in Indonesia's foreign policy], paper presented at the Syarif Hidayatullah State Islamic University, Jakarta, 5 September.

Anwar, Dewi Fortuna (2009) 'A journey of change: Indonesia's foreign policy', *Global Asia* 4(3), available at http://www.globalasia.org/V4N3_Fall_2009/Dewi_Fortuna_Anwar.html.

Budianto, Lilian (2010a) 'RI to focus on Myanmar elections at summit', *Jakarta Post*, 6 April.

Budianto, Lilian (2010b) 'UN Myanmar probe gains RI support', *Jakarta Post*, 20 August.

Freedom House (2012) *Freedom in the World 2012*, available at http://freedomhouse.org.

Heath, Michael (1987) *Indonesian Foreign Policy: Towards a More Assertive Style*, Griffith University, Nathan.

Leifer, Michael (1983) *Indonesia's Foreign Policy*, George Allen & Unwin, London.

MacIntyre, Andrew and Douglas Ramage (2008) *Seeing Indonesia as a Normal Country: Implications for Australia*, Australian Strategic Policy Institute, Canberra, May.

Murphy, Ann-Marie (2009) 'Indonesia returns to the international stage: good news for the United States', *Orbis* 53(1): 65–79.

Natalegawa, Marty M. (2009) 'Remarks by H.E. Dr. Marty Natalegawa, Foreign Minister of the Republic of Indonesia on the occasion of the 7th general conference of the Council for Security Cooperation in the Asia Pacific, 16 October 2009', Jakarta, available at http://www.cscap.org/index.php?page=general-conference-reports.

Natalegawa, Marty M. (2010) 'Indonesia and the world 2010', abridged version of the minister's annual policy statement on 8 January 2010, available at http://embassyofIndonesia.it/opinion-foreign-minister-marty-m-natalegawa-on-Indonesia-and-the-world-2010/.

Sukarnoputri, Megawati (2001) 'State address by H.E. Excellency the President of the Republic of Indonesia Megawati Soekarnoputri before the House of People's Representatives on the occasion of the 56th Independence Day 16 August 2001', Jakarta.

Sukma, Rizal (1995) 'The evolution of Indonesia's foreign policy: an Indonesian view', *Asian Survey* 35(3): 304–15.

Sukma, Rizal (2003) *Islam in Indonesian Foreign Policy*, Routledge, London.

Sukma, Rizal (2011a) 'Soft power and public diplomacy: the case of Indonesia', in S.J. Lee and J. Melissen (eds) *Public Diplomacy and Soft Power in East Asia*, Palgrave Macmillan, New York.

Sukma, Rizal (2011b) 'Indonesia finds a new voice', *Journal of Democracy* 22(4): 110–23.

Suryodiningrat, Meidyatama (2007) 'Soft power needs hard thinking to get results', *Jakarta Post*, 21 March.

Suryodiningrat, Meidyatama (2009) 'ASEAN 9, human rights 1', *Jakarta Post*, 24 July.

Sutrisno, Elvan Dany (2011) 'Pimpinan DPR minta Mendagri tertibkan LSM asing' [DPR leaders ask Minister of Home Affairs to discipline foreign NGOs], *detik.com*, 9 September.

Thannhauser, Sara E. (2006) 'Southeast Asia's democratic challenge: strength (and weakness) in diversity', Democracy Series Working Paper III, Georgetown University, Washington DC, July.

Vatikiotis, Michael (1993) 'Indonesia's foreign policy in the 1990s', *Contemporary Southeast Asia* 14(4): 352–67.

Vatikiotis, Michael (1995) 'A giant treads carefully: Indonesia's foreign policy in the 1990s', in R.S. Ross (ed.) *East Asia in Transition: Toward a New Regional Order*, M.E. Sharp, New York.

Williamson, Lucy (2008) 'Indonesia: Muslim bridge-builder?', *BBC News*, 28 February, available at http://news.bbc.co.uk/go/pr/fr/-/2/hi/asia-pacific/7269017.stm.

Wirajuda, N. Hassan (2002) 'The democratic response', *Brown Journal of World Affairs* 9(1): 15–21.

Wirajuda, N. Hassan (2005) 'Indonesian foreign policy: strategy and objectives', *DUTA: Indonesia and the World*, Indonesian Council on World Affairs, August.

Yudhoyono, Susilo Bambang (2005) 'Indonesia and the world', keynote address to the Indonesian Council on World Affairs (ICWA), Jakarta, 19 May.

6 CAN INDONESIA LEAD ON CLIMATE CHANGE?

Frank Jotzo

Indonesia's environment matters not only to the quality of life of its people, but also to its neighbours and the world. Indonesia is among the world's largest emitters of carbon dioxide, but it has good opportunities to reduce those emissions to the benefit of future generations everywhere. Better management of the environment could also have more tangible benefits, such as saving Indonesia's neighbours from haze pollution, reducing flooding, increasing agricultural productivity and protecting Indonesia's globally important reservoirs of biological diversity.

There is a fundamental tension between the environment and development in Indonesia (Resosudarmo and Jotzo 2009). The country is exceptionally well endowed with natural resources, the exploitation of which accounts for a large share of economic activity. Conversion of natural forests to oil palm plantations brings jobs and infrastructure to backward areas. It also creates large profits for industry as well as substantial tax revenues. So does mining for minerals and coal, and the extraction of oil and gas. Meanwhile, growth in service and manufacturing industries together with rising household incomes mean ever-increasing demand for electricity and other forms of energy.

Managing the environmental effects of economic development is a challenge for all countries. Sustainability entered mainstream global strategic thinking with the 1992 Rio Earth Summit and today finds its expression in the ambition for 'green growth'. Climate change is the emblematic issue in the quest for green growth, as rapid global economic growth using the conventional, greenhouse gas-intensive model could result in dangerous changes to the world's climate. The issue is not to slow development and economic growth but to achieve such growth in a manner that puts less stress on the environment.

Indonesia could play an important role in the global effort to put economies on a more environmentally sustainable footing. On climate change in particular, Indonesia might be able to take a leadership role among developing countries, because of its potential to change its trajectory in deforestation and energy supply, and because of its strategic position as a large, fast-growing developing country that tends to look for a middle way in international affairs.

Indonesia has been a positive influence in international climate change negotiations, reflecting its desire to be a responsible and constructive player on the global stage. President Susilo Bambang Yudhoyono made a significant pledge to reign in Indonesia's greenhouse gas emissions, choosing a G20 summit as the venue for his announcement.

But pledges do not equal action. In Indonesia as in other democracies, substantive reform tends to meet resistance from entrenched interests. The owners of resources tend to oppose new laws that would force them to operate with more regard to the environment, even if it serves the overall national interest. As Chatib Basri points out in Chapter 3 of this volume, in the context of market reform, powerful vested interests can hold sway over the highest levels of politics. Local communities that rely on forest conversion generally see little benefit in contributing to a national or global ambition to reduce carbon emissions. Line ministries in the resource sectors tend to look after their industrial clients, and are often looked after by those industries in turn.

This chapter is organized as follows. The next section discusses international climate change policy, and Indonesia's role in it. This is followed by an examination of Indonesia's greenhouse gas emissions profile and its emission reduction target. The chapter then looks at ways to meet that target before discussing political and institutional constraints.

INDONESIA'S ROLE IN INTERNATIONAL CLIMATE CHANGE POLICY

Climate change as a global strategic and policy issue

Climate change has been a top-level item on the agendas of international forums and national governments, following a number of influential reports that pointed out its dangers and charted ways of addressing the challenge. Among the most influential were the 2007 report by the Intergovernmental Panel on Climate Change (IPCC 2007) and a review of the economics of climate change commissioned by the British government and led by Lord Nicholas Stern, a prominent economist who had formerly worked for the World Bank (Stern et al. 2006).

The IPCC report summarized the increasingly firm insights from climate change science and helped establish the case for urgent government action to reduce greenhouse gas emissions. These findings were subsequently popularized by former US vice-president Al Gore by way of a documentary movie, *An Inconvenient Truth,* which further elevated the issue in public debate, in Indonesia as elsewhere.

Stern, meanwhile, made a powerful argument that addressing climate change was primarily a matter of good economics. He argued that the cost of cutting emissions now was much lower than the likely adverse economic impacts later on, and presented analysis on how countries could change their greenhouse gas trajectories without sacrificing much economic growth.

This helped elevate the issue in the consideration of many governments, as it was no longer considered 'just' an environmental issue. Climate change was a key subject of discussion among finance ministers of the G20 group of nations, especially during 2008 and 2009. It was the topic of the *Human Development Report 2007/2008* (Watkins 2007) and the *World Development Report 2010* (World Bank 2010), and the subject of comprehensive strategy reviews by national governments (see, for example, Garnaut 2008).

Responding to climate change is increasingly seen not just as an issue that requires cooperative action to limit the risk of future damage, but also as an opportunity for strategic leadership. Attaining leadership in clean energy technologies has been spelled out as a strategic goal by both China and the United States.

Indonesia has no prospect of technological leadership. Moreover, international action to cut greenhouse gas emissions poses a strategic challenge for its exports of fossil fuels, in particular coal, the most carbon-intensive fuel. Indonesia is now the largest exporter globally of coal for electricity production, and the second-largest coal exporter overall (just behind Australia) after annual increases of more than 10 per cent over the last five years (EIA 2012; see also Figure 6.1 below). Demand for such thermal coal is strong in the short term, but depending on the extent of global action to mitigate climate change, it may tail off in the future (IEA 2011). This would have serious implications for Indonesia's export revenues. However, Indonesia has a strong interest in fostering global action in order to minimize adverse impacts from future climate change.

International climate change policy and Indonesia's interests

The scale of effective global action to mitigate climate change would be enormous. The ambition enshrined in the 1992 United Nations Framework Convention on Climate Change, ratified by practically all countries, is to avoid dangerous climate change. The mainstream scientific view is that this necessitates keeping the rise in global average temperatures to less than 2 degrees above the pre-industrial average (that is, before the time that fossil fuels started to be burned on an industrial scale). It would require a drastic turnaround in global emission trajectories to achieve sizeable annual reductions in the next decade (Steffen 2011) and to reduce the annual level of emissions to perhaps half their current level by 2050.

This is a massive challenge in the face of rapid economic growth in developing countries and the fast expansion of energy use it brings with it (Garnaut et al. 2008). Current policy settings will fail to achieve this goal. However, following the 2009 UN climate conference in Copenhagen, most nations have now made pledges to constrain or cut their emissions (Jotzo 2010; McKibbin, Morris and Wilcoxen 2011). Negotiations to make these pledges binding have been slow, but many countries are preparing or implementing policies to help put their pledges into action – including Indonesia, as examined further below.

Indonesia has a strong self-interest in fostering an effective global response to climate change. The country is highly vulnerable to the effects of climate change: sea-level rise threatens to inundate its coastal cities and agricultural areas; intensification of rainfall patterns may cause more frequent flooding as well as more pronounced periods of low rainfall; and higher temperatures and the spread of mosquito-borne diseases would have adverse effects on human health (Jotzo et al. 2009; Yusuf and Francisco 2009). It is also in Indonesia's interest to develop effective coping (adaptation) mechanisms, and for the international community to assist Indonesia where appropriate, for example through support for research and development, exchange of experiences and funding for infrastructure.

Indonesia has substantial opportunities to cut its emissions and become one of the few developing countries that manages to reduce its absolute level of emissions in the short to medium term. As laid out in more detail below, important savings in emissions could be achieved at little or no economic cost, or could even carry a net benefit quite apart from their effect on greenhouse gas emissions. Better environmental management and improved policy and regulatory settings are the key to such savings. Other options to cut emissions would have economic costs because they would involve more costly production processes or mean foregoing other economic opportunities. In many cases implementation would require compensation to stakeholders or interest groups; in most it would require sound institutional foundations.

International financing

International financing for climate change mitigation may help make many of these emission reduction options economically feasible and politically more attractive. A limited amount of project-based financing already exists under the Kyoto Protocol's Clean Development Mechanism, where carbon credits are created from projects such as retrofitting cement plants, capturing gases from landfills and producing electricity from hydropower, geothermal plants or palm oil residue. The credits are bought by investors in Europe and Japan to help them fulfil their emission reduction obligations under the Kyoto Protocol.

Climate change financing is becoming increasingly available from multilateral agencies. The Clean Technology Fund administered by the World Bank and Asian Development Bank, for example, has provided $400 million in co-financing for renewable energy and energy efficiency in Indonesia. The fund aims to mobilize an additional $2.7 billion from other sources (ADB 2010).

Looking ahead, the hope and expectation is that large-scale climate change financing will become available to support reductions in deforestation, improvements in land management and investments in clean energy alternatives. Over time, market-based financing may gain in importance as developed countries make investments in developing countries to help meet their own climate change commitments.

Under the banner of reducing emissions from deforestation and forest degradation (REDD), there have been many years of UN negotiations and preparations by civil society and business groups to establish such financing mechanisms. Alongside Brazil, Indonesia could potentially become the largest supplier of REDD credits.

Norway has promised to provide up to $1 billion to Indonesia to improve forest management, and as a reward for curbing deforestation (Governments of Norway and Indonesia 2010; Jupesta et al. 2011; Ardiansyah 2012). This is the single largest initiative to date aimed at driving REDD forward in Indonesia. By all indications it has been successful at least in catching the attention of policy makers and instigating some changes to land-use policy, as discussed further below.

Substantial progress has been made on the technical aspects of creating international REDD mechanisms, but the problem now lies in limited demand for such credits from developed countries. At present no developed country has domestic policies in place that would create demand for the credits. This may change, depending in part on whether the implementation of REDD schemes inspires sufficient trust among developed countries that the credits do in fact represent true reductions in emissions.

Indonesia's positioning in the climate negotiations

Indonesia has long played a progressive role in international climate policy. In climate negotiations as in other international forums, it is generally seen as a moderate voice, contributing constructively to technical work, helping to build consensus among developing countries and making efforts to bridge the gap between developing and developed countries. Indonesia was the first OPEC country to ratify the Kyoto Protocol (in 2004)[1] and has made various joint submissions with other countries, for example Australia.

But Indonesia has taken charge of the agenda only on rare occasions. One such occasion was the 2007 UN climate conference in Bali, as highlighted by Garnaut in Chapter 2 of this volume. As host and president of the conference, Indonesia had a significant hand in engineering the official start of a new process for international negotiations. The Bali Roadmap sketched out the agenda towards the infamous 2009 Copenhagen conference where world leaders met to discuss climate change but no real agreement could be struck. The principles agreed in Bali still reverberate in the ongoing climate negotiations.

Another notable instance was President Yudhoyono's announcement in 2009 that Indonesia would adopt a unilateral emissions target of potentially significant stringency (Yudhoyono 2009). The announcement was made at a meeting of G20 leaders in the United States, and it was made earlier than corresponding pledges by many other major developing countries. It was thus calibrated for maximum international visibility (Aspinall 2010).

Despite Indonesia's central position in shaping the Bali Roadmap and its highly visible voluntary national pledge, Indonesia did not end up being one of the main protagonists at the Copenhagen conference. Among the developing countries, this role fell to the so-called BASIC group, the name given to the alliance of Brazil, South Africa, India and China in the climate negotiations. The BASIC group has continued to set the agenda on many aspects of the global climate change regime until the time of writing in early 2012, while Indonesia's role has been much less pronounced. Indonesia would be a logical member of this group given its size and global importance for addressing climate change – it is far larger in population and greenhouse gas emissions than South Africa.

Why did Indonesia not become part of the BASIC group? Does the well-worn cliché of Indonesia 'punching below its weight' apply? Part of the answer may lie in the fact that Indonesia's weight in international climate negotiations is less than its size might suggest. Each of the four

1 Indonesia withdrew from OPEC in 2008 after becoming a net importer of oil.

BASIC member states has much greater institutional capacity on climate change and each has a much longer history of strong engagement in the climate negotiations. In South Africa's case, an additional factor is that the country tends to be seen as a de facto representative of African interests as a whole, with few other African nations having the capacity to represent their interests by themselves. So Indonesia may simply not have been viewed as a rightful member of the club.

On the other hand, in early 2010 there were reports that Indonesia had received informal offers to join BASIC (Simamor and Nurhayati 2010). If this is so, then strategic considerations may have played a role in its decision not to become a member. Indonesia has expressed its desire to make 'a million friends and zero enemies' (see page 61). Joining BASIC would put it in the camp of countries that have pursued a much more hard-line approach to the international negotiations than Indonesia has done. It would run counter to Indonesia's role as a moderate and conciliatory influence, and might be seen to jeopardize its position of soft influence not just in climate change but in other areas of international affairs. Some developed countries might view a decision to join as an affront, even if Indonesia sought to become a moderating force within the group.

A Southeast Asian leadership role?

Indonesia is of course free to take a leadership role on its own, or in conjunction with other countries. A promising bilateral alliance would seem to be with Brazil. Both countries are dominant in their respective regions of the world, and significant in global economic terms. Both are rich in resources and in forested land that is being converted to plantations and agriculture. Together they would account for the vast majority of global opportunities to cut forest-related emissions. If they could agree on a common approach, this would give the bilateral partnership substantial leverage in negotiations with developed countries.

The strongest potential for Indonesian leadership, however, may be in the Southeast Asian region – in line with the government's stated foreign policy objective 'to demonstrate leadership in ASEAN cooperation' (Ministry of Foreign Affairs 2012). Indonesia is the dominant country in Southeast Asia, not just in terms of population but also in terms of greenhouse gas emissions. Its physical, social and economic diversity means that most climate change issues of importance to other Southeast Asian countries are also, in one form or another, domestic issues of importance to Indonesia. Hence, it should have little trouble speaking for the region as a whole.

On the face of it, these factors would suggest a natural leadership role for Indonesia in Southeast Asia on climate change – not necessarily by way of a formal group within the international negotiations, but possibly by way of an informal role as champion of Southeast Asian interests in the climate negotiations. Against this vision of regional leadership stands the fact that several Southeast Asian countries – especially the Philippines and Thailand – have been playing significant roles of their own in the international climate negotiations. Papua New Guinea has made its mark in negotiations on forestry issues and Singapore is also actively pursuing its own agenda. It therefore appears unlikely in the near term that Indonesia would assume a unilateral leadership position in the UN negotiations. Similarly, there appears to be little prospect in the short term that Southeast Asia would come to a common negotiating position – with Indonesia playing a key role in defining it – in light of the experience within the Association of Southeast Asian Nations (ASEAN) (see Chapter 5 by Sukma).

Nevertheless, Indonesia may find itself in a natural leadership role in the region with regard to an Asia–Pacific carbon-trading scheme. Such a scheme might comprise a number of Southeast and East Asian developing countries as sellers of emission reductions, and countries such as Australia, South Korea and Japan, and North American states such as California, as buyers. As the largest potential destination for investment to cut emissions, Indonesia would have a natural role in establishing such a regional trading scheme, and in defining the rules.

Domestic prerequisites

Any international leadership role must be built on the foundation of domestic action on climate change; without effective implementation at home, external leadership ambitions remain hollow. This means creating the necessary institutions, putting in place suitable policy frameworks and ensuring thorough and sustained implementation. It also means encroaching on entrenched economic interests and cutting across established patterns of political power in managing the economy, both at the central and regional government levels. As discussed below, this will require significant effort, including political leadership and well-managed transitional arrangements. Without such domestic policy resolve, Indonesia's international leadership ambitions would likely falter.

INDONESIA'S EMISSIONS PROFILE AND EMISSIONS TARGET

Resources and environment

Agriculture and mining play an important role in the Indonesian economy. Together they account for around a quarter of GDP – slightly more

Figure 6.1 *Value of Indonesia's exports of wood and pulp, palm oil and coal, 1999–2010 ($ billion, current)*

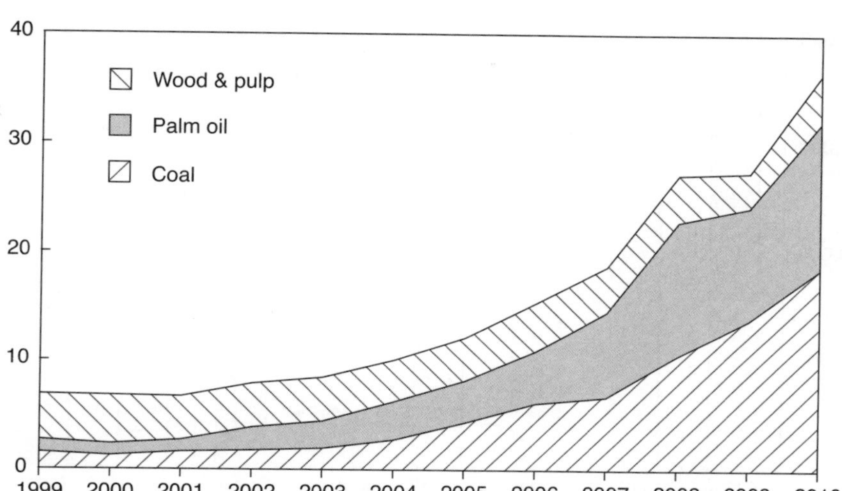

Source: CEIC Asia database.

than the entire manufacturing sector – and they make up roughly half the value of the nation's exports (Bank Indonesia 2012).

Within mining, fossil fuels (coal, oil and gas) make the dominant contribution to the economy, and to exports. Coal production and exports have increased dramatically in recent years (Figure 6.1) at the same time as oil production has shrunk and Indonesia has become a net importer of oil. Coal has a larger environmental impact than other fuels because it is the most carbon-intensive form of energy. In most cases the mining activities also have greater local impacts than either oil and gas extraction or renewable energies.

Within agriculture, plantations are playing a sharply increasing role in production and exports, with palm oil production a particularly lucrative business due to high global demand and prices. The strong demand for palm oil has been driving large-scale conversion of forests to plantations, which in turn releases large amounts of carbon dioxide.

Indonesia's greenhouse gas emissions in context

Indonesia is one of the world's most populous nations, and also one of the largest emitters of human-induced greenhouse gases. According to the most recent comparable estimates, Indonesia was the world's fifth-

Figure 6.2 Annual greenhouse gas emissions of the largest emitting countries, 2005 (million tonnes CO_2 equivalent)

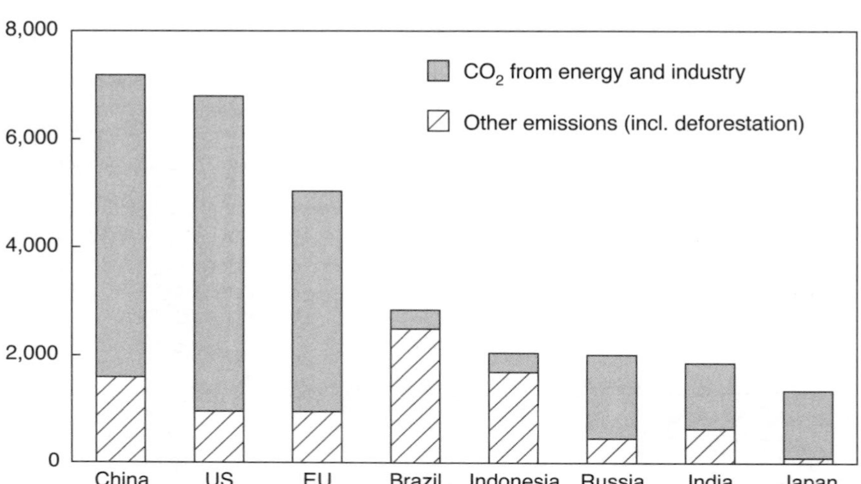

Source: World Resources Institute, Climate Analysis Indicators Tool (CAIT), version 8, available at http://cait.wri.org/.

largest emitter of greenhouse gases in 2005 (Figure 6.2), or the fourth largest if considering the European Union as individual countries. In an earlier, widely reported study (PEACE 2007), Indonesia was described as the world's third-largest emitter. This was because the estimates were for 2000, a year in which Indonesia's land-based emissions were estimated to exceed those of Brazil.

The largest share of Indonesia's greenhouse gas emissions comprises carbon dioxide from the land sector. This is mostly due to deforestation, that is, the conversion of forests to make way for agricultural land or simply the removal of trees without replanting. Indonesia had one of the world's highest rates of deforestation during the 1990s, with forests in Kalimantan and Sumatra disappearing particularly rapidly. The rate has since decelerated, but is still high globally (Table 6.1). It should be noted, though, that deforestation data are notoriously uncertain. Different data sets and estimation methodologies can yield very different estimates.

Peatlands also make a major contribution to Indonesia's land-based carbon dioxide emissions. Peatlands are naturally covered by water but are often drained to make the land available for agriculture. The ground is then susceptible to burning, which can release enormous quantities of carbon dioxide into the atmosphere. This is particularly prone to happen during La Niña years when the rains arrive late. Large and protracted

Table 6.1 Deforestation in Indonesia, Malaysia, Brazil and the world, 1990–2010

	1990–2000	2000–2005	2005–2010
Rate of reduction (% p.a.)			
Indonesia	1.6	0.3	0.7
Malaysia	0.4	0.6	0.4
Brazil	0.5	0.6	0.4
World	0.2	0.1	0.1
Absolute reduction (million hectares p.a.)			
Indonesia	1,914	310	685
Malaysia	79	140	87
Brazil	2,890	3,090	2,194
World	8,323	4,841	5,580

Source: FAO (2010).

peat fires occurred during 1997–98, when Indonesia may temporarily have been the world's largest carbon dioxide emitter (Page et al. 2002), and during several years in the early 2000s.

The combustion of coal, oil and gas is another important part of Indonesia's emissions profile (Figure 6.3). Oil is used predominantly for transport, while coal and gas are used for electricity generation and in industrial applications. Over the period 2000–2005, emissions from energy use accounted for only an estimated one-fifth of Indonesia's total emissions, a much lower share than in most other countries, reflecting the relative importance of land-based emissions. However, this source of emissions has been growing very fast, at around 6 per cent per year. That growth rate implies a doubling of levels every 12 years.

Unless measures are taken to dampen demand and shift to lower-carbon energy sources, fossil fuel use and the resulting carbon dioxide emissions are likely to continue to grow at similar rates in the years and decades to come (Garnaut et al. 2008). That is because, at Indonesia's stage of development, energy use tends to rise at roughly the same rate as overall economic growth. At current prices, the cheapest ways of providing the required energy in most locations is to use coal to produce power, and petrol, diesel or gas for transport. As discussed below, there are alternatives, but these are generally more expensive or face other hurdles.

Other sources of greenhouse gas emissions include methane from agriculture, particularly the cultivation of paddy rice, and waste decom-

Figure 6.3 Indonesia's greenhouse gas emissions by source, 2000–2005, and 2020 target (million tonnes CO_2 equivalent)

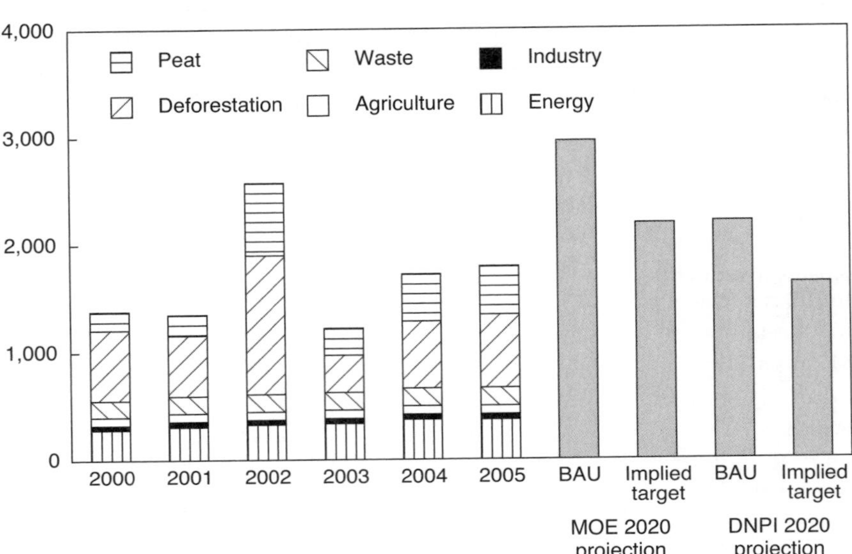

Note: BAU = business as usual; MOE = Ministry of Environment; DNPI = Dewan Nasional Perubahan Iklim (National Climate Change Council). Deforestation includes emissions from land use, land-use change and forestry. The 2020 targets are for 26 per cent below business as usual.

Source: Ministry of Environment (2010); DNPI (2011); author's calculations for target levels.

position in landfills. Various industrial processes, such as chemical and cement production, also make a contribution. Emissions from these sources tend to grow more slowly than energy emissions, and in some cases may even decline of their own accord as cleaner technologies and production practices become the norm.

Taken together, these trends imply that Indonesia's emissions profile is likely to change fundamentally over time, with the current dominance of deforestation emissions being replaced by emissions from an ever-growing, fossil fuel-intensive energy sector. Longer-term efforts to reign in emissions growth therefore need to focus not just on forests, but also on energy supply.

Indonesia's 2020 emissions target

In the lead-up to the UN climate conference in Copenhagen at the end of 2009, all major countries made pledges to cut emissions or to reign in emissions growth. Indonesia's target, like the pledges of several other developing countries, was framed relative to the level of business-as-usual emissions – that is, the level of emissions that would be reached if no effort was made to check them. Indonesia pledged a reduction of 26 per cent below the baseline at 2020, and up to 41 per cent with international assistance (Yudhoyono 2009).

This means that annual emissions would need to be lowered by almost three percentage points each year from what they would otherwise have been. This is a significant effort in absolute terms and broadly comparable to the deviations from business as usual that are explicit or implicit in the pledges of other countries, including the major developed countries, newly industrialized countries such as South Korea and Mexico, and major developing countries such as China, Brazil and South Africa (Jotzo 2010; McKibbin, Morris and Wilcoxen 2011).

To be operational, however, the target needs a baseline, that is, a counterfactual estimate of the emissions trajectory into the future that would prevail without climate policy action (under business as usual). If, for example, the baseline were for emission levels to stay constant over time, then a 26 per cent reduction below the baseline would be a 26 per cent reduction below current emission levels. But if it involved a doubling of emissions, then a 26 per cent reduction from the counterfactual would amount to a 48 per cent increase over current levels.

The baseline is subject to assumptions and judgment. Energy use will keep growing fast, and with it carbon dioxide emissions. Yet the trajectory for emissions from deforestation and the loss of peatlands, which are thought to account for as much as two-thirds of Indonesia's total emissions in an average year, is unclear. Will they stay roughly at the same annual level or will they fall as forest cover declines and fire management practices improve? Or might they even increase as rising resource prices make forest conversion ever more profitable?

Two reports released in 2010 by two different government agencies – the Ministry of Environment and the National Climate Change Council (DNPI) – project business-as-usual emissions growth between 2005 and 2020 to be 65 per cent (Ministry of Environment 2010) and 23 per cent (DNPI 2011). The '26 per cent below business as usual' target then translates either to a roughly one-quarter increase, or a slight decrease, relative to 2005. This is a very large difference in terms of the actual effect on emission levels (Figure 6.3).

The national emissions baseline that will be used to underpin the target therefore defines the ambition of Indonesia's target, and matters greatly for the international credibility of the climate commitment. Hence the issue will need to be revisited by the government. The best way to do this would be to put forward a quantitative baseline for emissions that is based on sound analysis and open to outside scrutiny. It needs to be well balanced to ensure its assumptions provide international credibility without creating a target that is very costly to achieve. The baseline would then need to be coupled with sound systems to monitor actual emissions.

Alternatively, the emission savings from individual programs and policy interventions could be estimated. However, this would not give a picture of the overall effect of those policies. Also, the process might be open to manipulation: it would be easy to exaggerate the savings from specific interventions; to count measures that would have been implemented anyway for reasons unrelated to climate change; and to leave out of the accounting any policy interventions that increased rather than decreased emissions.

OPTIONS AND MECHANISMS TO CUT EMISSIONS

How and where could the emission reductions be achieved? Most of the near-term potential is in the forestry and land-use sector, where emission levels are high and where successful policy interventions could lead to relatively fast reductions. To enable longer-term cuts, however, Indonesia would need to support reforms in the energy sector. In neither case would implementation be easy, despite the substantial side benefits.

Curbing deforestation and improving land management

Reducing deforestation and improving land management offer the most immediate and promising opportunities for Indonesia to cut its greenhouse gas emissions. When trees are removed and soils disturbed, carbon dioxide is released. Protecting forests, developing plantations on degraded rather than prime forest land, using gentler methods of logging in production forests and planting new forests could all make a big difference to emissions.

The greatest scope for fast improvement, however, is in peatlands. In parts of the islands of Sumatra and Kalimantan in particular, the top layer of soil consists of peat. It releases vast amounts of carbon dioxide when it burns, or when it decomposes after coming into contact with air. Many peat swamps have been drained to allow conversion to agricultural land, and fires occur frequently in these regions, sometimes lasting for months. Stopping the conversion of peat swamps, and reflooding previously drained peatlands, could prevent very large amounts of greenhouse gas emissions.

In Singapore and Malaysia as well as Indonesia, the smoke from forest and peat fires has adversely affected people's health and on occasion disrupted air transport. Better fire management and prevention of peat fires would therefore have benefits not only for global climate change mitigation, but also for Indonesia's neighbours and some parts of Indonesia (Tacconi, Jotzo and Grafton 2008).

Many of the measures outlined above could be implemented at relatively low cost compared with the cost of avoiding greenhouse gas emissions in other sectors of the economy. For example, a study commissioned by the National Climate Change Council has estimated that emissions of up to 500 million tonnes of carbon dioxide per year could be avoided at a cost of under $1 per tonne through fire prevention and better water management in peatlands alone (DNPI 2011).[2] This would amount to almost one-sixth of the estimated national total in 2030 under the study's business-as-usual scenario. The per unit cost is many times lower than the prices already being paid by European emitters for emission offsets. According to the estimates, a further 800 million tonnes of carbon dioxide emissions per year could be avoided at low cost through improved forest management and reforestation. In contrast, avoiding deforestation emissions by not allowing conversion of forests to oil palm or pulp wood plantations would carry a much higher cost because of the foregone profit opportunities.

But in practice making these kinds of changes is difficult. In many cases the reforms would threaten the profits of established business interests; in others they would run counter to local economic interests as perceived by local elites or local people. Often, local players simply ignore national laws and regulations – a decree issued in Jakarta may not have much effect at the forest frontier.

To be effective, schemes to cut emissions need to overcome entrenched interests in the bureaucracy where it is an open secret that officials may benefit financially from land conversion activities; to buy out or otherwise bring on board established business interests; and to serve local interests by creating alternative economic opportunities and helping to improve local conditions. This means linking climate change objectives with overall economic reform and good governance, and with broader development objectives. This is a large agenda requiring policy and institutional reform on many levels.

Changes to the regulatory framework governing land-use change are one important avenue available to the Indonesian government. It has already embarked on this road by placing a moratorium on new

2 Such estimates are subject to great uncertainty; they make assumptions about future economic developments and about the feasibility and cost of measures that are mostly untried on a large scale, and they ignore administrative costs (Schwarz 2010).

licences for forest conversion, motivated by the agreement with Norway discussed above. The moratorium is time limited, does not affect licences that have already been issued (including a large swathe granted just before it came into force) and excludes land that has been selectively logged (Edwards and Laurance 2011). Nevertheless it is sending a strong signal that the government intends to tackle the issue. This may well influence business investment decisions beyond the immediate effects of withholding some land conversion licences.

Changes to fiscal policy settings are another crucial set of policy options. Business taxes and subsidy schemes for the forestry, plantation and agricultural sectors could be reformed to discourage carbon-intensive operations, and to provide positive incentives for activities that create economic output with a lower environmental footprint.

Fiscal transfers from the central to local levels of government provide another tool to create incentives for the latter to act in accordance with national goals. The central government routinely makes large budgetary payments to the district governments, where many of the practical decisions about land-use change are made. Some of these fiscal transfers could be allocated to support climate-related activities. Ultimately the central government could create a system of financial incentives to implement climate-friendly measures, leaving flexibility to local entities about what actions to take and how to implement them (Ministry of Finance 2009: Ch. 5; Jotzo and Mazouz 2010).

A National Action Plan for the Reduction of Greenhouse Gas Emissions - Rencana Nasional Penurunan Emisi Gas Rumah Kaca - was enacted by presidential decree in September 2011 (Wang-Helmreich et al. 2011). It consists of a catalogue of measures to be taken in different sectors and regions, with various ministries responsible for implementation. The plan quantifies expected reductions in emissions, the vast majority of which would be achieved through better forestry and peatland management. To what extent the broad plan is underpinned by detailed analysis and provision for implementation is unclear.

Reforming the energy sector

Emissions from the energy sector - principally the use of coal, oil and gas for transport, electricity generation, industrial purposes and household use - currently account for around one-quarter of Indonesia's emissions. Energy use in Indonesia is still far below the per capita global average, and even further below per capita energy consumption levels in developed countries. But it is catching up fast. Aggregate energy use is growing roughly in line with GDP, and a growing share of energy is supplied by high-carbon coal, especially through the expansion of coal-fired power plants (Narjoko and Jotzo 2007). If left unchecked, Indonesia's emissions profile could be dominated by emissions from fossil fuel use within a few decades.

The options to curb emissions growth include improving energy efficiency and so using less energy to supply the same services, and taking the carbon out of the energy supply by shifting to lower-carbon energy sources. Indonesia has plentiful opportunities to do both. To achieve these outcomes, however, it would need to make significant changes to the institutional, regulatory and fiscal settings for the energy sector. Many of these reforms would be politically difficult or face significant practical hurdles in implementation.

A prime example is the expansion of geothermal power, that is, electricity generated using underground volcanic heat. This is a well-established technology, and some geothermal fields can produce electricity at lower cost than coal, especially when the explicit and implicit subsidies for coal-fired generation, and the costs imposed by local pollution, are taken into account (Ministry of Finance 2009: Ch. 4). Indonesia has 40 per cent of the world's geothermal resources, but only around 3 per cent of the resource is developed. A number of geothermal power plants came on line in the 1990s before progress was halted by the 1997–98 financial crisis. The government has an ambitious plan to ramp up geothermal power production, but to date the rate of development of new capacity is slower than would be needed to attain its target.

Geothermal development is hampered by a number of specific factors. They include cumbersome regulatory arrangements that compromise incentives for businesses to invest as independent power producers and to enter into contracts with the state electricity company, PLN. High up-front investment costs coupled with an inflexible system for determining the rates that PLN will pay independent power producers also increase the risk to project developers (Jotzo and Mazouz 2010). More fundamentally, retail electricity pricing does not adequately reflect the cost of producing power. Moreover, as a state monopolist subsidized from the budget, PLN does not face the right incentives to pursue efficient investments and minimize costs. Addressing the underlying distortions in the electricity sector would yield broader economic benefits beyond carbon emission reductions, by enhancing the efficiency of the sector.

Ultimately, the best way for Indonesia to shift investment onto a lower-carbon pathway is to put a tax on emissions. This is widely regarded as the most efficient way of creating economy-wide incentives to cut carbon emissions (Stern et al. 2006). Making high-emission activities relatively more expensive creates the incentives for lower-emission investments. In addition, a carbon tax could be a source of substantial fiscal revenues that could be used to compensate poor people for the added impost in terms of higher energy costs, and to offset other, more distorting, taxes. Modelling exercises suggest that, in Indonesia's case, a carbon tax could increase economic output as measured by GDP and at the same time reduce poverty (Yusuf and Resosudarmo 2007; Ministry of Finance 2009).

A carbon tax is thus a highly attractive option from the viewpoint of economic policy reform. However, as the experience in other countries has shown, it is also highly politically contentious because it may mean substantial changes to the patterns of profitability in the energy industry as well as higher household prices for energy. Energy pricing reform is a prerequisite for a carbon tax to work as intended; otherwise the price signal cannot work its way through the economy (Howes and Dobes 2010).

It could also be argued that Indonesia should first wind back its subsidies for transport fuels and domestic electricity, which would result in large fiscal savings and provide incentives to cut back on wasteful energy use. These subsidies overwhelmingly benefit middle and higher-income Indonesians, so removing them would not disproportionately penalize the poor, and could actually benefit them if the removal were coupled with income support measures such as the cash transfer program that accompanied the fuel subsidy reductions of 2005 (Beaton and Lontoh 2010). But removing energy subsidies is politically difficult because of its highly visible effect on prices, so phasing in carbon pricing in parallel with energy subsidy removal may be warranted.

POLITICAL ECONOMY OF CLIMATE POLICY REFORM

Reorienting the economy towards more environmentally friendly ways of operating is likely to be a long and windy road of policy reform, driven by the opportunity for economic as well as environmental outcomes, but with political roadblocks all along the way. The experience in most democracies is that entrenched economic and political interests make reform difficult. The difficulties are exacerbated by the fact that the ultimate benefit from climate change policy is a global and long-term one, intangible to local actors and subject to the actions of other countries. Nevertheless, Indonesia has a strong intrinsic interest in limiting climate change and its adverse effects on development, and this could provide an ongoing impetus for reform.

Climate policy reform takes place in a complex system of interwoven interests in society, as sketched below.

Economy and business

The political economy of reform that affects business interests is often characterized by a situation where the likely 'losers' from the reform are highly visible and concentrated, and may have strong political influence based on their existing positions of financial strength or political importance. Potential 'winners', meanwhile, tend to be businesses that are not yet large and well connected. In many cases, winners represent a broad or diffuse set of businesses and individuals ahead of the reform taking place, and sometimes it is not even possible to clearly identify who the winners will be. As a result, the political pressure from business in favour of the status quo tends to be much stronger than the pressure for reform.

This situation is not unique to Indonesia, but also prevails in most other democracies. In the case of climate change policy, the political trade-offs with established industry interests have been evident in both Australia and the European Union, where large amounts of the fiscal revenue from putting a price on emissions have been offered to industry, in large part to buy off opposition from business (Pezzey, Mazouz and Jotzo 2010).

The primacy of self-interest is clearly at work in Indonesia as well (McCarthy and Tacconi 2011). In the land-use sector, existing business practices are geared towards maximizing profits using a business model that takes little or no heed of environmental objectives. A typical model is to convert timber-rich lands to plantations, sell the timber and use the proceeds to finance the establishment of oil palm plantations that are geared for quick returns rather than maximum yield per hectare. An alternative, more environmentally friendly, model would minimize land use by maximizing yield, and seek to establish plantations on degraded land rather than by cutting down natural forests. This model would probably require payments or tax concessions to make it financially attractive, or regulatory interventions to prohibit the conventional way of doing things, coupled with reliable enforcement provisions.

Such a model would clash with the established business models of industry players, who could be expected to resist measures to shift to the alternative path. A typical symptom of this process is that businesses will complain to government about problems with the new model, but will not be prepared to enter into discussions about how their specific concerns might be addressed.

For example, the energy sector is characterized by large investments in long-lived capital and infrastructure, such as power stations, railways and ports, and mines. Changes in policy could reduce the value of those investments, and would therefore meet resistance from large, established business interests. A case in point is Indonesia's coal-fired electricity sector. Large operations have been developed to mine and transport coal that is not of sufficient quality for export markets, and so is used solely to supply domestic power. A significant portion of these mines, as well as a number of coal-fired power stations, is owned by Bumi Resources, Indonesia's largest coal-producing company. Bumi Resources is majority owned by Aburizal Bakrie and his brother. Bakrie was Coordinating Minister for the Economy and then Minister for People's Welfare in the first Yudhoyono administration, and is now the chairman of the Golkar party. He is widely considered one of Indonesia's most politically influential figures.

Governments and bureaucracy

Entrenched interests can also be found in the Indonesian public service. Line ministries, such as the Ministry of Forestry or the Ministry of Energy, tend to represent the interests of their existing business clienteles. This occurs in other countries as well, but the potential for adverse effects on policy making from a national interest perspective are more pronounced where governance is weak and corruption in its many forms is more prevalent.

In contrast, central agencies and ministries with an over-riding brief tend to champion reform. One example is the Presidential Unit for Development Supervision and Control (UKP-PPP), headed by Kuntoro Mangkusubroto who previously oversaw the post-tsunami reconstruction in Aceh. The unit has a REDD implementation task force. Another example is the Ministry of Finance, which has an interest in overall sound management of government finances and strong influence over budget allocations. As pointed out by former finance minister Sri Mulyani, its fiscal policies offer a range of options to support climate change policy objectives (Indrawati 2009), although the shaping of sector-specific policies is not within its remit. There have been tensions between government agencies, for example between the Ministry of Forestry and the UKP-PPP over the moratorium on land conversion, and between the ministries of forestry and finance over a decree on revenues from REDD projects.

The over-riding factor influencing policy decisions in democracies is usually the effect on the popularity of the sitting government and its prospects for re-election. This often precludes difficult policy reform unless there is an externally imposed imperative for it, and tends to make reform harder towards the end of the electoral cycle. As Basri points out in Chapter 3, the Indonesian government is currently hesitant to make further reductions in fuel subsidies, possibly in anticipation of the next presidential election in 2014.

Similar dynamics are at play at the local government level, with the added complication that the incentives for local leaders obviously lie in serving their local constituencies. In the case of climate change, local objectives do not automatically align with national objectives. For example, the national government has an interest in fulfilling its international climate change commitments in order to increase Indonesia's standing and influence in the global community. But achieving this aim relies in part on the actions of local governments, which have no direct interest in the outcome. Hence, the central government needs to create incentive structures or effective regulatory instruments to bring local and national objectives into line.

Civil society

Non-government organizations have traditionally played an important role in promoting the case for environmental policies in Indonesia. Activism on environmental issues started under Suharto, and today is among the most powerful agents for domestic change on environmental issues. Climate change has also been covered extensively in Indonesia's media. Coverage of specific environmental issues can act as a counterweight to the influence of business interests.

NGOs are an important source of human capital. A number of today's senior government officials and advisers on climate change cut their teeth working for NGOs, and representatives of environmental organizations have frequently been included as official members of Indonesia's delegations to UN climate negotiations.

CONCLUSION

How Indonesia deals with the climate change challenge is important for the world. As one of the most populous countries with a fast-growing and resource-intensive economy, Indonesia contributes a sizeable share of the world's annual greenhouse gas emissions. It also has ample opportunities to cut its emissions – in the forestry and land-use sector in the short term and in the energy sector over the long term. Addressing climate change is part of a broader paradigm where economic growth is less dependent on the exploitation of non-renewable resources and causes fewer adverse environmental impacts. The 'green growth' agenda may become relevant to developing countries that are gaining the economic, social and institutional prerequisites to improve not just the quantity, but also the quality, of their economic growth. Indonesia is one such country.

With its global ramifications and the need for action by most if not all countries, climate change is an important field of international diplomacy. Indonesia's traditional role has been as a moderating force in the developing world, speaking with a quiet voice and rarely occupying centre stage – except for one or two forays by President Yudhoyono in recent years. As in other areas of international life, Indonesia can be said to have been looking for 'a million friends and zero enemies'.

Given its size and its centrality on the climate change issue, Indonesia could over time grow into a leadership role as a second-tier global power. Taking more of a leadership role within the Southeast Asian region would also be logical. International leadership starts with action at home, however. To take a greater role in international affairs will require boosting the country's capacity to monitor and analyse the issues in play, and continued visible political commitment. Above everything else, it will require successful implementation of measures to cut emissions in Indonesia, on a large enough scale to be appreciated internationally.

This will not be an easy task. A thicket of entrenched interests in business and the bureaucracy acts as a brake on reform, with the interplay between central and local government interests creating additional complexity. Electoral politics in many instances precludes reforms that would be beneficial not just to the environment but also to the economy. But Indonesia has shown on more than one occasion that it can manage difficult reforms, and the environment could join the list of successes. If so, it will provide an unusually good opportunity for the country to play an international leadership role.

REFERENCES

ADB (Australian Development Bank) (2010) *Clean Technology Fund Investment Plan for Indonesia*, ADB, Manila.

Ardiansyah, F. (2012) 'Revisiting the global role of tropical forest nations', *Strategic Review* 2(1): 56–67.

Aspinall, E. (2010) 'Indonesia in 2009: democratic triumphs and trials', in D. Singh (ed.) *Southeast Asian Affairs*, Institute of Southeast Asian Studies, Singapore.

Bank Indonesia (2012) *Economic and Financial Data for Indonesia*, Bank Indonesia, Jakarta.

Beaton, C. and L. Lontoh (2010) *Lessons Learned from Indonesia's Attempts to Reform Fossil-Fuel Subsidies*, International Institute for Sustainable Development, Winnipeg.

DNPI (Dewan Nasional Perubahan Iklim) (2011) *Indonesia's Greenhouse Gas Abatement Cost Curve*, DNPI, Jakarta.

Edwards, D.P. and W.F. Laurance (2011) 'Carbon emissions: loophole in forest plan for Indonesia', *Nature* 477: 33.

EIA (Energy Information Administration) (2012) *International Energy Statistics*, EIA, Washington DC.

FAO (Food and Agriculture Organization) (2010) 'Global forest resource assessment 2010', FAO Forestry Paper No. 163, FAO, Rome.

Garnaut, R. (2008) *The Garnaut Climate Change Review: Final Report*, Cambridge University Press, Cambridge and New York.

Garnaut, R., S. Howes, F. Jotzo and P. Sheehan (2008) 'Emissions in the Platinum Age: the implications of rapid development for climate-change mitigation', *Oxford Review of Economic Policy* 24(2): 377–401.

Governments of Norway and Indonesia (2010) 'Letter of intent between the Government of the Kingdom of Norway and the Government of the Republic of Indonesia on "Cooperation on reducing greenhouse gas emissions from deforestation and forest degradation"', Oslo.

Howes, S. and L. Dobes (2010) *Climate Change and Fiscal Policy: A Report for APEC*, World Bank, Washington DC.

IEA (International Energy Agency) (2011) *World Energy Outlook 2011*, IEA, Paris.

Indrawati, S.M. (2009) 'Policy instruments to influence climate change mitigation and adaptation policies', in *Turning Words into Action: Advancing Reform and the Economic Agenda*, Fiscal Policy Office, Ministry of Finance, Jakarta.

IPCC (Intergovernmental Panel on Climate Change) (2007) *Climate Change 2007: The Physical Science Basis*, Cambridge University Press, Cambridge.

Jotzo, F., (2010) 'Comparing the Copenhagen emissions targets', research report, Centre for Climate Economics and Policy, Australian National University, Canberra, available at http://ideas.repec.org/p/ags/eerhrr/107577.html.

Jotzo, F. and S. Mazouz (2010) 'Indonesia's climate change challenge: economic policy for effective and efficient mitigation', *Indonesian Quarterly* 38(1): 23–40.

Jotzo, F., I.A.P Resosudarmo, D.A. Nurdianto and A.P. Sari (2009) 'Climate change and development in eastern Indonesia', in B. Resosudarmo and F. Jotzo (eds) *Working with Nature against Poverty*, Institute of Southeast Asian Studies, Singapore.

Jupesta, J. et al. (2011) 'Managing the transition to sustainability in an emerging economy: evaluating green growth policies in Indonesia', *Environmental Innovation and Societal Transitions* 1(2): 187–91.

McCarthy, S. and L. Tacconi (2011) 'The political economy of tropical deforestation: assessing models and motives', *Environmental Politics* 20(1): 115–32.

McKibbin, W.J., A.C. Morris and P.J. Wilcoxen (2011) 'Comparing climate commitments: a model-based analysis of the Copenhagen Accord', *Climate Change Economics* 2(2): 79–103.

Ministry of Environment (2010) *Indonesia Second National Communication under the UN Framework Convention on Climate Change*, Ministry of Environment, Jakarta.

Ministry of Finance (2009) *Green Paper: Economic and Fiscal Policy Strategies for Climate Change Mitigation in Indonesia*, Ministry of Finance, Jakarta.

Ministry of Foreign Affairs (2012) *Direction of Indonesian Foreign Policy*, Ministry of Foreign Affairs, Jakarta.

Narjoko, D.A. and F. Jotzo (2007) 'Survey of recent developments', *Bulletin of Indonesian Economic Studies* 43(2): 143–70.

Page, S.E., F. Siegert, J.O. Rieley, H.V. Boehm, A. Jaya and S. Limin (2002) 'The amount of carbon released from peat and forest fires in Indonesia during 1997', *Nature* 420: 61–5.

PEACE (PT Pelangi Energi Abadi Citra Enviro) (2007) *Indonesia and Climate Change*, PEACE, Jakarta.

Pezzey, J.C.V., S. Mazouz and F. Jotzo (2010) 'The logic of collective action and Australia's climate policy', *Australian Journal of Agricultural and Resource Economics* 54(2): 185–202.

Resosudarmo, B.P. and F. Jotzo (2009) 'Development, resources and environment in eastern Indonesia', in B.P. Resosudarmo and F. Jotzo (eds) *Working with Nature against Poverty*, Institute of Southeast Asian Studies, Singapore.

Schwarz, A. (2010) 'Low carbon growth in Indonesia', *Bulletin of Indonesian Economic Studies* 46(2): 181–5.

Simamor, A.P. and D. Nurhayati (2010) 'Indonesia may join Basic group on climate talks', *Jakarta Post*, 2 March.

Steffen, W. (2011) *The Critical Decade: Climate Science, Risks and Responses*, Climate Commission, Canberra.

Stern, N.H. et al. (2006) *Stern Review: The Economics of Climate Change*, HM Treasury, London.

Tacconi, L., F. Jotzo and R.Q. Grafton (2008) 'Local causes, regional co-operation and global financing for environmental problems: the case of Southeast Asian haze pollution', *International Environmental Agreements: Politics, Law and Economics* 8(1): 1–16.

Wang-Helmreich, H., W. Sterk, T. Wehnert and C. Arens (2011) 'Current developments in pilot nationally appropriate mitigation actions of developing countries (NAMAs)', JIKO Policy Paper 01/2011, Wuppertal Institute, Wuppertal.

Watkins, K. (2007) *Human Development Report 2007/2008. Fighting Climate Change: Human Solidarity in a Divided World*, Palgrave Macmillan, Houndmills, and New York NY.

World Bank (2010) *World Development Report 2010: Development and Climate Change*, World Bank, Washington DC.

Yudhoyono, S.B. (2009) 'Intervention by HE Dr Susilo Bambang Yudhoyono on climate change at the G-20 Leaders' Summit, Pittsburgh PA, available at http://forestclimatecenter.org/.

Yusuf, A.A. and H. Francisco (2009) 'Climate change vulnerability mapping for Southeast Asia', Economy and Environment Program for Southeast Asia, Singapore, available at http://web.idrc.ca/uploads/user-S/12324196651Mapping_Report.pdf.

7 INDONESIAN MUSLIMS AND THEIR PLACE IN THE LARGER WORLD OF ISLAM

Martin van Bruinessen

With over 220 million Muslims, Indonesia has the largest community of Muslims in the world. Nevertheless, Indonesian Muslims do not play a role in global Muslim thought and action that is commensurate with their numbers. Indonesian Muslims have been eager to learn from Arab as well as Indian, Turkish and Persian thinkers, but do not seem to think they may have something valuable to offer in return. In Indonesian bookshops one finds the translated works of classical and modern Arabic authors, as well as studies of and by major Indian, Pakistani, Iranian and Turkish authors. But Malaysia is the only other country where one can find works by Indonesian Muslim authors, and there are virtually no serious studies of Indonesian Islam by scholars of other Muslim nations. The Arab world has shown a remarkable lack of interest in Asia in general, let alone in the social and cultural forms of Islam in Southeast Asia.[1] Though more outward looking, other Muslim

* The author wishes to thank Martin Slama, Ulil Abshar-Abdalla, Mona Abaza and Tony Reid for their comments on an earlier version of this paper.

1 The sole Egyptian academic to have published serious studies on Malaysian and Indonesian Islam, as well as on the relationship between the Middle East and Indonesia, is the German-trained sociologist Mona Abaza. Her overview of Arabic writing on Asia reveals how shallow and uninformative most of the existing literature is (Abaza 2011; see also Abaza 2007). She makes an exception for an encyclopaedic work on Islam among non-Arabic speakers by Ahmad Shalabi (1983), who spent many years teaching in Indonesia in the 1950s and 1960s.

regions of Asia have not taken a serious interest in their Southeast Asian co-religionists either.[2]

Indonesians are pursuing Islamic studies in India, Pakistan, Iran and Turkey, as well as in the Arab world and in the West. Indian and Turkish Muslims travelling to Indonesia, on the other hand, are not going there as students but as teachers and missionaries. Missionary movements such as the Ahmadiyya and the Tablighi Jama'at (both originating in India) and the Nur and Gülen movements (which started in Turkey) are active all over the world, as are the various transnational movements originating in the Arab world. But no corresponding Indonesian movement is attempting to spread its message beyond the confines of the country.

The apparent lack of interest in Indonesia as a great Muslim nation, and the reluctance of Indonesian Muslims to make their religious culture better known in the wider world, calls for an explanation. Indonesian Islam has a number of traits that have struck outside observers as unique and even enviable. One such observer was the late Pakistani-American scholar Fazlur Rahman (d. 1988). He was the intellectual mentor of a number of prominent young Indonesian intellectuals, most notably Nurcholish Madjid and Syafi'i Ma'arif. His rationalistic and analytical approach caused him problems in Pakistan but seemed to appeal to many Indonesians, and he was invited to the country several times. He liked what he saw in Indonesia, and certainly did not consider Indonesian Islam to be inferior to or less authentic than Arab or Indian Islam.

Fazlur Rahman made friendly comments about Pancasila as an Indonesian exegesis (*tafsir*) of Islam that was suited to Indonesian society and culture.[3] The Pancasila state, he said, provided precisely the climate of religious tolerance that would enable free development of religious thought. He was very pessimistic about the state of intellectual debate in the Muslim world in general but saw two exceptions that gave reason for hope: Indonesia and Turkey. He was convinced that if there were to be a renaissance of the Muslim intellectual tradition, it would begin in those countries.[4] Another critical reformist scholar of Islam was the Egyptian Nasr Hamid Abu Zayd (d. 2010). Like Fazlur Rahman he had to leave his country of birth and spend his last years in exile, but he too found dedicated groups of admirers in Indonesia and Turkey and regularly visited both countries.

---

2 One exception is Göksoy's (1995) work on Islam in Indonesia under the Dutch. Originally a dissertation submitted to the School of Oriental and African Studies in London, the book was later published in Turkish by a publishing house associated with Turkey's Directorate of Religious Affairs.

3 The Pancasila are the five guiding principles of the Indonesian state, namely belief in God, humanitarianism, national unity, democracy and social justice.

4 Conversations with Fazlur Rahman, Jakarta, 15–17 August 1985.

This raises again the question of the relative invisibility of Indonesian Islam. If it is the case that Turkey and Indonesia share certain conditions that allow or even stimulate the development of an original and daring Muslim intellectual discourse, why is it that we see Turkey and Turkish Muslim movements projecting themselves confidently in the wider world whereas Indonesia and Indonesian Muslims do not? Is it just a matter of modesty or lack of confidence, or are other factors at play?

IS INDONESIAN LEADERSHIP IN THE MUSLIM WORLD THINKABLE?

There was a time when Indonesian Muslims felt more confident about their role in the world, and other Muslims, even in the Middle East, appeared to notice something worth emulating in them. Allow me to reconstruct from memory a conversation I had in the late 1980s with Kiai Abdullah Abbas, the head of the large *pesantren* of Buntet near Cirebon.[5] He was one of the most prominent members of Nahdlatul Ulama (NU) in West Java, and one of Abdurrahman Wahid's staunchest (and most crucial) supporters.[6] A man of broad views and rich experience, he enjoyed sharing his memories of the closing years of Dutch colonial rule, the Japanese occupation, the struggle for independence and stormy years of the young republic, the violent inauguration of the New Order and the years of development under Suharto. The best years, the period when he felt most alive, were apparently the Sukarno years:

> We are more prosperous now, but in those days we were proud of being Indonesian. When we went to Arabia on the *hajj* and told people where we were from, they always responded positively. They would say, 'Ah! Indonesia! Ahmad Sukarno!' and give us a thumbs-up. We felt that we counted for something in the world. Nowadays we don't get that sort of response any more when we travel abroad; something important has been lost ...[7]

Kiai Abdullah admittedly was a Sukarnoist and Indonesian nationalist, and one of those who felt that Indonesia, as a large Muslim nation recently liberated from the colonial past, should rightly play a leading role in a third bloc between the capitalist (and largely Christian) bloc

---

5 A *pesantren* is a traditional Islamic boarding school. The religious scholar or leader in charge of the *pesantren* is called a *kiai*.

6 Abdurrahman Wahid was the head of NU from 1984 to 1998 and the president of Indonesia from 1999 to 2001.

7 Conversations with K.H. Abdullah Abbas, Pesantren Buntet, Cirebon, 10–11 October 1987.

and the communist (and presumably atheist) bloc. The Bandung Conference (1955) and succeeding conferences confirmed Sukarno's – and by implication Indonesia's – leading role in the ensuing Non-Aligned Movement (Mackie 2005). By performing the pilgrimage to Mecca (in 1955) and adopting the name 'Ahmad', Ir. H. Ahmad Sukarno emphasized his identity as a Muslim leader and as a leader of Muslims. Kiai Abdullah's nostalgic memories suggest that many Muslims of other nations recognized Indonesia's leading role and shared the hopes of a shift in the global balance of power.

Half a century ago, the idea of the secular Muslim nation of Indonesia leading what came to be known as the Third World was not only thinkable but briefly appeared to become a reality. As we know now, the dream was not to last: the Non-Aligned Movement fell apart, Sukarno was brought down and under Suharto Indonesia renounced its revolutionary vanguard role. Since the demise of the New Order in 1998, there have been a few attempts to raise Indonesia's international profile as a leading Muslim nation (about which more below) but so far these have not been very successful. Indonesia's visibility has increased and its significance is being recognized, but it is not (or not yet?) a country that others look to for leadership.

Indonesian leadership in international organizations has not been entirely absent in the post-Sukarno period, however. The most prominent example is Mohamad Natsir, a former head of Masyumi (the largest political party in Indonesia in the late 1940s and 1950s), prime minister from 1950 to 1951, and a staunch critic of Sukarno's who spent the last years of the latter's rule in jail and was still not allowed to return to formal politics under Suharto. He was given leading positions in various Saudi-sponsored international bodies, notably the Muslim World League (Rabita). The league was established by Saudi Arabia in 1962 to counter the revolutionary influence from Nasser's Egypt, which threatened to undermine the monarchies of the Gulf region. Ideologically it was at the opposite end of the political spectrum from the Non-Aligned Movement. Natsir, a product of the puritan reformist Muslim movement Persis, was liked and trusted by the Saudis. He was for many years a member of the 'council of founders' of the Muslim World League and a board member of various associated bodies. The organization for Islamic propagation that Natsir founded in 1967, the Indonesian Council for Islamic Propagation (DDII), doubled as the de facto Jakarta office of the Muslim World League as long as Natsir was alive – only after his death in 1993 was a Saudi sent to Jakarta to represent it.[8]

---

8 Natsir appears in various roles in a major study of the Muslim World League by Schulze (1990). See also Schulze (1983).

Natsir obviously owed his position not only to his personal qualities but also to the perceived demographic importance of Indonesian Islam. He never used the position to draw attention to specifically Indonesian Muslim thought or cultural expressions, which probably had no religious legitimacy for him.[9] Indeed, in an early debate on Indonesia's national culture pitting nativists against Westernizers in the 1930s, Natsir contributed a booklet on 'Muslim culture' in which he spoke exclusively of the golden age of Muslim civilization in the Middle East and made no reference at all to any Indonesian contribution.[10]

It was through Natsir and the DDII that Islamist and later Salafi ideas spread from the Arabian peninsula to Indonesia, carried by young Indonesians selected for study in Saudi Arabia.[11] Natsir was influential, but his influence remained restricted largely to getting the Saudi authorities to pressure Indonesia to adopt domestic policies that conformed to Saudi perceptions of the furtherance of Islamic interests. He kept his prominent position in the Muslim World League until the late 1980s, when the Suharto regime successfully lobbied the Saudis for him to be replaced by a more pliable figure, H.M. Rasjidi.

Even in the heyday of Indonesia's leading role in the Non-Aligned Movement, the respect accorded Indonesian Muslims by fellow believers of other nationalities reflected the country's political role in the world and appears not to have been translated into interest in, let alone appreciation of, Indonesian Muslim culture(s) and learning. Foreign Muslims who came to study in Indonesian *pesantren* were typically from other parts of Southeast Asia (Malaysia, Thailand, Cambodia) and rarely if ever from South Asia, the Middle East or Africa. Indonesians seeking advanced knowledge of Islam, on the other hand, would spend years in *madrasah* in Mecca,[12] at Al-Azhar University in Cairo or occasionally in India or Pakistan. Religious scholars (*ulama*) from those places also travelled to Indonesia as teachers, but only very rarely were learned Indonesians invited to teach in the Middle East.

Religious authority is by definition an unequal relationship, and Indonesians were almost always on the receiving end. Indonesian Muslims

---

9 However, an anonymous book on the political position of Muslims in New Order Indonesia and Christian conspiracies to undermine Islam in the archipelago is commonly attributed to him; see Al-Andunisi (1984).

10 See Mujiburrahman (2006: 207–11) for an analysis of the debate, which has become known in retrospect as Polemik Kebudayaan – the Polemic on Culture.

11 Salafism seeks a return to the teachings and example of the early generations of Muslims; the term usually refers to the most strictly fundamentalist and puritanical stream of Islamic thought.

12 A *madrasah* – or *medrese* (see below) – is an Islamic school or college.

have developed a wide range of unique expressions of Islam, but they have shown no great zeal in propagating them to other parts of the Muslim world.

INDONESIAN *ULAMA* AND TRANSNATIONAL SCHOLARLY NETWORKS

The preceding observation about the apparent one-way nature of religious authority and teaching requires qualification. Indonesians studying in Mecca or Cairo often did so under teachers who were, like themselves, of Southeast Asian origin. Linguistic competence in Malay and/or Javanese no doubt played a part in bringing teachers and students together, but we know that some of these teachers did in fact also have non-Southeast Asian students. Azyumardi Azra has drawn attention to the fact that the eighteenth-century scholar from Palembang, Abdussamad al-Jawi (al-Falimbani), who taught for many years in Medina and Yemen, had numerous Arab as well as Malay students (Azra 2004: 112–17). Michael Feener and Michael Laffan (2005) have found references to a much earlier Sufi scholar in Aden with probable Southeast Asian connections who influenced well-known contemporary Arab scholars.[13]

Abdussamad and other Southeast Asian scholars active in Arabia were connected by teacher–student links and correspondence with numerous other *ulama* in scholarly networks that spanned the Middle East, Asia and Africa. In such networks, ethnicity and place of origin were almost by definition irrelevant, since the main criterion for membership was the recognition of learning. Southeast Asians who enjoyed peer recognition as accomplished scholars could be chosen as teachers by students of diverse ethnic origins. However, it was residence in Mecca, Medina or Cairo that made it possible for them to become internationally recognized. I do not know of any great scholar permanently based in Indonesia whose name drew students from abroad to his feet. Apart from teaching in the Arabian heartland, writing learned books in Arabic was another possible way of gaining renown and authority in the wider world. All Indonesian authors of major Arabic Islamic texts of whom I am aware, however, were residents of Mecca or Medina and also taught there.

Perhaps I may add a minor observation here. While browsing in an Islamic bookstore in Diyarbakir, in Turkish Kurdistan, I came across a book whose author I recognized as Indonesian: Ihsan bin Muhammad Dahlan of Jampes, Kediri (d. 1952). Enthusiastically I showed it to the

---

13 Sufism is the mystical dimension of Islam; a Sufi is a Muslim mystic.

bookseller, saying: 'This author is an Indonesian, and he is very famous in East Java'. The man was not impressed but politely asked a few things about Indonesia and complimented the Indonesians he had encountered during the *hajj* on their modest and polite behaviour. He did not think, however, that the author's nationality was relevant to the authority of the book (Dahlan n.d.), a commentary – probably the most recent of many – on a well-known eleventh-century Sufi text by Ghazali. The discursive world of commentaries, supercommentaries and glosses on classical texts that constitute the main material of study in traditional *madrasah* all over the world is largely deterritorialized.

Some of the most prolific Southeast Asian *ulama* based in Mecca in the late nineteenth century appear to have written their works not as contributions to the global scholarly discourse, but as popularizing summaries and commentaries intended for Southeast Asian audiences. Muhammad bin Umar Nawawi of Banten and Da'ud bin Abdullah of Patani wrote numerous books in Arabic and Malay respectively, which were originally printed in Mecca or Cairo and later reproduced cheaply in such places as Singapore and Surabaya (van Bruinessen 1990; Bradley 2010). This phenomenon underscores the prestige and authority that association with Arabia attaches to books as well as persons in the eyes of ordinary Southeast Asians. No matter how impressive one's lineage or scholarship, one does not become a respected *kiai* in Java unless one has spent a few years studying in Mecca or, nowadays, Cairo. The process of Islamization of the archipelago over the past six centuries, and of Islamic reform over the past three, has been powered less by foreign preachers and missionaries arriving from abroad than by local people travelling to Arabia in search of knowledge and prestige.

HADRAMAUT AND SOUTHEAST ASIA

A group of Islamic scholars who have been of special significance for Southeast Asian Islam are the Sayyid (presumed descendants of the Prophet) of Hadrami origin.[14] Hadrami traders and scholars, Sayyid as well as commoners, have been travelling to Southeast Asia from the Middle East for many centuries. We find such men occasionally mentioned in the seventeenth and eighteenth centuries – Abdussamad al-Jawi of Palembang and the famous Acehnese scholar and mystic Nuruddin Raniri were both of Hadrami descent on the father's side, though born in Sumatra and Gujarat respectively of local women. Hadrami migration to

14 Hadramaut is a region in South Arabia, in the east of the present state of Yemen.

Indonesia increased massively in the nineteenth and twentieth centuries. Some of the men who had made their fortunes in trade with Indonesia later resettled in Hadramaut. As travel became easier, Indonesianized Hadramis also revisited the old country, resulting in increasing cultural exchange between the two regions.[15]

Hadrami society, in Indonesia as well as in Hadramaut itself, was highly stratified, with the Sayyid occupying the upper stratum and carefully maintaining the social boundary separating them from other Hadramis. All commoners (including indigenous Indonesian Muslims) were expected to kiss the hand of a Sayyid when meeting, and whereas Sayyid freely took indigenous women as their wives, they never allowed anyone but another Sayyid to marry their sisters and daughters. Existing tensions between the Sayyid and other Hadramis came to a head in the early twentieth century over a series of conflicts sparked by a reformist teacher originally from Sudan, Ahmad Soorkatti. He arrived in Java in 1911 to teach in the schools of Indonesia's first modern Muslim association, Jamiat Khair, which was dominated by the Sayyid. He held that all men were equal and that the Sayyid claim to superiority because of their genealogy was spurious. Soon the entire Hadrami community of Java was divided over the issue. The anti-Sayyid faction split from Jamiat Khair, establishing the Muslim reformist association Al-Irsyad, led by Soorkatti; the Sayyid withdrew to a fiercely anti-reformist, mystically tinged traditionalism and cultivation of their families' hereditary charisma.[16]

Natalie Mobini-Kesheh (1999) has described how the conflict between the two groups, which was fought out with theological arguments, was transplanted from Java back to Hadramaut, where it again led to challenges to the dominant position of the Sayyid (see also Kostiner 1984). This is the only major case of which I am aware where a development in Indonesian Islam had an impact in the Middle East. The conflict hardly affected indigenous Indonesians, however; by and large, membership of Al-Irsyad has remained restricted to Indonesian Arabs. It is therefore more appropriate to speak of a conflict in the Hadrami diaspora having an impact on power struggles in the homeland. Conditions in Indonesia were at best a catalyst for the conflict – no indigenous Indonesians were directly involved.

---

15 In recent years there has been considerable academic interest in the Hadrami diaspora and its relations with the homeland, resulting in several important publications. A particularly insightful study is Ho (2006).

16 On the complex stratification of Hadrami society, see Heiss and Slama (2010). On Soorkatti's interventions, see Pijper (1977: 109–20) and Mobini-Kesheh (1999).

THE SINGULARITY OF INDONESIA'S ISLAMIC ORGANIZATIONS

Indonesian Islam can boast a number of unusual features that have drawn the admiration of foreign Muslim observers. The pattern of associational life is one of them. Indonesianists may take the existence of the largest associations – the modernist Muhammadiyah and the traditionalist NU – for granted, because they have been there so long (since 1912 and 1926 respectively) and appear to be such an inevitable part of the societal landscape. But nowhere else in the Muslim world do we find anything quite like them.[17] Both have various affiliated unions and institutions (women's, youth and students' associations, and a wide range of NGOs) and are organized at the national, provincial and district levels, with elected boards at each level. Their five-yearly congresses, where new leaders are elected and general policies established, are massive exercises in democratic decision making. Heavy-handed government intervention in these congresses has been the rule rather than the exception, especially under Suharto, but the organizations have always shown considerable resilience and maintained a degree of autonomy.

Muhammadiyah has established thousands of schools and dozens of universities, hospitals and orphanages in most major cities, and even a few banks, all of them run by a well-organized bureaucracy. NU is less professionally organized, reflecting the different social backgrounds of its membership; it represents the world of the *pesantren*, a broad segment of the rural masses and small-town businesspeople. It does not control the *pesantren*, as Muhammadiyah controls its schools – the *kiai* tend to guard their independence and are extremely wary of external intervention in their schools – but functions as a forum for communication and mutual consultation, and in various ways represents the interests of its constituency.

Muhammadiyah and NU enjoy strong legitimacy as representatives of broad segments of the Islamic community (*ummah*), and they have remained the largest and strongest embodiments of civil society throughout the twentieth century. Surveys show that their members tend to be more active than average in other societal activities such as neighbourhood associations and charitable work. These associations have arguably been a stabilizing force, helping to enable the democratic transformation of the country.

---

17 The Muslim Brotherhood, which was established in Egypt in 1928 and later spread to other Arab countries, has never attained the same level of organization, transparency or societal penetration, though it developed more systematic methods of disciplining its cadres.

Though both have their regional centres of gravity, they have long been organized throughout the country and have played an important part in strengthening a common national awareness among Muslims. Like similar but smaller associations such as Persis, Muhammadiyah and NU have never attempted to expand their activities to non-Indonesian Muslim populations; their few foreign branches serve only Indonesian residents abroad. Leaders of the two organizations – most conspicuously Abdurrahman Wahid – have been invited to various international conferences, but until recently neither played a leading role on the world stage.

Since the demise of the New Order, both associations have shown increasing confidence and have taken some initiatives to make their mark internationally. Under former chairman Hasyim Muzadi, NU organized the first International Conference of Islamic Scholars in Jakarta, in which prominent *ulama* from across the world took part. This initiative was not unrelated to Muzadi's personal ambitions – he was Megawati Sukarnoputri's running mate in the 2004 presidential elections, and the first conference conveniently took place in early 2004 – but it also reflected a broadly shared desire to make Indonesia and NU more visible internationally. Megawati delivered an opening speech that appeared to allude to the spirit of the Bandung Conference, calling for cooperation in the face of the great challenges faced by all Muslim nations. Follow-up conferences took place in 2006 and 2008, again with considerable international participation. Muzadi's successor, Said Aqiel Siradj, deliberately broke with many of his predecessor's policies but continued the effort to make NU more internationally prominent by organizing a large meeting of Sufi orders in July 2011.

THE STRENGTH OF LIBERAL AND PROGRESSIVE RELIGIOUS THOUGHT

Indonesia has produced some remarkable Muslim thinker-activists, men as diverse as Tan Malaka, Haji Misbach, Tjokroaminoto, Agus Salim, Mohamad Natsir, Kartosuwiryo, Nurcholish Madjid, Dawam Rahardjo, Kuntowijoyo and Abdurrahman Wahid. With very few exceptions, their writings have not been translated into Arabic or English, and their thinking has therefore never made the impact in other parts of the world that many would judge it deserves. One may adduce a number of possible explanations for this state of affairs, although none of them is entirely satisfactory.

It is doubtless the case that Muslim activists in the Middle East have been more interested in the demographic and political weight of the

Indonesian *ummah* than in its possible contribution to Islamic thought. Besides the general bias towards the Middle East, this may be due to the widespread perception that Indonesian Islam tends to be syncretistic and less than rigorous (which is exactly what many Westerners find attractive about it). But although similar perceptions have long existed concerning Indian Islam, South Asian Muslim thinkers such as Mohammad Iqbal, Abu'l A'la Maududi, Fazlur Rahman and Asghar Ali Engineer have had a major influence beyond their own region.

Another possible explanation is that much Indonesian Muslim writing specifically concerns the Indonesian context and responds to conditions that do not prevail elsewhere, making it less relevant to other nations. Indonesian Muslim thinkers have moreover typically been people of action whose thinking was expressed in the context of, and in a format appropriate to, social and political struggles. Much of their energy went into organizing, teaching, and establishing associations or NGOs.[18] Their intellectual output took the form of numerous speeches, essays and short articles, and rarely if ever a substantial synthesizing work. An Indonesian Muslim intellectual's book typically consists of a collection of heterogeneous articles, many of them addressing specifically Indonesian concerns.[19]

This does not detract from the fact that the Islamic discourse developed by the Muslim intellectuals who flourished during the New Order and after – the religious 'renewal' (*pembaruan*) movement associated with Nurcholish Madjid since 1970 and the various 'liberal' and 'progressive' currents of the 1990s and 2000s – was unique in the Muslim world. I lived in Indonesia myself during much of the 1980s and early 1990s and regularly attended the public discussions of Muslim intellectuals. The freedom of debate, the courage to think 'out of the box', the intellectual curiosity with which young Indonesian Muslims sought, and acquainted themselves with, ideas beyond the Muslim mainstream and creatively adopted and disseminated them, struck me as highly unusual and unlike anything I knew of elsewhere in the Muslim world. Like other

---

18 It is no coincidence that Pramoedya Ananta Toer's famous quartet of novels – based on the life of Tirtoadisoerjo, founder of the first indigenous newspaper and the first Muslim association in the Dutch Indies – emphasizes the importance of organizing as essential to the struggle for liberation, giving it priority even over writing. An anecdote related to me by Ulil Abshar-Abdalla may also be relevant here: an Egyptian visitor to Indonesia jokingly observed that the Qur'an was revealed in Saudi Arabia, is recited in Egypt and is put into practice in Indonesia (*'Al-Qur'an nazal fi al-Sa'udiyya, wa yutla fi Masr, wa yu'malu bihi fi Indonesia'*).

19 See, for example, Salim (1954), Natsir (1955), Rakhmat (1986), Madjid (1987), Madjid and Roem (2000), Kuntowijoyo (2001) and Wahid (2006).

observers, Indonesian as well as foreign, I often wondered with regret why this intellectual creativity, yielding theological arguments in support of inter-religious understanding, human rights, democracy, gender equality and greater religious freedom, remained almost unknown and made no impact abroad.[20]

Much of what was most attractive in the ideas of the *pembaruan* and later liberal and progressive movements was in fact borrowed from thinkers based elsewhere. But it was only in Indonesia (and to some extent Turkey) that the works of these thinkers found a warm reception. The Pakistani Fazlur Rahman, the Indian Asghar Ali Engineer, the Sudanese Mahmoud Muhammad Taha and Abdullahi An-Na'im, the Egyptians Hassan Hanafi and Nasr Abu Zayd, the Moroccan Muhammad Abed al-Jabri – all have found a much wider following in Indonesia than in their own countries.[21] Indonesia was the only Muslim country to allow the Pakistani-American Muslim feminist theologian, Riffat Hassan, to address students in an Islamic university.[22] It was also the first country where Abdullahi An-Na'im was able to find allies to carry out his project to develop a locally grounded Muslim secularist discourse.[23] Both Hassan and An-Na'im greatly influenced the emerging Indonesian-Muslim feminist movement and Muslim human rights activism, although these movements soon developed well beyond the ideas of their original inspiration.

It was not, then, originality that made Indonesia's liberal and progressive Muslim discourse unique, but its broad degree of acceptance of critical Islamic thought, and perhaps the eagerness with which young Muslim intellectuals sought out foreign authors who could offer interesting ideas that might help them reconstruct Islamic thought. The broad acceptance of such ideas and the widespread participation in relevant

20 For an overview of the ideas developed in such circles, see van Bruinessen (2011). On the *pembaruan* movement, see Barton (1995).

21 Three of them (Rahman, An-Na'im and Abu Zayd) were forced to live in exile; one (Taha) was sentenced to death for his ideas and hanged.

22 Hassan was invited to Indonesia in 1992 by a small group of women's rights activists and students who had read an article by her published in the Muslim intellectual journal *'Ulumul Qur'an* (Hassan 1990). She met mostly with small groups, but was also invited to speak at IAIN Sunan Kalijaga in Yogyakarta, where her talk provoked heated discussion. Hassan's article and her visit were major events in the emergence of an Indonesian Muslim feminism.

23 The first results of this project, carried out by a team of Indonesian collaborators under An-Na'im's supervision, were published as An-Na'im (2007). Similar projects were to follow in other countries. An-Na'im was already known in Indonesia for his book on the thought of Mahmoud Muhammad Taha (An-Na'im 1990), which had been translated into Indonesian and had sold surprisingly well.

debates had much to do with the institutional support for rational analysis provided by the State Islamic Institutes (IAIN), established by the government to train a class of enlightened religious officials. Most of the interesting thinkers were affiliated with the Jakarta or Yogyakarta institutes, where the rectors, Harun Nasution and Mukti Ali, provided protection and an atmosphere of free intellectual debate.[24]

INDONESIA'S MUSLIM WOMEN ACTIVISTS AND ISLAMIC FEMINISM

Of the various liberal and progressive trends, Indonesia's Muslim feminist movement is the most dynamic and diverse.[25] It is also the one intellectual trend in Indonesian Islam that has become well known and admired elsewhere in the Muslim world and is gaining some traction there. Like the other strands of critical Islamic thought in Indonesia, Muslim feminism was nurtured by foreign thinkers and activists but developed into a broad-based movement – a loose coalition of women's groups and individual activists taking up various gender-related and women's issues, both at the grassroots level and within the large associations and the state bureaucracy. Indonesian feminists have been especially successful in translating ideas into action, both at the village and small town levels and in the legislative process. They have engaged in debate with male Muslim authorities, from the national to the local levels, and they have been able to bring their concerns to the floor of Muhammadiyah and NU congresses, through the women's wings of those organizations. Their writings explore the gamut of Muslim women's issues, from reproduction, humans rights and education to inheritance laws, jurisprudence and the case for legal reform.[26]

In the past two decades Muslim feminism has become a global movement, with regular meetings between thinkers and activists from many countries. Within this movement, there is a broad awareness of the special significance and achievements of Indonesian women (in addition to those of Iranian women, who were the true pioneers). Unlike in most other countries, in Indonesia Muslim feminism is not an elite movement.

24 See Suminto (1989), Munhanif (1996), Effendy (1999) and Jabali and Jamhari (2002).

25 I use the term 'Muslim feminism' in a broad sense that includes the whole range of Muslim women's rights activism (although many of the women concerned would reject the label 'feminist'). It subsumes Islamic feminism, which seeks to ground arguments for women's rights in Islamic scripture.

26 See, for example, Marcoes-Natsir and Hasyim (1997), Assegaff (2005), Marcoes-Natsir (2005), Muhammad et al. (2006) and Mulia (2004).

Aided by more elite-based groups such as Malaysia's Sisters in Islam and the transnational network Musawah, whose working language is English, the Indonesian activists have grabbed international attention and are regarded as role models to be emulated.[27]

Like other thinkers, activists and organizers, Indonesia's Muslim feminists have never sought international attention or thought of spreading their ideas beyond the confines of their own country. It was thinkers and activists elsewhere who 'discovered' them, found their work valuable, and turned them into role models and major participants in the international networks.

INDONESIA AND TURKEY COMPARED

The reluctance of Indonesian Muslims to seek the international limelight, their modesty (or is it lack of confidence?) and their conviction that they have more to learn from than to teach others, are remarkable and become even more so when we compare them with their Turkish counterparts. In the light of Fazlur Rahman's comments on Indonesia and Turkey as the two countries offering hope for the future of an enlightened Islam, a comparison of the international impact of Muslim thought and action in these two countries may be apt. Both represent great civilizations at the edge of the Arab world, and both have developed forms of expression of Islam that are quite different from those of the Arab heartlands. Turks, however, have been much more confident than Indonesians about the value, validity and relevance to others of their Muslim culture.

Under Mustafa Kemal Atatürk (d. 1938), republican Turkey was the first Muslim state to disestablish the authority of the *ulama* and put in place a form of secular regime in which the state defined what proper and acceptable Islam was. Most colonized Muslim nations, including semi-colonies like Egypt, were led to independence by secular elites who adopted lighter versions of Turkish Kemalism. Meanwhile, Turkey's secular bureaucratic and military elite, which has led the country for three-quarters of a century, is being replaced by a new, socially conservative middle class steeped in Islamic piety. Not only is the ruling Justice and Development Party (AKP) held up by the United States as a shining example of how Islam and democracy may be compatible, but Islamist movements all over the world are studying the party's rise and develop-

---

27 See http://www.sistersinislam.org.my/ and http://www.musawah.org/. Indonesian Muslim feminism has also drawn increasing scholarly attention; see, for example, Feillard (1997), Rinaldo (2008), Robinson (2008) and Brenner (2011).

ment in the hope of emulating its successes.[28] Prime Minister Erdogan and his team are very confident of the leading role their country has to play in the world of Islam.

While Sufi orders remain officially banned in Turkey, the music and dance of the Mevlevi 'Whirling Dervishes' have conquered the world, and the annual commemoration in Konya of their founder, the great poet Mevlana Jalaluddin Rumi, is an event that draws numerous pilgrims from all over the globe. Turkey's most influential Muslim thinker of the twentieth century, the Kurdish mullah Bediüzzaman Said Nursi, wrote works in an archaic style that modern Turks have difficulty understanding. *Risale-i Nur* [Treatise on the Divine Light], a collection of his main works, is pervaded by dreams and visions, and rooted in Persian and Kurdish mystical traditions. At the same time, however, Nursi advocates modern education and the cultivation of modern science as compatible with personal piety (Mardin 1989). Selections from his work have been translated into many languages and there is an active mission, the Nur movement, spreading his teachings and worldview. The Fethullah Gülen movement, which is also based on Nursi's teachings, is even more active in carrying out its Turkish-Islamic mission worldwide, establishing schools, centres of religious dialogue, charities and centres of Turkish culture in over a hundred countries worldwide, including Indonesia and Australia (Yavuz and Esposito 2003; Agai 2007; Osman 2007).

Turkish Muslims do not share the Indonesians' eagerness to learn from the Arabs; on the contrary, there is a widespread conviction that Turkish Islam is in many ways superior to the ways in which Arab Muslims practise their faith. This striking difference in attitude reflects the countries' different histories. Turkey was the heart of the Ottoman Empire, which for four centuries (1520s–1910s) ruled much of Arabia. The major centres of education, the *medrese*, were administered from Istanbul and their professors were appointed and paid by the central administration. There were of course autonomous centres of excellence elsewhere, such as Cairo's Al-Azhar University and the Great Mosque of Mecca, and in the late nineteenth century more private *medrese* emerged in Mecca offering a different curriculum. Nevertheless, most Turkish Muslim intellectuals at the time the new Turkey was established were the products of Ottoman *medrese* and interaction with the West, rather than of the Arab world. (Some of them went into exile in Egypt after the republic was established, but this did not contribute significantly to improving the communication of ideas.)

---

28 This includes Indonesia's Prosperous Justice Party (PKS) and Malaysia's Pan-Malaysian Islamic Party (PAS), both of which have – in vain – made efforts to establish closer relations with the AKP.

The history of Indonesian Muslims' connection with Arabia is a very different one. The search for wisdom, knowledge and power in hard-to-reach spiritual centres had long been a core element of Indonesian religiosity, and after the onset of Islamization Mecca replaced forest and mountain hermitages as the most prestigious centre. In the seventeenth century, several Javanese rulers sent envoys to Mecca asking the Grand Sharif to grant them the title of sultan and requesting spiritual endorsement of their rule. Seekers of knowledge and power travelled to Mecca to perform the *hajj* and stayed on for years to study Islamic law and mysticism. By the end of the nineteenth century, Southeast Asians constituted the largest immigrant community in Mecca. With only a little exaggeration one might say that the Indies had two capitals: Batavia, where the heart of Dutch commerce and administration was located, and Mecca, to which pious Muslims looked for guidance.

Under colonial rule, many pious Indonesians preferred to live in Mecca. Dutch fears of pan-Islamic propaganda and action from Mecca, targeting the Indies, were largely unfounded, but for the pious, Mecca and Arabia at large represented a free haven where religious practice was not impeded and where knowledge flourished. The *pesantren*, which from the nineteenth century onward were rapidly increasing in number, could succeed only if their founders and major teachers could show that they had spent at least some years in Mecca studying under famous *ulama*. In the twentieth century, Cairo's Al-Azhar also attracted many Indonesian students.[29] Even today, there is widespread awareness that the level of learning attained in Indonesian *pesantren* remains well below that offered by Al-Azhar or the Mecca-based teachers.

The history of the continuing process of Islamization of Indonesia is one of generation after generation of reformers, educated in Mecca or Cairo, returning to their homeland and 'correcting' Islamic belief and practice in accordance with what they had observed in the Middle East (Laffan 2003; Azra 2004). In the eyes of those reformers, the specifically Indonesian forms of expression that had developed were deviations needing correction. The reformist, 'Arabizing' urge was always contested and gave rise to various forms of cultural resistance, including the production of obscene Javanese texts mocking scripturalist Islam, the emergence of syncretistic esoteric (*kebatinan*) movements, the cultivation of nominal or less observant (*abangan*) culture as 'true Islam', efforts to develop an Indonesian school of Islamic law (*madhhab*), the advocacy of 'cultural' as opposed to 'political' Islam during the New Order period,

---

29 For an analysis of how Mecca and Cairo contributed to shaping Indonesia's *pesantren* tradition, see van Bruinessen (1994). On Indonesians in Cairo, see Abaza (1994) and Laffan (2003).

and the rise of 'liberal Islam' and various movements supporting the use of local artistic traditions in Islamic teaching and devotions (van Bruinessen, forthcoming). All these types of resistance emphasized and celebrated local forms and expressions, and almost by definition had no ambition to be relevant to other cultural contexts.

As an afterthought, one might observe that the relations of Indian Islam with the Arab Middle East have been different from those of both Southeast Asia and the Ottoman Turks. The Muslim culture of the southern coastal regions, especially Kerala and Tamil Nadu, owes much to the Indian Ocean trade and is similar to that of Southeast Asia. All of the most prominent Indian Muslim thinkers and movements, however, hail from northern India, where Islam was established by invasion from the north. A considerable proportion of Indian Muslims are (or believe themselves to be) the descendants of invaders, notably the nobility (*ashraf*), many of whom claim descent from the Prophet or his Companions. Until being replaced by Urdu in the nineteenth century, the dominant language of scholarship among Indian Muslims was Persian, and for a long time relations were closer with the Persianized regions to the north and west than with Arabia.

Indian Muslims did perform the *hajj*, of course, and we find Indian *ulama* teaching in Mecca and Medina even before the first prominent Southeast Asians arrived there. For the Indians, however, Arabia was never the sole source of Islamic learning. Following the demise of the Mughal Empire and the extension of British rule to all of India by the mid-nineteenth century, some *ulama* opted for exile in Mecca, like their Indonesian counterparts. The most illustrious of the Indian *ulama*, Rahmat Allah Kairanawi, established Mecca's first modern *madrasah*, the Sawlatiyya, which attracted Indonesian as well as Indian students. In the long term, however, it proved to be more significant for Indonesian than for Indian Islam. It was the *madrasah* of Deoband in north India rather than any Meccan institution that contributed most to shaping contemporary Indian Islam.[30]

INDONESIA AS A MARKET AND NEW HOME BASE FOR MOVEMENTS ORIGINATING ELSEWHERE

Indonesian Islam may not (yet) be 'export oriented', but a wide range of Islamic movements views Indonesia as a huge and attractive market,

30 On Rahmat Allah Kairanawi and other Indian *ulama* and the role of Mecca, see Alavi (2011). On the significance of the Sawlatiyya for Indonesian Islam, see van Bruinessen (1994). On Deoband and its significance for Indian Islam, see Metcalf (1978).

and carries out active missions there. As observed above, Natsir's DDII was actively supported by Saudi Arabia and the Muslim World League in bringing Indonesian belief and practice into greater conformity with those on the Arabian Peninsula. Both the Muslim Brotherhood and, later, the Salafi movement gained their first foothold in Indonesia through the good offices of the DDII (van Bruinessen 2002).

After the Iranian revolution, many young Indonesians converted from Sunni to Shi'a Islam. This movement was self-generated, and the Iranian embassy was reluctant to be seen supporting it. However, it quickly met a massive counteroffensive from Saudi Arabia and other Gulf countries, which felt threatened by Iran's revolutionary rhetoric. Initially they used Natsir and the DDII as their vehicles, but soon these were circumvented by Saudi-controlled institutions in Jakarta such as the Institute for Arabic and Islamic Studies (LIPIA) and the Muslim World League. Indonesia's Salafi movement, the most recent and dynamic of its various Islamic movements, is actively supported and supervised by foundations and individuals in Saudi Arabia, Kuwait, Yemen and Qatar (Hasan 2006, 2010).

The Indonesian chapter of Hizb ut-Tahrir, Hizbut Tahrir Indonesia (HTI), may have emerged more or less accidentally after its chief organizer was invited to leave Australia to teach Arabic in a *pesantren* in Bogor. Its spectacular growth and great visibility since 1998 have made HTI the strongest 'national' chapter of this anti-nationalist, avowedly global caliphate movement (Osman 2009, 2010). Indonesia is, moreover, one of the few Muslim countries where the organization is not banned, making it of crucial importance to the central leadership. Given the strong Arab bias in the movement, in spite of its global pretensions, it is unlikely that Indonesians will come to lead it any time soon, or that the movement will adapt itself to Indonesian peculiarities. However, this is probably the first transnational Muslim movement that has had to take serious account of its Indonesian followers.

A transnational movement of a very different kind, for which Indonesia has also become increasingly important, is the Naqshbandiyya Haqqaniyya Sufi order. Its charismatic grand sheikh, Nazim al-Qubrusi, was born in the Turkish part of Cyprus (where he has now retired), but the order has become truly global, with branches in many Muslim countries and converts across Europe and North America. The current de facto leader is the grand sheikh's representative in North America, Hisham Kabbani, who among other things has made the order the central pillar of a worldwide anti-fundamentalist alliance. In the 1990s, Sheikh Nazim and Sheikh Hisham began directing their activities towards Southeast Asia, in what was seen by some as an effort to find a permanent base in a major Muslim region. In the 2000s the latter has made annual visits to Indonesia, establishing connections with existing Sufi networks and founding branches of Haqqaniyya among the urban middle class. The Indonesian connection is now of central importance to the order (Laffan 2006: Nielsen, Draper and Yemelianova 2006).

Other transnational movements that have recently intensified their activities in Indonesia include Tablighi Jama'at and Fethullah Gülen. Both initially restricted their international expansions to culturally related populations (the South Asian diaspora in the case of the former and the Turkish diaspora and Turkic peoples of Central Asia in the case of the latter) but in the past decade have succeeded in making major inroads among non-related populations. Indonesia is a significant, though not the most important, field of mission for them. Their activities have, however, contributed to the increased visibility of Indonesians among Muslim populations elsewhere.

CONCLUSION

Indonesia has not regained the leading position it held briefly among Muslim nations in the 1950s, but its visibility has increased significantly since the fall of the Suharto regime, and there is a new confidence among the country's leaders to take initiatives in the international arena. The role of Indonesia in such international Muslim forums as the Organisation of the Islamic Conference has not been remarkable so far, and its efforts to mediate in international conflicts (the southern Philippines, the Middle East) have been relatively modest, but at least the government has been positioning itself for a new international role in the Muslim arena (Perwita 2007). NU's first major international initiative, the International Conference of Islamic Scholars, may have had more to do with Hasyim Muzadi's bid for the country's vice-presidency than with the association's international ambitions, but NU has continued to project itself in the international arena. Indonesia's growing confidence is also evident in the increased charitable activity directed towards Palestine, in which several Indonesian Muslim charities have been competing for attention (Latief 2009, forthcoming).

The increased visibility of the Indonesian *ummah* has drawn a broad range of transnational Muslim movements to the country, for some of which Indonesia appears to be becoming the most important field of action. In this sense, too, the Indonesian *ummah* may be seen to be moving from a peripheral to a more central position, corresponding to its demographic weight.

Indonesian Islam is characterized by a vibrant intellectual discourse, a remarkable openness to alternative views and a broad acceptance of religious pluralism, in spite of a strong anti-liberal and anti-pluralist reaction during the past six or seven years. Although the uniqueness and attractiveness of Indonesia's Muslim intellectualism have been noticed by visiting Muslims, its impact beyond Indonesia has been minimal, especially when compared with that of other major cultural regions such as Turkey and South Asia. Indonesia's Muslim thinkers have been eager to draw inspiration from a wide variety of sources, many of them foreign, but they have remained remarkably reluctant to disseminate their own work abroad.

Part of the explanation for the lack of international impact of Indonesian Muslim thought, as suggested above, lies in the fact that most Indonesian Muslim thinkers have been activists whose writing has served a social or political purpose. They have not written great synthesizing works but rather numerous shorter pieces, often in response to questions or circumstances that may not immediately make sense to foreign audiences, even if inspired by universal ideas. The thrust of much of their discourse concerns the defence of pluralism, variety and local colour in the cultural expressions of Islam, against the homogenizing tendencies of transnational Islamism. It is perhaps too inherently local to be exportable.

REFERENCES

Abaza, Mona (1994) *Indonesian Students in Cairo: Islamic Education, Perceptions and Exchanges*, Association Archipel, Paris.

Abaza, Mona (2007) 'More on the shifting worlds of Islam. The Middle East and Southeast Asia: a troubled relationship?', *Muslim World* 97(3): 419–36.

Abaza, Mona (2011) 'Asia imagined by the Arabs', in K. Bustamam-Ahmad and P. Jory (eds) *Islamic Studies and Islamic Education in Contemporary Southeast Asia*, Yayasan Ilmuwan, Kuala Lumpur.

Agai, Bekim (2007) *Zwischen Netzwerk und Diskurs: Das Bildungsnetzwerk um Fethullah Gülen (geb. 1938): Die Flexible Umsetzung Modernen Islamischen Gedankengutes* [Between Network and Discourse: The Educational Network around Fethullah Gülen (b. 1938): The Flexible Transformation of Modern Islamic Thought], EB-Verlag, Berlin.

Al-Andunisi, Abu Hilal (1984) *Ghara Tabshiriyya Jadida 'ala Andunisya* [The New Missionary Invasion of Indonesia], Dar al-Shuruq, Jeddah.

Alavi, Seema (2011) '"Fugitive mullahs and outlawed fanatics": Indian Muslims in nineteenth century trans-Asiatic imperial rivalries', *Modern Asian Studies* 45(6): 1,337–82.

An-Na'im, Abdullahi Ahmed (1990) *Toward an Islamic Reformation*, Syracuse University Press, New York NY. (Published in Indonesian in 1994 as *Dekonstruksi Syari'ah: Wacana Kebebasan Sipil, Hak Asasi Manusia dan Hubungan Internasional dalam Islam* [Deconstructing the Shariah: The Discourse of Civil Liberties, Human Rights and International Law in Islam], LKiS, Yogyakarta.)

An-Na'im, Abdullahi Ahmed (2007) *Islam dan Negara Sekuler: Menegosiasikan Masa Depan Syariah* [Islam and the Secular State: Negotiating the Future of the Shariah], Mizan, Bandung.

Assegaff, Farha Abdul Kadir (2005) 'Islamist feminism? Syariah for the empowerment of women: the case of Indonesia's Pesantren Al-Firdaus', Islam, Syari'ah and Governance Background Paper No. 5, Melbourne Law School, University of Melbourne, Melbourne.

Azra, Azyumardi (2004) *The Origins of Islamic Reform in Southeast Asia: Networks of Malay–Indonesian and Middle Eastern 'Ulama' in the Seventeenth and Eighteenth Centuries*, KITLV Press, Leiden.

Barton, Gregory James (1995) 'The emergence of neo-modernism: a progressive, liberal movement of Islamic thought in Indonesia. A textual study examining the writings of Nurcholish Madjid, Djohan Effendi, Ahmad Wahib and Abdurrahman Wahid, 1968–1980', PhD thesis, Monash University, Clayton.

Bradley, Francis R. (2010) 'The social dynamics of Islamic revivalism in Southeast Asia: the rise of the Patani school', PhD dissertation, University of Wisconsin, Madison WI.

Brenner, Suzanne (2011) 'Private moralities in the public sphere: democratization, Islam, and gender in Indonesia', *American Anthropologist* 113(3): 478–90.

Bruinessen, Martin van (1990) '*Kitab kuning*: books in Arabic script used in the *pesantren* milieu', *Bijdragen tot de Taal-, Land- en Volkenkunde* 146: 226–69.

Bruinessen, Martin van (1994) '*Pesantren* and *kitab kuning*: continuity and change in a tradition of religious learning', in W. Marschall (ed.) *Texts from the Islands: Oral and Written Traditions of Indonesia and the Malay World*, University of Berne Institute of Ethnology, Berne.

Bruinessen, Martin van (2002) 'Genealogies of Islamic radicalism in Indonesia', *South East Asia Research* 10(2): 117–54.

Bruinessen, Martin van (2011) 'What happened to the smiling face of Indonesian Islam? Muslim intellectualism and the conservative turn in post-Suharto Indonesia', RSIS Working Paper No. 222, S. Rajaratnam School of International Studies, Singapore, 6 January, available at http://www.rsis.edu.sg/publications/workingpapers/wp222.pdf.

Bruinessen, Martin van (forthcoming) '*Ghazwul fikri* or Arabization? Indonesian Muslim responses to globalization', in K. Miichi (ed.) *Muslim Responses to Islam and Globalization in Southeast Asia*.

Dahlan, Ihsan M. (n.d.) *Siraj al-Talibin, Sharh 'ala Minhaj al-'Abidin* [Guidance for Seekers, a Commentary on the Path of Worshippers], al-Haramayn, Jeddah.

Effendy, Edy A. (ed.) (1999) *Dekonstruksi Islam: Mazhab Ciputat* [Deconstructing Islam: The School of Ciputat], Zaman Wacana Mulia, Bandung.

Feener, R. Michael and Michael F. Laffan (2005) 'Sufi scents across the Indian Ocean: Yemeni hagiography and the earliest history of Southeast Asian Islam', *Archipel* 70: 185–208.

Feillard, Andrée (1997) 'Indonesia's emerging Muslim feminism: women leaders on equality, inheritance and other gender issues', *Studia Islamika* 4(1): 83–111.

Göksoy, Ismail Hakki (1995) *Endonezya'da Islam ve Hollanda Sömürgeciligi* [Islam in Indonesia and Dutch Colonialism], ISAM Yayinlari, Ankara.

Hasan, Noorhaidi (2006) *Laskar Jihad: Islam, Militancy and the Quest for Identity in Post-New Order Indonesia*, Cornell Southeast Asia Program, Ithaca NY.

Hasan, Noorhaidi (2010) 'The failure of the Wahhabi campaign: transnational Islam and the Salafi *madrasa* in post-9/11 Indonesia', *South East Asia Research* 18(4): 675–705.

Hassan, Riffat (1990) 'Teologi perempuan dalam tradisi Islam: sejajar di hapadan Allah' [The theology of women in Islamic tradition: equal before God], *'Ulumul Qur'an: Jurnal Ilmu dan Kebudayaan* 1(4): 48-55.

Heiss, Johann and Martin Slama (2010) 'Genealogical avenues, long-distance flows and social hierarchy: Hadrami migrants in the Indonesian diaspora', *Anthropology of the Middle East* 5(1): 34–52.

Ho, Engseng (2006) *The Graves of Tarim: Genealogy and Mobility across the Indian Ocean*, University of California Press, Berkeley CA.

Jabali, Fuad and Jamhari (2002) *IAIN dan Modernisasi Islam di Indonesia* [The IAIN and the Modernization of Islam in Indonesia], Logos, Jakarta.

Kostiner, Joseph (1984) 'The impact of the Hadrami emigrants in the East Indies on Islamic modernism and social change in the Hadramawt during the 20th century', in R. Israeli and A.H. Johns (eds) *Islam in Asia. Volume 2: Southeast and East Asia*, Westview Press, Boulder CO.

Kuntowijoyo (2001) *Muslim Tanpa Masjid: Esai-esai Agama, Budaya, dan Politik dalam Bingkai Strukturalisme Transendental* [Muslims without Mosques: Essays on Religion, Culture and Politics in the Framework of Transcendental Structuralism], Mizan, Bandung.

Laffan, Michael F. (2003) *Islamic Nationhood and Colonial Indonesia: The Umma below the Winds*, RoutledgeCurzon, London.

Laffan, Michael F. (2006) 'From alternative medicine to national cure: another voice for the Sûfî orders in the Indonesian media', *Archives de Sciences Sociales des Religions* 135: 91–115.

Latief, Hilman (2009) 'Internationalising domestic aid: charity activism and Islamic solidarity movement in contemporary Indonesia', paper presented at the International Graduate Student Conference, Gadjah Mada University, Yogyakarta, 23 November.

Latief, Hilman (forthcoming) 'Islamic charities and social activism: welfare, *da'wa* and politics', PhD dissertation, Utrecht University, Utrecht.

Mackie, Jamie (2005) *Bandung 1955: Non-alignment and Afro-Asian Solidarity*, Didier Millet, Singapore.

Madjid, Nurcholish (1987) *Islam, Kemodernan dan KeIndonesiaan* [Islam, Modernity and Indonesian-ness], Bandung: Mizan.

Madjid, Nurcholish and Mohamad Roem (2000) *Tidak ada Negara Islam: Surat-surat Politik Nurcholish Madjid – Mohamad Roem* [The Islamic State Does Not Exist: Political Correspondence of Nurcholish Madjid and Mohamad Roem], Djambatan, Jakarta.

Marcoes-Natsir, Lies (2005) 'Abortion and the Qur'an: a need for reinterpretation in Indonesia?', in A. Saeed (ed.) *Approaches to the Qur'an in Contemporary Indonesia*, Oxford University Press, Oxford.

Marcoes-Natsir, Lies and Syafiq Hasyim (1997) *P3M dan Program Fiqh an-Nisa untuk Penguatan Hak-hak Reproduksi Perempuan* [P3M and a Program of Women's *Fiqh* for Strengthening Women's Reproductive Rights], P3M, Jakarta.

Mardin, Serif (1989) *Religion and Social Change in Modern Turkey: The Case of Bediuzzaman Said Nursi*, State University of New York Press, Albany NY.

Metcalf, Barbara D. (1978) 'The *madrasah* at Deoband: a model for religious education in modern India', *Modern Asian Studies* 12: 111–34.

Mobini-Kesheh, Natalie (1999) *The Hadrami Awakening: Community and Identity in the Netherlands East Indies, 1900–1942*, Cornell Southeast Asia Program, Ithaca NY.

Muhammad, K.H. Husein et al. (2006) *Dawrah Fiqh concerning Women: Manual for a Course on Islam and Gender*, Fahmina Institute, Cirebon.

Mujiburrahman (2006) *Feeling Threatened: Muslim–Christian Relations in Indonesia's New Order*, Amsterdam University Press, Amsterdam, available at http://igitur-archive.library.uu.nl/dissertations/2006-0915-201013/.

Mulia, Siti Musdah (2004) 'Modernisation of Islamic law. Counter legal draft: the compilation of Indonesian Islamic law', Gender Mainstreaming Team, Ministry of Religious Affairs, Jakarta.

Munhanif, Ali (1996) 'Islam and the struggle for religious pluralism in Indonesia: a political reading of the religious thought of Mukti Ali', *Studia Islamika* 3(1): 79–126.

Natsir, Mohamad (1955) *Capita Selecta* [Selected Writings], Bulan Bintang, Jakarta.

Nielsen, Jørgen S., Mustafa Draper and Galina M. Yemelianova (2006) 'Transnational Sufism: the Haqqaniyya', in J. Malik and J. Hinnells (eds) *Sufism in the West*, Routledge, London.

Osman, Mohamed Nawab (2007) 'Gülen's contribution to a middle way Islam in Southeast Asia', paper presented at a conference on the Muslim World in Transition: Contributions of the Gülen Movement, London School of Economics, London, 25–27 October, available at http://www.fethullahgulen.org/conference-papers/302-contributions-of-the-gulen-movement/2465-gulens-contribution-to-a-middle-way-islam-in-southeast-asia.html.

Osman, Mohamed Nawab (2009) 'Reviving the caliphate in the Nusantara: Hizbut Tahrir Indonesia's mobilization strategy and its impact in Indonesia', RSIS Working Paper No. 171, S. Rajaratnam School of International Studies, Singapore, February, available at http://www.rsis.edu.sg/publications/WorkingPapers/WP171.pdf.

Osman, Mohamed Nawab (2010) 'The transnational network of Hizbut Tahrir Indonesia', *South East Asia Research* 18(4): 735–56.

Perwita, Anak Agung Banyu (2007) *Indonesia and the Muslim World: Islam and Secularism in the Foreign Policy of Soeharto and Beyond*, NIAS Press, Copenhagen.

Pijper, G.F. (1977) *Studiën over de Geschiedenis van de Islam in Indonesië 1900–1950* [Studies on the History of Islam in Indonesia, 1900–1950], Brill, Leiden.

Rakhmat, Jalaluddin (1986) *Islam Alternatif: Ceramah-ceramah di Kampus* [Alternative Islam: Campus Lectures], Mizan, London and Bandung.

Rinaldo, Rachel (2008) 'Envisioning the nation: women activists, religion and the public sphere in Indonesia', *Social Forces* 86(4): 1,781–804.

Robinson, Kathryn (2008) 'Islamic cosmopolitics, human rights, and anti-violence strategies in Indonesia', in P. Werbner (ed.) *Anthropology and the New Cosmopolitanism*, Berg, Oxford.

Salim, H. Agus (1954) *Djedjak Langkah Hadji A. Salim: Pilihan Karangan, Utjapan dan Pendapat Beliau dari Dulu sampai Sekarang* [In the Footsteps of Haji A. Salim: Selected Writings, Lectures and Opinions of a Lifetime], Tintamas, Jakarta.

Schulze, Reinhard (1983) 'Der einfluss Islamischer organisationen auf die länder Südostasiens - von Mekka aus gesehen' [The influence of Islamic organizations on the countries of Southeast Asia, seen from Mecca], in W. Draguhn (ed.) *Der Einfluss des Islams auf Politik, Wirtschaft und Gesellschaft Südostasiens* [The Influence of Islam on the Politics, Economy and Society of Southeast Asia], Institut für Asienkunde, Hamburg.

Schulze, Reinhard (1990) *Islamischer Internationalismus im 20: Jahrhundert. Untersuchungen zur Geschichte der Islamischen Weltliga* [Islamic Internationalism in the 20th Century: Studies on the History of the Muslim World League], Brill, Leiden.

Shalabi, Ahmad (1983) *The Encyclopaedia of Islamic History: Islam and Non-Arabic-speaking Muslim Countries*, Maktabat al-Nahda al-Misriyya, Cairo.

Suminto, H. Aqib (ed.) (1989) *Refleksi Pembaharuan Pemikiran Islam: 70 Tahun Harun Nasution* [Reflections on the Renewal of Islamic Thought on the Occasion of Harun Nasution's 70th Birthday], Lembaga Studi Agama dan Filsafat, Jakarta.

Wahid, Abdurrahman (2006) *Islamku, Islam Anda, Islam Kita: Agama Masyarakat Negara Demokrasi* [My Islam, Your Islam, Our Islam: Religion, Society, State, Democracy], Wahid Institute, Jakarta.

Yavuz, M. Hakan and John L. Esposito (eds) (2003) *Turkish Islam and the Secular State: The Gülen Movement*, Syracuse University Press, New York NY.

8 INDONESIA'S QUIET SPRINGTIME: KNOWLEDGE, POLICY AND REFORM

Scott Guggenheim

Indonesia's recent emergence as a middle-income country carries with it significant implications for its overall development strategy and the role that knowledge and education play within it. Indonesia is increasingly operating in a highly competitive global economy, one that values not just the country's traditional economic strengths in natural resource extraction and low-cost labour, but also the ability to innovate and create economic value through knowledge. Development aid as a share of the national budget will continue to shrink, placing an ever-growing premium on the ability of policy makers to make smart choices about how best to spend national budgetary resources. Moreover, the continuing process of democratization carries with it demands for informed public participation through which public policy can be accessed, understood and debated by a broad range of stakeholders.

Where will the knowledge about policy options and their trade-offs come from? For a variety of reasons that will be discussed later, during the post-colonial and New Order years Indonesia did not develop the kind of domestic knowledge infrastructure that can currently be seen in other large developing countries such as China, India, Mexico or Brazil. Instead, it has always relied heavily on international technical assistance to help develop policy options that could be presented to high-level

* Special thanks are due to Kamala Chandrakirana, Benjamin Davis, Merry Ginting, Jessica Mackenzie, Debbie Muirhead, Patrick Barron, Diastika Rahiwidiarti, Idauli Tamarin and Beth Thomson. I am grateful to P.D. Hien for supplying data for two of the figures. This chapter draws on the design document for 'Revitalizing Indonesia's knowledge sector' (AusAID 2011).

government decision makers. Nor has Indonesia made much progress in providing an incentive framework for the private sector, universities or civil society to provide these services. However, with the country's growing wealth, the transition to democracy and associated rise in the importance of public policy debate, and the increasing complexity of policy choices facing the government at both the national and subnational levels of its operation, this strategy is no longer viable.

This contribution to the book will argue that after the long winter of New Order control of the institutions of independent thinking, there are signs that new shoots are pushing their way to the surface. Their survival is by no means guaranteed, however. The genius of the New Order's control system lay not in the instances of outright oppression of critical scholars, analysts and researchers, but in the use of bureaucratic incentives to undermine the production of knowledge from within the very institutions that created and used it. Young scholars, analysts and progressive policy makers today must find new ways to push past this legacy and the many people who have a vested interest in preventing the structural reforms that are needed to change the system.

The chapter, then, is an attempt both to describe the current state of Indonesia's knowledge sector and to develop a preliminary framework to understand what reforms are needed to improve it. Here, the 'knowledge sector' means the overall institutional landscape of government, private sector and civil society organizations that support the development of public policy. It includes think tanks, university institutes, specialized agencies within government ministries, certain types of private sector contractors and a range of non-government organizations.

In using the term, the objective is not to nail down with full precision the boundaries of the sector, but to focus attention on the overall landscape and the issues that reviewing it from a systems perspective can provide. To the extent that using the term offers up new ideas and approaches that can help Indonesia think through an agenda for reform, it is a useful way to frame a critical development challenge. While the term is meant to be used flexibly, it nevertheless builds on two important foundational concepts.

First, treating knowledge as a sector carries with it certain implications about what analytical issues deserve priority. Past approaches to knowledge development in Indonesia have for the most part consisted of efforts to build up individual institutes by providing them with direct assistance through grants, scholarships, twinning programs and other forms of direct support. By contrast, sectoral approaches move the overall structure of regulation, opportunities and constraints to the foreground. The problems of individual organizations' strengths, weaknesses, leadership, financing and so on remain important, but the driving argument for treating knowledge as a sector is that unless the overall environment for knowledge development improves, efforts to build a structure to use locally generated knowledge to drive development policy will be slow, painful and scattered.

The second benefit of defining the knowledge sector generically rather than with full classificatory precision is that it avoids the common pitfall of limiting the boundaries of the policy community to a small group of organizations located mostly in the national capital and closely identified with the national government. At least for the purposes of this study, Indonesia's framework for developing knowledge must be part and parcel of how it develops democracy. In a democratic model, better decisions come from more people contesting more ideas, using a broader range of institutional forums for debate. Knowledge is not just about better technical decision making, but about how the policy agenda that is developed between government, civil society and the public at large can be informed by analysis built from evidence. In the context of a country that is still emerging from a highly constrained political environment, keeping open the boundaries defining which individuals and organizations can become 'legitimate' members of Indonesia's emergent policy community will be of critical importance for some time to come.

This article is a hybrid document. It is built on a range of secondary analyses as well as primary research that seeks to identify the main causes of Indonesia's constrained knowledge sector development. The sources include original research commissioned for the Knowledge Sector Program, a joint initiative of the Australian and Indonesian governments.[1] But the study is also meant to provide the outline for a reform framework that can help Indonesian policy makers, intellectuals and civil society activists identify what types of reforms the country might pursue to overcome the anaemic legacy of the colonial and New Order years. To achieve that goal, the chapter is built around a model of how knowledge becomes policy. However, as with most policy-oriented papers, it is a lot easier to say what is wrong and must be fixed than what recipes Indonesia must follow to move past the problems. For the case of the reform agenda proposed here, that fuzziness about solutions is built into the knowledge sector action program itself. To the extent that knowledge sector reform is part and parcel of Indonesia's democratic transition, all that a policy paper such as this can hope to achieve is to clarify the nature of the problem and suggest options for public debate.

---

1 The papers in the series are available at http://www.ausaid.gov.au/publications/pubout.cfm?ID=6907_4230_9750_6366_1236&Type=.

Figure 8.1 Share of published research on a country carried out by domestic researchers (%)

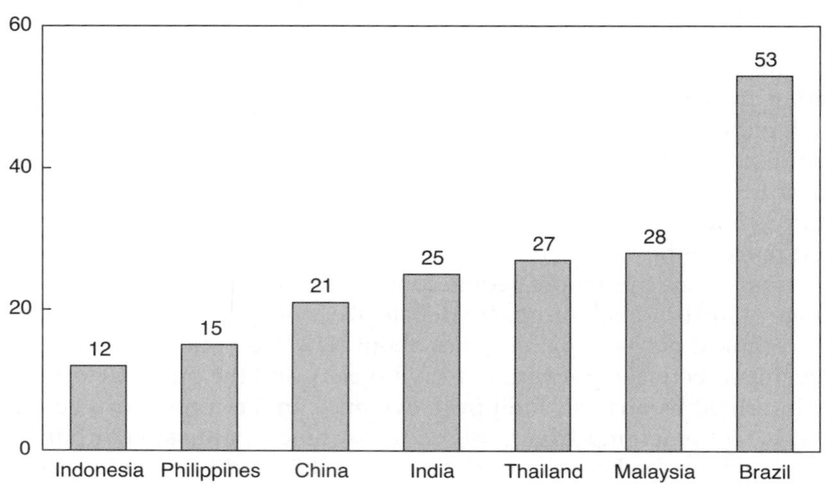

Source: Suryadarma, Pomeroy and Tanuwidjaja (2011: 3), based on SSCI database, Thomson Reuters Web of Knowledge, 1956–2011.

THE STATE OF INDONESIA'S KNOWLEDGE SECTOR

It is difficult to place a benchmark on the knowledge sector that would allow for fully rigorous comparisons across countries. Nevertheless, several international comparisons indicate that Indonesia performs well below other countries of comparable economic standing. This section uses a selected set of commonly accepted comparators to give a sense of why Indonesian policy makers and others are concerned with knowledge sector reform.

One simple if not entirely revealing indicator of the performance of a country's knowledge sector is the extent to which its research community publishes. According to SCImago Journal and Country Rank, during the period 1996–2010 Indonesia produced only 13,047 published scientific documents, placing its scientific productivity over the 15 years of record keeping below that of Bangladesh, Kenya, Lithuania and Nigeria – and far below that of neighbouring Thailand, Malaysia and Singapore.[2]

The Social Sciences Citation Index (SSCI), which covers international peer-reviewed journals, shows that only 12 per cent of social science research published on Indonesia is undertaken by authors based in the country, or less than half the share for Thailand and Malaysia (Figure 8.1).

2 See http://www.scimagojr.com, accessed 2 January 2011.

Figure 8.2 Research intensity of Asian countries, 2002–2008 (no. of international publications per 1 million people)

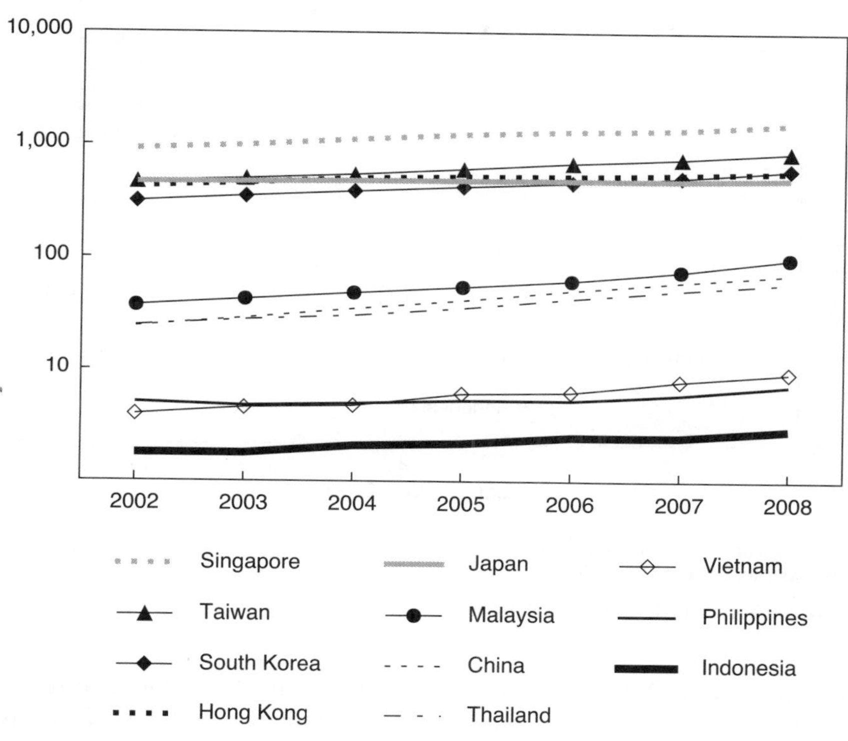

Source: Hien (2010), based on ISI database.

Although the number of international publications by Indonesians is growing, Indonesia still has the lowest number per million people when compared with the other large or relatively more developed Asian countries (Figure 8.2).

To a certain extent, research intensity is correlated with per capita GDP and a country's performance on the Human Development Index. Economic growth should allow for increased investment in higher education and better-quality research. However, Indonesia performs worse than other Asian countries on a comparison of research intensity (as measured by the number of publications per million people) and per capita GDP – even worse than Vietnam and the Philippines, which have lower per capita GDP (Figure 8.3).

More qualitative measurements of knowledge sector development tell the same story. According to the 2010 'Global "go-to think tanks"'

Figure 8.3 Correlation of research intensity with per capita GDP, Asia

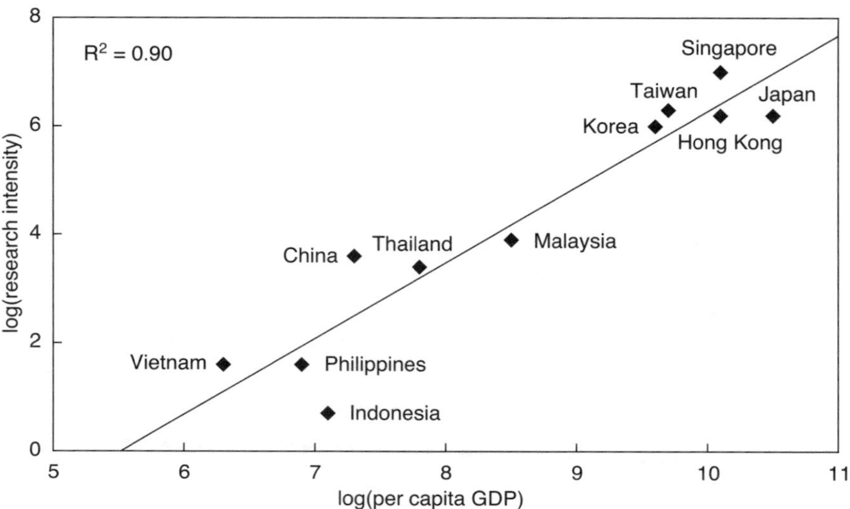

Note: Research intensity is measured by the number of international publications per 1 million people. Data are for 2004.

Source: Hien (2010), based on ISI database.

report (TTCSP 2011), only one Indonesian think tank, the Centre for Strategic and International Studies (CSIS), made it into the top 25 think tanks in Asia. However, even CSIS's lustre is fading as the institute goes through various efforts to renew its leadership, funding and staffing. Other organizations, such as the SMERU Research Institute, are likely to rise in the rankings as measurement catches up with output, but the larger point is that for such a large, relatively wealthy country, Indonesia has just a handful of independent institutes that can carry out internationally respected work on their own.

Indonesia's low research output compared with other developing countries is an indicator of the broader and systemic problems underlying the knowledge sector. But unlike in other developing countries where a weak or undeveloped knowledge sector can be attributed to extrinsic causes such as country-wide poverty or overt political repression, in Indonesia the current situation is the result of government policies that deliberately undermined the institutional preconditions needed for a healthy knowledge sector to develop. Overcoming that legacy is proving to be a very difficult challenge indeed.

Historical antecedents: why does Indonesia have a knowledge sector problem?

Indonesia's underdeveloped knowledge sector can be traced to the intellectual conformity imposed by past regimes. Despite some last-minute flourishes to educate the elite, the Dutch never built up a national university system to educate a large body of Indonesian administrators in the way that the British were doing in India or the Spanish had done in Latin America two centuries earlier. By the time World War II started, fewer than 1,000 Indonesians had a college degree, and while these graduates played a critical role in the country's independence movement,[3] they did not go on to form the backbone of a new intellectual class of technocrats, academics and policy makers.

After independence in 1949, Indonesia's incipient knowledge sector was supported by national leaders in ways that were common in many other newly independent countries. Broadening access to higher education for more than a handful of Indonesians was a top priority for the independence leaders now in power, who were anxious to do away with this very visible reminder of colonial oppression and who also needed to find a whole new source of administrators, engineers, teachers and health workers to carry out their plans for national development. At the same time, though, the increasing politicization of the campuses and their manipulation within the broader drama of Sukarno's various confrontations were the backdrop for the crackdown that followed.

The 1966 coup d'état saw General Suharto's rise to power and the dawn of the New Order regime. The regime's relationship to academic development was not quite as straightforward as simply repressing its critics by force. Whereas the Dutch had refused to provide broad-based higher education to Indonesians, the New Order government established over 20 state universities across the archipelago, allowing much greater access to tertiary education. But although the government encouraged narrowly defined technocratic input into its development strategies and programs, its education policies subjected universities to rigid centralized government control, which curtailed autonomy and academic freedom. New Order authoritarianism suppressed critical thinking and shut down virtually all public spaces for contestation that challenged government policies.

Understanding the mechanisms by which this was achieved is crucial for developing a reform agenda that can reach down to the roots of today's constraints. As Pompe (2005) has shown for the problems

---

3 See, for example, Mrázek (1994), especially Chapter 4 on the birth of Pendidikan Nasional Indonesia – the Indonesian National Education movement.

currently faced in the justice sector, the New Order government operated less by outright repression than by using the machinery of public administration and finance to bring presumptively independent institutions into the orbit and then the control systems of the bureaucracy. Promotion was based on the approval of bureaucratic superiors rather than on academic merit. Budgetary support for universities and the few think tanks that were allowed to operate was both highly centralized and extremely rigid, allowing civil servants to control allocations and apply punitive sanctions to institutions that allowed individuals to challenge government authority. Compressed salary structures gave further discretionary control to administrators and, as in other parts of the civil service, encouraged a working environment in which researchers depended heavily on consulting contracts and off-budget income sources to complement their grossly inadequate salaries.

A second, less well-understood factor that helps to explain the deficits in today's knowledge sector lies in the New Order's extreme centralization. It is important not only to be able to produce high-quality, independent policy knowledge, but to have an audience that is able and willing to use it. During the New Order period, the main development function of subnational governments was to execute national policies, not to develop their own policies and programs based on local assessments. Compared with countries such as Colombia, India or the Philippines, where local officials and administrations were accountable for autonomous policy decisions and obtained tailored assessments and feasibility studies from universities, think tanks and consulting groups, Indonesian legislators and administrators had little discretion and did not develop procedures to commission or review high-quality, locally generated research. Nor, for the most part, did the government encourage local participation or debate about policy alternatives, as often happens in other centralized countries such as China. Lacking both demand for their products and accountability, universities and independent institutes had few reasons to develop systems for quality control, policy responsiveness or applied research.

Finally, while the extent is difficult to quantify, there is little question that international technical assistance produced displacement effects that provided top-level decision makers with a viable source of policy knowledge without them having to develop potentially threatening capacities within the country. Affirmative action programs that required local partnerships probably exacerbated rather than solved the problem since, while there were unquestionable benefits for some younger Indonesians to work with global experts, such programs also created too many incentives for box ticking on the donor side and pro forma, low-quality work by overstretched academic consultants on the other, as famously described by Clifford Geertz in a review of the state of the social sciences in Indonesia at the beginning of the 1970s (Geertz 1971).

New opportunities for reform

A number of factors suggest not just that this model is no longer sustainable, but that the ownership and commitment needed to drive a reform program are now present. First, the sheer size and complexity of the Indonesian economy mean that the demand for high-quality policy analysis is rising. Decentralization will accelerate this trend, creating demand over time for affordable local sources of analysis. Second, demand for university education is soaring, with more than 4 million Indonesians enrolled in national universities in 2010 (Hill and Thee 2011). Third, the lifting of New Order authoritarian controls has been accompanied by a big increase in exposure to global media. The current generation of college graduates will be the first to have grown up in an environment of uncensored press, competitive elections and expectations that they will eventually play a leadership role in shaping national institutions. Professionally trained Indonesian analysts are not likely to accept passively career paths that are overly dependent on bureaucratic patronage and conformity. Fourth, with public policies now being openly and vigorously contested, the demand for evidence to back competing claims can only grow. In 2008 Indonesia passed a comprehensive Freedom of Information Law, Law No. 14/2008, which came into effect on 1 May 2010. If implemented, it will provide a compelling mechanism to increase the amount of government information released into the public domain, where its quality and accuracy can receive critical review.

There are also several encouraging signs at the more 'micro' level. First, both the government and international donors have made large and still rising investments in overseas scholarships.[4] Studies show that returning students continue to face structural problems that deter them from pursuing careers in public policy, but the overall availability of potential contributors is a necessary precondition for successful reform. Second, while the Supreme Court has invalidated a bill that would have expanded university autonomy, the push to reform the tertiary sector remains strong and follow-up action is already being planned. Third, individual sectors are also undertaking knowledge-driven reform initiatives, such as the 2007 masterplan to make the National Development Planning Agency (Bappenas) a knowledge-based institution, the continual upgrading of the national statistical agency (BPS) and the efforts

4 Statistics are still being gathered but a rough estimate suggests that there are approximately 45,000 Indonesians studying abroad.

of the ministries of health and education to improve their in-house research institutes. Fourth, civil society institutes are both increasing in number and diversifying their activities, with many of the older and better-established groups now undertaking a much needed program of revitalization and renewal. Finally, while the point is diffuse, it is nevertheless important: despite the New Order's failure to develop a formal apparatus of think tanks, universities and policy institutes, Indonesia benefits from a rich tradition of critical dialogue on national and local policy issues through its arts and cultural performances, social networks, news media, and religious institutions and organizations.

A continuous domestic production of research for policy purposes would give Indonesian decision makers and civil society access to a ready supply of evidence-based options for timelier, better-targeted and more responsive policy decisions (Carden 2009). However, the availability of evidence is only one element in the complicated mix of factors and forces behind governmental policy decisions. Decision making also depends on other considerations, such as political feasibility assessments, negotiations among interest groups, popular pressures for action on politically contentious issues and so on. For all the talk about evidence-based policy making that is so popular in the global development discourse today, no country on earth operates in so straightforward a manner. But if there is no direct path that leads from evidence to policy, the converse argument that knowledge has at best a tenuous basis in policy making is not valid either. Understanding how knowledge can influence policy requires taking a step back to conceptualize what moving parts must fit together for knowledge and policy making to become friendly partners rather than distant neighbours.

IMPROVING THE KNOWLEDGE-TO-POLICY CYCLE

One useful model for thinking about how high-quality knowledge is generated, and then used by policy makers to make decisions, comprises:

- the *research organizations* that produce the knowledge and evidence that influence policies (referred to here as the supply side);
- the *policy makers* who demand and use evidence in formulating policies (generally referred to as the demand side);
- the *intermediary* functions and bodies that communicate between policy makers and research organizations; and
- the *enabling environment* where policies govern how the supply and demand sides interact, and the research systems operate (Lindqvist 2000, 2001; Lavis et al. 2006).

Figure 8.4 A functioning knowledge-to-policy cycle

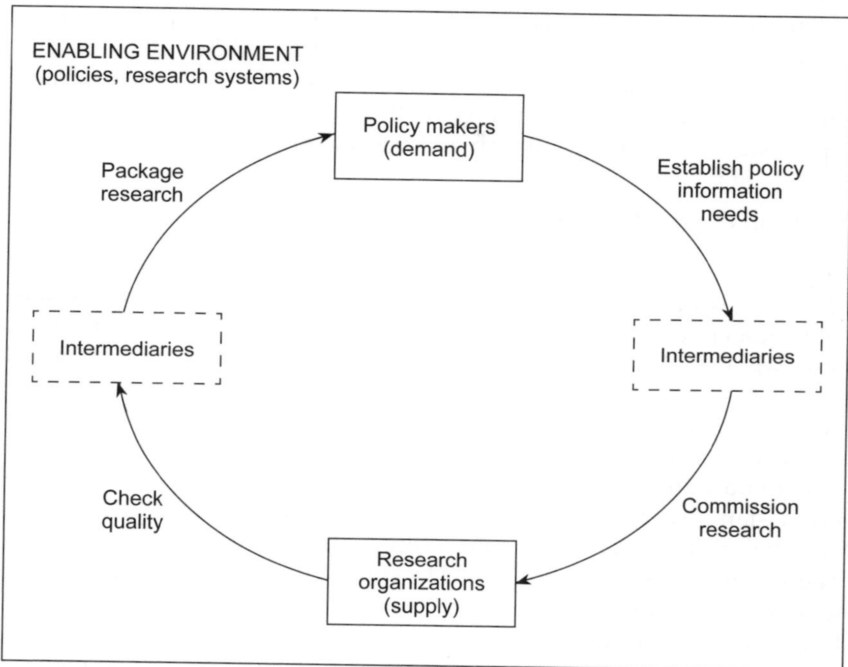

Source: AusAID (2011: 9).

Taken together, these elements construct a *knowledge-to-policy cycle* (Figure 8.4). It is by improving the elements and interactions within the knowledge-to-policy cycle that a healthier, more effective public policy-making process can be achieved. By breaking down the knowledge sector into functional roles, the model provides a useful basis for developing a reform program tailored to the specific constraints faced by different players.

It should be noted, however, that this is just a model, not a rigid empirical description. Categories can be porous. Often, the intermediary function is carried out directly by the supply and the demand sides. For example, research organizations may produce policy briefs to communicate their research findings directly to government decision makers without going through a notional intermediary. In other cases, the intermediary can indeed stand alone as a separate entity. For example, civil society organizations that use evidence to advocate for policy change are intermediaries that neither produce research (are not part of supply) nor make policies (are not part of demand). What matters for the model is that translating research findings into formats that are accessible to policy makers involves a deliberate act of brokerage.

The first section of this chapter provided an initial picture of the constraints facing Indonesia's knowledge sector and how they became embedded in the incentive environment for the sector. These constraints will now be discussed according to the framework described above: supply side, demand side, intermediaries and enabling environment.

Issues on the supply side

Very few research organizations in Indonesia are producing applied policy knowledge. This poses a first-order problem of volume: in most fields, not enough evidence is being gathered and analysed to contest or inform policy at the national level, let alone the subnational provincial or district levels. Indonesian research organizations commonly struggle with a number of constraints that reduce their effectiveness and their ability to produce quality research over time.

Foremost among these constraints - and the one most often cited by Indonesian researchers - is the lack of stable sources of funding (Asia Foundation 2011). Adequate core funding allows organizations to set an independent research agenda and to choose projects that fit with their mandate. However, this is a luxury that most Indonesian organizations do not have. With limited core funding, the majority of contracts that research groups receive are short term and rarely cover their ongoing costs, overheads and institutional capacity building.

Over-reliance on contract-based projects limits opportunities for staff to secure expertise in their main areas of interest, leading to high turnover of short-term researchers. Pay structures for organizations and individual researchers also produce perverse incentives that dictate against the production of quality research. At the level of the organization, most think tanks and research institutes are paid by the number of research projects they undertake, leading to an over-reliance on short-term or low-difficulty contracts. At the level of the individual, remuneration systems drive researchers to become overextended or to take on non-research activities (Box 8.1).

But the dominant and at times exclusive focus on funding issues as the explanation for poor-quality research can also mask other problems that are only partially related to the precariousness of funding. Controlling the quality of the research that is produced is a recurring problem that cuts across virtually all research organizations. Interviews with the national and international consumers of research products from a broad range of Indonesian research groups reveal recurrent patterns of poor writing, unfocused analysis and subjective assertions not backed by

BOX 8.1 How remuneration systems drive performance incentives for research

To understand the economic constraints that affect knowledge organization in Indonesia, Suryadarma, Pomeroy and Tanuwidjaja (2011) interviewed representatives from 27 Indonesian knowledge organizations: 20 suppliers and seven users. They found that there were two main types of salary structure, both of which impeded the production of high-quality research.

For most non-government researchers, salaries were *variable*, with a high positive correlation between salary level and the number of concurrent research projects. Researchers thus gravitated towards taking on large numbers of short-term research projects. Researchers in government offices received *fixed* but very low base rates of pay – on average just Rp 4 million (approximately A$440) per month. As a result, these researchers often took on other jobs to supplement their incomes. Also, a review of their time allocations showed that they tended to spend a large share of their time on non-research-related activities.

Source: Suryadarma, Pomeroy and Tanuwidjaja (2011).

objective evidence. Most organizations do not have a monitoring and evaluation mechanism to assess the organization as a whole, although they do monitor discreet donor projects. There are few professional standards for quality or clear regulations regarding research ethics. Peer review is not an institutional mechanism and, in those cases where it does take place, reviewer selection and follow-up nearly always depend on individual preference and professionalism.

Working conditions in most organizations also militate against quality improvements. The quality of organizational leadership is nearly always equated with the presence of charismatic individuals rather than with institutionalized systems to support staff development and ensure organizational continuity. This works well when the leader is charismatic and respected, but it fails badly during leadership transitions, which far too often produce large-scale breakdowns in research institutions. Also wanting are basic principles for organizational success, such as merit-based promotion, long-term career development and work planning to ensure that researchers are able to focus on their primary tasks.

In contrast to countries where think tanks and policy institutes contribute to public discourse on policy issues, in Indonesia there is an overall lack of investment in building linkages between research groups and the potential users of research in both government and civil society. Fostering alliances takes time and significant effort. Resources for other activities (looking for funding, implementing projects) are already spread too thin, so many organizations opt to give less priority to networking with potential users of their information, who in turn therefore do not provide the feedback that could lead to a virtuous circle of improvement.

Issues on the demand side

Several studies have pointed out that one of the main problems impeding knowledge-to-policy transfer is the lack of demand from policy makers for quality evidence (Suryadarma, Pomeroy and Tanuwidjaja 2011; Sutmuller and Setiono 2011). This can be traced back to the civil service culture inherited from the New Order. Although there are regulations that stipulate the use of evidence, policy makers frequently consider the commissioning of studies as a 'tick-the-box' exercise and do not assess or use the studies. For example, local governments often hire consultants to carry out studies as part of preparations for the medium-term development plans they are required to formulate. However, a review of some of those plans confirms that it is common for consultants to re-use studies from other areas and simply change the name of the location to suit the particular contract (Box 8.2).

Not all countries rely on think tanks and universities for their knowledge resources, and even those that do usually have a division within each ministry that is in charge of commissioning and interpreting research. In Indonesia this is the role notionally played by the Office for Research and Development (Balitbang), the division within each sectoral ministry that is responsible for developing and executing research and development according to the needs of the agency.

It is not unfair to say, however, that across government agencies the Balitbang are consistently among the most deeply marginal structures. They struggle to mediate between research and policy making for three main reasons, only one of which has to do with their ability to carry out research. First and most importantly, few if any ministries have a clear organizational system to let mid-tier or operational managers commission research or receive reports from the research division. Instead, these managers have to go through a lengthy and cumbersome chain of approvals until they reach a director-general or higher official who can authorize the review or officially receive the report. Second, the career advancement criteria for policy analysts working in ministries and government offices not only lack any direct connection to the utility of what researchers do for their internal clients, but often reward them for

BOX 8.2 Understanding subnational governments' limited demand for knowledge

Based on a survey of 21 regional governments (six provinces, five cities and 10 districts), case studies of 11 city and district governments, interviews with more than 200 people (representing executives, legislatures, universities, the business community and civil society) and a review of over 100 local public policy documents, Sutmuller and Setiono (2011) identified the following core issues related to the use of knowledge to formulate local public policies.

- The excessive detail and prescriptiveness of government directives curtails creativity and innovation by regional governments in formulating public policies.
- Regional governments do not have the funds to pay for quality research. The general purpose grants (*dana alokasi umum*) made available by the central government are generally sufficient to pay only for local government operations, and most local governments are able to raise very little additional funding from local sources of revenue such as taxes, fees and charges. Most are therefore dependent on special purpose grants (*dana alokasi khusus*) to fund development. However, the use of these funds is prescribed, with the projects eligible for funding sometimes only coincidentally coinciding with local needs and policy priorities.
- Local governments hire consultants to undertake research and to prepare their medium and long-term development plans. However, they allocate little or no funding to the preparation of sectoral strategies, annual plans and budgets. Instead, they formulate these policy plans in-house, without external support.
- There is no habit of involving stakeholders (practitioners, experts, academics, businesspeople, civil society activists) in the policy formulation and decision-making process, and therefore no established channels for regional governments to benefit from outside knowledge and expertise.
- Sectoral strategies tend to be copied without change from the equivalent national strategies, while annual plans and budgets are copied from previous years' plans and budgets without any evaluation of their effectiveness.

Source: Sutmuller and Setiono (2011).

producing knowledge of no immediate relevance. As much a product of the first two reasons as a cause of the poor take-up of in-house research is the general lack of technical capacity among government staff in core areas such as research methodology, reviewing research products or developing policy briefs.

As a result of the inability of the Balitbang to produce timely, quality analysis, the directorates often commission their own research, without coordinating with the Balitbang. This further undermines the role of these bodies in government agencies.

Despite the overall lack of demand for the use of evidence to inform policy making, there is nevertheless a growing number of reformers who are demonstrating real interest in using evidence and, perhaps even more importantly, in developing healthy partnerships with independent providers of information. Interviews with national and subnational policy makers point to a number of changes introduced in the 2001–2006 reform period that are starting to provide new incentives for officials to demand quality research (Box 8.3).

Often to the consternation of public policy specialists, planners and other lovers of administrative efficiency, Indonesia's political system is proving to be strikingly open to new entrants and resistant to the type of political consolidation that would provide more orderliness to government. But on the positive side, the country's enthusiasm for political competition and its endemic political fractiousness are proving to be important drivers of knowledge sector reforms.

Competition changes the dynamic between knowledge and policy in several ways. Democratically elected heads of local government generally want to improve their chances of re-election by showing results that can be published in newspapers and brandished by their campaign teams in their encounters with other candidates and the media. Political competition is also spurring demand for knowledge to inform confrontations between executive and legislative bodies. The growing interest of legislatures in using facts and figures pressures executives to back the claims they make during parliamentary commission hearings with research; parliamentarians too are beginning to seek help from research bodies that can reinforce their stature when confronting officials. Civil society organizations that have better access to data on such matters as budgets and expenditures may pressure the government (executive or legislative) for better policies. This in turn requires policy makers in both branches to defend existing policies or to justify future policy choices by using evidence that, for the first time, may also be subject to challenge and review.

Within the government administration, policy makers are willing to use research if it allows them to demonstrate progress that results in an

BOX 8.3 Accounting for change

Sutmuller and Setiono (2011) studied how subnational governments obtain research and use it to make policy decisions. This question is of particular concern given the continuing process of decentralization. The authors found that only a minority of local governments and local government agencies base their public policies on research or evidence. Which ones are they, and what triggers their eagerness to use research to achieve better public policy outcomes?

- Health and education agencies are more used to collecting and analysing data and searching for evidence to improve their policies. The resultant policies may not be perfect, but in general they are more likely to be based on research than the public policies of most other sectors.
- In jurisdictions where an elected leader is visionary, brave and willing to do things differently, and encourages staff to be creative and innovative, sectoral agencies are more likely to search for the causes of problems and adopt research-based solutions.
- A capable head of a planning agency (where most public policy originates) is more likely to be motivated – and to motivate staff – to develop quality public policies and, when financial resources permit, to encourage staff to collect data and evidence to assist in the preparation of public policies.
- Professional heads of sectoral agencies are far more engaged and feel far more responsibility for their sectors than their non-professional colleagues. They tend to search for the causes of problems in order to develop public policies that are backed up by as much data and evidence as possible.
- Where better public policies provide better access to funding, local governments are willing to allocate funds to the preparation of public policies. Where good staff performance is rewarded by performance-based incentives, many more civil servants are likely to put extra effort into preparing research or evidence-based public policies.

Source: Sutmuller and Setiono (2011).

increased budget. There is a growing appetite to use evidence-based planning and budgeting techniques to improve performance and demonstrate success. Some of Indonesia's national and international development commitments are actually translating into a perceived need for government agencies to deliver results. The central government's introduction of the Millennium Development Goals (MDG) as a barometer for public policy, for example, has obliged local governments to use the MDG indicators either as part of their situation analyses and targets or to be able to describe the current situation in their reports to the budget ministries. The reporting requirements have proven to be particularly potent for the health and education ministries, although both cases illustrate well the earlier point that the path from more knowledge through better policy to improved performance can follow a slow and winding route.

Issues with mediation

Intermediary organizations are those that communicate between the research community and policy makers. An intermediary can:

- collate and package research findings in a friendly format for policy makers;
- communicate the government's research needs to the research community (including commissioning research for policy purposes); and
- advocate for policy changes based on research findings.

Interviews and research carried out for this study pointed to a number of interesting reasons why the communication between policy makers and the research community does not meet the needs of either side.

Limited access to reliable information. Researchers commented extensively on the difficulty that independent research groups have in gaining access to basic government data and planning documents. Even within government, because information is often not shared across agencies, quality controls to correct for inconsistencies do not operate well.

Disincentives for government researchers to respond to policy makers' needs. Oversight by the Indonesian Institute of Sciences (LIPI) of advancement procedures for functional researchers reinforces the disconnect between civil service researchers and policy makers, as researchers are more inclined to adhere to LIPI's advancement procedures than to listen and respond to internal feedback on the usefulness of their research to their own institutions.

Lack of multi-stakeholder policy journals and other media. Compared with developing countries such as India, the Philippines, Mexico or Brazil, Indonesia has very few journals where researchers and policy makers can openly discuss and critique policy issues. Lack of English-language competence or familiarity with professional journals further hinders access to regional and global dialogue on policy-relevant issues.

Poor communication skills and procedures. Researchers everywhere produce long reports that are not read by policy makers unless someone produces a summary that extracts the main points and assesses their implications. This function is almost entirely absent in Indonesia. Government staff and research departments do not provide this service, and the number of think tanks and policy journals that could play this role is extremely limited.

Inadequate monitoring. Because the gap between the research community and policy makers is so large, it is almost impossible for organizations to monitor whether their activities are achieving policy influence.[5] With only one exception, none of the organizations interviewed during preliminary work on the design of the Knowledge Sector Program had any monitoring systems in place; across the sector, no agreed definitions of how to assess impact are in use. Instead, organizations appear to rely primarily on their success in attracting media attention and, to a lesser extent, on their ability to raise funds. While these are not the worst proxies imaginable, they do not provide especially useful ways to assess whether the findings and recommendations of researchers are actually understood or used by the policy community.

Corruption. Studies and interviews point repeatedly to endemic problems of corruption and the problems that ensue from it. Several of the best research organizations simply refuse to take contracts from government offices. Given the extremely limited funding base for research groups, however, this is a solution open to only a small group of organizations, primarily those with connections to international agencies. For Indonesian researchers as a whole, the costs of corruption are high: crony organizations can repeatedly win contracts regardless of their merit or past performance; poor-quality research can be submitted without correction; qualified researchers can be replaced by unqualified consultants; and so on. Field interviews suggest that as much as 40 per cent of a government research contract gets diverted into leakage, with devastating effects for the quality of the product.

Issues in the enabling environment

Many of the challenges that research organizations, policy makers and intermediaries face stem from systemic barriers in the knowledge sector's authorizing and enabling environment. These systemic barriers can be found in:

- Indonesia's rigid and restrictive procurement regulations;
- the structure and administrative procedures of the civil service;

5 For an example of an effort to measure policy influence by Latin American think tanks, see Lardone and Roggero (2008).

- the limited government funding for policy research; and
- the roles and functions of knowledge intermediaries, especially LIPI.

Such barriers are very difficult to address and changing them will take considerable time. But if they are not lifted and the ground rules for knowledge development are not changed, then any effort to revitalize the knowledge sector is unlikely to be sustainable. While a full reform program would require a comprehensive review of the country's laws and regulations, an inventory of the main policy barriers to knowledge sector development can be summarized briefly.

For many officials in government, the single biggest obstacle to better interaction with Indonesia's universities and think tanks is the rigid and restrictive regulations on government procurement. Public procurement – the process by which public funds turn into contracts for goods, works and services – is always complex because of the need to ensure fair competition, prevent corruption and justify the use of public money, but in Indonesia it has become particularly convoluted across broad swathes of development. New Order procurement rules were, arguably, designed as much to protect Indonesian firms and allow government manipulation of contracts as they were to provide a fair and level playing field. Numerous reforms since the fall of the New Order have tried to overcome this heritage by modifying procurement rules. However, without some fundamental economic restructuring to promote more rather than less competition, and a better legal system to enforce compliance, the result has been a continuous patchwork of amendments.

The main legislation relating to knowledge procurement is Presidential Decree No. 54/2010, which replaced Presidential Decree No. 80/2003. Initially the main purpose of both pieces of legislation was to safeguard against corruption in government procurement. The procurement legislation has been amended eight times since 2003, yet many users still consider procurement processes and regulations to be overly complex, inconsistent and confusing. The decree is open to multiple interpretations, and while high-level officials continue to insist that nothing in it prevents government from procuring services from universities and think tanks, there is a widespread perception on both sides of the procurement equation that it prohibits the government from directly purchasing research from not-for-profit institutions, including most research organizations (Sherlock 2010).

A second set of issues concerns the structure of the civil service and the administrative procedures associated with it. At present, the core architecture of the civil service does not support effective interaction between policy makers and researchers. First, the distinction between 'functional' staff, who are assigned to research roles, and 'structural' staff, who operate in managerial positions, creates an overall disconnect between the two types of staff, as demonstrated by the (dysfunctional) relationship between the Balitbang and other operational units within ministries. The reality in many workplaces is that functional research staff work under structural staff, who then task them with non-technical (that is, non-research-related) assignments.

The civil service only allows staff to enter at a base level with minimal work experience. It does not permit the recruitment of people from outside the civil service to middle and senior positions. Once a person enters the civil service, it is very hard to exit, let alone re-enter. This limits the ability to recruit high-calibre individuals with extensive experience outside the civil service who could provide knowledge-to-policy expertise. These individuals can only be hired as contractors with no decision-making authority. Moreover, the procedures for hiring experts tend to be cumbersome, politicized and not based on merit.

A third set of issues concerns the level and availability of government funding for research. It is not clear how much the government actually invests in research, particularly in those areas that are most relevant for development policy. The government distributes its research funds through several channels, such as the Ministry of Research and Technology, the National Research Council and LIPI, the line ministries (Balitbang and policy units), subnational agencies, government research institutes and state universities. These funds are used not only to finance research activities, but also to cover institutional overheads and other costs, without any disaggregation. This makes it difficult to determine the level of investment in actual research activities. However, even with these cautions, it is clear that Indonesia's investment in research is very low compared with that of other developing countries, and particularly that of other middle-income countries. For example, using common indicators, UNESCO found that Indonesia recorded the lowest level of government expenditure on research of any of the roughly equivalent economies. Equally significant is that its business sector makes virtually no significant contribution to policy research for development, unlike in other middle-income countries such as India or Brazil, where public support for research is supplemented by policies to draw in private sector support (Figures 8.5 and 8.6).

Inadequate funding for the government's own research programs is matched by inadequate mechanisms to obtain high-quality research from outside providers through grants that build up the national research community as a whole. There are very few channels for the government to allocate grant funding to non-government research organizations. Keeping in mind the complexity of Indonesian budget mechanisms, which may yet reveal some undiscovered sources, there appear to be only two

Figure 8.5 Government expenditure on R&D as a share of GDP, selected countries (%)

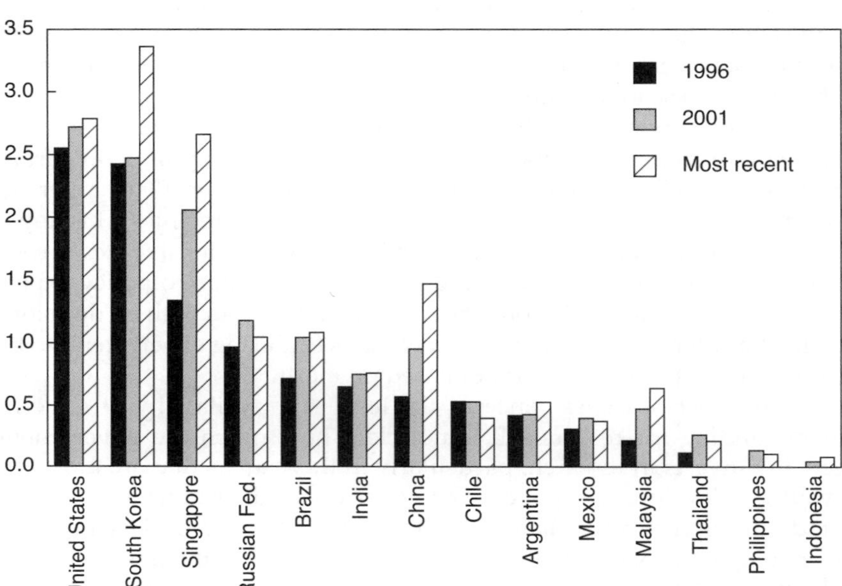

Note: No data are available for Indonesia and the Philippines in 1996. The 2001 data for Malaysia and the Philippines are for 2000 and 2002 respectively. The most recent data are for 2008, with the exception of Malaysia (2006), India, Mexico, the Philippines and Thailand (2007) and Indonesia (2009).

Source: UNESCO Institute of Statistics, 'Science and technology', Table 26, available at http://stats.uis.unesco.org/unesco/ReportFolders/ReportFolders.aspx.

types of competitive government grants for research: one by the Ministry of Research and Technology focusing on the natural sciences; and the other by the Ministry of National Education for universities. There are no known avenues for the government to provide grants for non-government research in the social sciences and humanities, let alone core funding for independent research organizations.

The fourth set of constraints in developing an effective knowledge-to-policy cycle can be found in the role played by knowledge intermediaries. Not only is the current level of government funding inadequate, but research funds are channelled through just a small number of government agencies and research institutions that set the research agenda and provide funding for research. While the legislative intent in founding these institutions was to enable the strategic development of a national knowledge sector, these institutions themselves are often a key constraint

Figure 8.6 Share of R&D expenditure performed by government, higher education and business, selected countries (%)

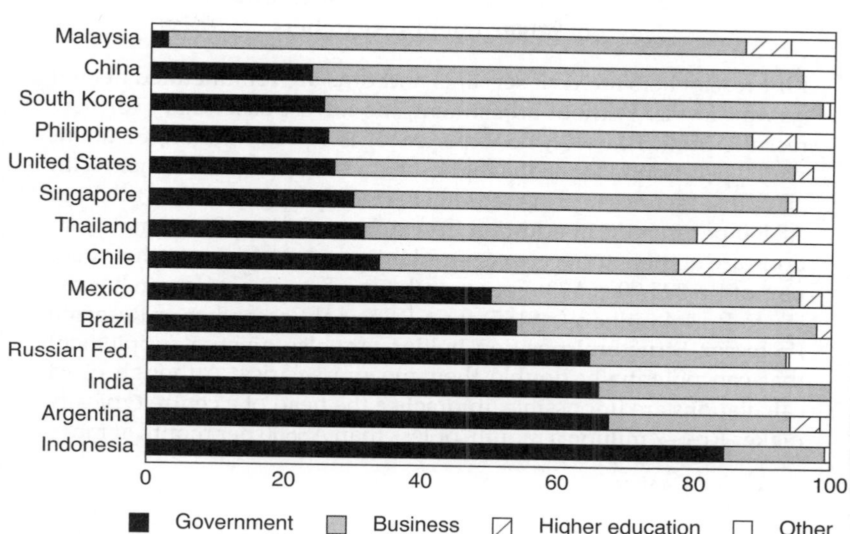

Note: The data are for 2008, with the exception of: (for business and government) Indonesia (2001), Thailand (2005), Malaysia (2006) and India, Mexico and the Philippines (2007); (for higher education) Indonesia (2001), Thailand (2005), Malaysia (2006) and Mexico and the Philippines (2007). No higher education data are available for China and the figure is negligible for India.

Source: UNESCO Institute of Statistics, 'Science and technology', Table 28, available at http://stats.uis.unesco.org/unesco/ReportFolders/ReportFolders.aspx.

to forming a functioning knowledge sector. They do not provide incentives for policy-targeted research; they do not provide reliable funding schemes; they do not prioritize social science or economic research; and they do not have a sufficiently strong legal basis or enough funding to play an effective intermediary role even for the government.

LIPI, however, is an indeterminate case. While the majority of government research institutions lack the financial resources, funding systems and mandates to be a key part of the knowledge sector – a situation that is unlikely to change without dramatic alterations to their organizational mandates, structures and modes of operations – LIPI still has a potentially critical role to play in revitalizing the knowledge sector. Its researchers may be underpaid (see Box 8.4), but it is nevertheless the only government institution with a long history of research, arguably dating back to the Dutch botanical research programs of the nineteenth century. More importantly, reinforced by former president Habibie's 2001 reforms, LIPI

BOX 8.4 The systematic underfunding of government researchers

LIPI researchers are civil servants and thus are remunerated at civil servant levels. Without adjustment, the lowest base salary for new recruits (rank IIIa with no experience) is Rp 1.7 million, or about A$200 per month, while the highest base salary (for researchers with 32 years of service nearing retirement) is only Rp 3.6 million, or about A$400 per month. In addition, researchers holding functional positions are eligible to receive a supplement to complement their base pay, of Rp 325,000 (A$36) per month for a First Class Researcher rising to Rp 1.4 million (A$155) for a Principal Researcher or Research Professor. Structural position holders are also given a supplement that can potentially double their meagre salaries. Although exact calculations are impossible, in practice the head of a centre typically makes Rp 6–7 million a month, or less than A$800 per month at most.

Source: Oey-Gardiner (2011).

can count on significant assets provided through the budget, a critical mass of its own researchers and, most significantly for the topic at hand, the authority to determine accreditation and advancement procedures for government researchers stationed in the Balitbang and non-ministry agencies.

At present this accreditation system is tedious, based on an intricate method of accumulating points for publications, training, seminar attendance and so on. It shows little regard for quality. It assigns the same number of points for publication in any journal, whether peer reviewed or not, with no more points given for publishing in, say, a peer-reviewed international publication than in a national one. This quantitative system protects seniority rather than rewarding merit. Moreover, the fact that LIPI is responsible both for self-financed research by its own staff and for developing a national research capacity means that it often ends up competing for funds with the same organizations it is meant to support.

There have been several attempts to reform LIPI, both from outside the organization and by reform-minded leaders. To date each wave of reform has been beaten back or foundered on the contradictory incentives built into the institute's structure and the lack of a defined clientele for its products. At present, even enthusiastic LIPI supporters carefully hedge their support by saying that it is for the *idea* of the institute rather than the institute itself, at least as it operates today. Nevertheless, the jury remains out on LIPI's long-term potential role in knowledge sector revitalization. Given its structural similarity to other countries' national strategic research bodies, it may well be better to work with the clay that is there than to presume that starting over would produce less unfortunate results.

Weak supply, minimal demand, misguided incentives backed by counterproductive regulations … how realistic is it to hope for the kind of large-scale structural reform that Indonesia's knowledge sector needs? The conclusion to this chapter will argue that while the state of the knowledge sector today may seem somewhat grim, there are nevertheless credible signals that the winter cloud hanging over the sector may soon begin to lift.

IS IT SPRINGTIME FOR INDONESIA'S KNOWLEDGE SECTOR OR JUST ANOTHER GROUNDHOG DAY?

When do countries undertake reforms to their knowledge sectors? Most development agencies operate from a model that is best described as the modern-day version of Europe's Enlightenment: visionary leaders backed by clever reformers and supportive financiers confront new challenges through masterplans for transforming their national institutions. The diagnosis presented in this chapter suggests that while there is indeed growing awareness among high-level policy makers that without significant reform Indonesia will find it increasingly difficult to manage a highly complex and competitive economy, by now there are also deeply embedded interests that will push back against reform. As with other apparently similar arguments about how a growing Indonesia will 'naturally' reform its judicial system, transform its bureaucracy or reduce corruption to less destructive levels, an 'Enlightenment' approach to reform may well produce many good diagnostics and fascinating seminars, but by itself will not succeed in dislodging the status quo.

The global literature suggests that while there is no single driver that can categorically provoke the kinds of significant changes needed in a country such as Indonesia, there are a number of generally accepted enabling conditions that make reform more likely to happen.[6] Of these, the most important are external pressures that shift the balance of power in favour of the reformers. This chapter has argued that such externally induced changes are well under way in Indonesia, but it is worth summarizing the main items inducing such an optimistic assessment.

6 This discussion draws on Sabatier (1988), Lindquist (2001), Ahmed (2005), Stone (2005) and Porter (2010).

First, there is no question that Indonesia's highly competitive, democratic elections are driving a reconsideration of the role to be played by knowledge institutions. New leaders increasingly turn to their own sources of advice rather than take on faith arguments provided by their bureaucracies and traditional sets of advisers and consultants. Even within ministries, pressure from parliament and senior officials to demonstrate results is strengthening the power of certain reformist bureaus and creating an interest in drawing in help from outside research groups.

Second, it is axiomatic to assume that Indonesia's overall growth, complexity and increasing integration with regional and global economies will provide strong incentives to strengthen the country's knowledge sector. While such trends are clearly under way, it should not be forgotten that the New Order government was quite successful at simultaneously shutting down critical inquiry and public contestation of its policies while at the same time educating a sufficient number of high-quality economists to manage its development agenda. But times have changed. It seems reasonable to assume that the rising middle class, the continuing decentralization agenda and Indonesia's increasing engagement with regional and global issues on trade, rights, environment and diplomacy will create pressures to improve higher education and policy-oriented research.

Third, the tertiary education system is becoming increasingly competitive. A corollary of this competition has been a rise in the formal and informal fees being charged to parents, who in turn are putting pressure on schools to improve quality. As Hill and Thee (2011) note in their review of tertiary education, while the elite public sector universities remain the first choice of upwardly mobile students, private universities are growing in leaps and bounds, and both public and private universities are themselves piloting a wide range of reforms that should improve their quality and allow them to attract more students.

Fourth, it would be difficult to overstate the importance that the opening up of Indonesia's media has had on providing the forums as well as the incentives to break free of the New Order development model. Under the New Order virtually all topics for public debate were directly or indirectly defined by the government, as were the forums in which policies could be discussed. This is no longer the case. Various interest groups and even individuals can now define what makes for a significant policy issue. Government officials are increasingly challenged by and through the national media; this in turn forces them to prepare more facts and better presentations rather than rely on their official authority alone to carry them through.

Fifth, while the track record of technological innovations that have reduced the cost of information is still too short for its effect on policy research to be assessed, there are encouraging signs that Indonesian policy researchers are beginning to use modern information technology to gain access to global discourse and scientific research. If in the past blockages such as lack of English-language competence, libraries and access to global events prevented researchers living outside the major urban centres from joining policy dialogues, today even those living in remote regions can easily take part in national and international discussions and join policy coalitions with a fraction of the difficulty that previous generations faced. Also, while no formal study appears to have been done on the extent to which researchers and policy makers are linking up with each other on social media, impressionistic data suggest that this is already happening on a surprisingly significant, albeit highly uneven, scale. Computer literacy, internet penetration and the consolidation of research networks such as the Eastern Indonesia Researcher Network (JiKTI) are providing both the means and the forums to diversify the nature of organizations involved in all aspects of the knowledge-to-policy cycle.

Finally, without overdoing the extent to which the bureaucracy is changing its core views on its role in society, official views towards external knowledge providers are clearly in flux. Organizations such as the SMERU Research Institute or the Partnership for Governance Reform (Kemitraan), which began largely as donor experiments developed in tandem with Indonesian civil society groups, are now invited to high-level government meetings. The Indonesian Forum for Budget Transparency (Fitra), Indonesia Corruption Watch and other organizations that advocate for budgetary transparency within government are being consulted by parliament and the political parties. Even at the sub-national level, the planning agencies of provinces such as Aceh or South Sulawesi now host monthly meetings of university and non-government research groups to discuss development issues and agree on joint topics for research. While the structural barriers identified earlier in this chapter – rigid procurement procedures, outdated civil service rules, a lack of appropriate budgetary mechanisms, an insufficient number of policy intermediaries and so on – remain in force, increasing the comfort levels of officials with these new alliances may well be the precursor needed to generate reform.

Nevertheless, if an analysis of the overall environment suggests that the time is ripe for knowledge sector reform, there is still no guarantee that it will succeed. Indonesia's development history is littered with promising initiatives to establish think tanks, government research groups and university institutes that initially seemed full of promise, only to fizzle out as their funding came to an end or their government champions changed jobs.

This chapter has attempted to go beyond a review of the individual successes and failures of Indonesia's knowledge-based organizations to understand why the knowledge sector so often appears to be stuck in a low-level equilibrium trap. The analysis has been built around five main propositions. The first is that fixing Indonesia's weak knowledge institutions is not just a matter of providing more scholarships, better financing or improved management skills, important though these may be. At least as important as improving the overall supply is addressing the lack of demand for policy-related knowledge and the multiple structural barriers embedded in the rules governing the bureaucracy that prevent policy makers from gaining access to high-quality evidence. The second argument is that reform will not come from within the bureaucracy, nor will donors be able to identify a sufficient number of reform 'champions' to overcome bureaucratic resistance and the maintenance of the status quo. Reform must instead develop through what Sabatier (1991) has called 'advocacy coalitions' that cross the traditionally rigid boundaries between government reformers, civil society organizations and self-interested research groups. However, even advocacy coalitions need to find the forums where evidence, argument, policy and reform can all be brought forward for debate, review and assessment. The fourth argument is that the new freedom of the media and its embrace of information technology are providing those public spaces to an extent never previously experienced. The fifth and final argument is that while knowledge sector reform is sure to be a slow, grinding process, there are many good reasons to believe that the conditions are finally ripe for Indonesia's budding knowledge sector to finally burst into bloom.

REFERENCES

Ahmed, M. (2005) 'Bridging research and policy', *Journal of International Development* 17: 765–73.

Asia Foundation (2011) 'Enhancing knowledge on the knowledge sector: report to AusAID', diagnostic for AusAID's Tertiary Education and Knowledge Sector Unit, Canberra.

AusAID (Australian Agency for International Development) (2011) 'Revitalizing Indonesia's knowledge sector for development policy', draft design document for AusAID's Tertiary Education and Knowledge Sector Unit, Canberra, August.

Carden, F. (2009) *Knowledge to Policy: Making the Most of Developmental Research*, SAGE Publications and International Development Research Centre, New Delhi.

Geertz, C. (1971) *A Report to the Ford Foundation Concerning a Program for the Stimulation of the Social Sciences in Indonesia*, Institute for Advanced Study, Princeton NJ.

Hien, P.D. (2010) 'A comparative study of research capabilities of East Asian countries and implications for Vietnam', *Higher Education* 60: 615–25.

Hill, H. and Thee Kian Wie (2011) 'Indonesian universities in transition: catching up and opening up', diagnostic for AusAID's Tertiary Education and Knowledge Sector Unit, Canberra, October.

Lardone, M. and M. Roggero (2008) 'Study on monitoring and evaluation of the research impact in the public policy of policy research institutes (PRIs) in the region', GDNet/CIPPEC, Buenos Aires.

Lavis, J., J. Lomas, M. Hamid and N. Sewankombo (2006) 'Assessing country-level efforts to link research to action', *Bulletin of the World Health Organization* 84(8): 620–28.

Lindqvist, E. (2000) 'Think tanks and the ecology of policy inquiry', in D. Stone (ed.) *Banking on Knowledge: The Genesis of the Global Development Network*, Routledge, London.

Lindqvist, E. (2001) 'Discerning policy influence: framework for a strategic evaluation of IDRC-supported research', unpublished paper, School of Public Administration, University of Victoria, Victoria BC.

Mrázek, R. (1994) *Sjahrir: Politics and Exile in Indonesia*, Studies on Southeast Asia No. 4, Cornell Southeast Asia Program, Ithaca NY.

Oey-Gardiner, M. (2011) 'Study of the role of the Indonesian Institute of Sciences (LIPI) in bridging between research and development policy: final report', diagnostic for AusAID's Tertiary Education and Knowledge Sector Unit, Jakarta, August.

Pompe, Sebastiaan (2005) *The Indonesian Supreme Court: A Study of Institutional Collapse*, Cornell Southeast Asia Program, Ithaca NY.

Porter, C. (2010) 'What shapes the influence evidence has on policy? The role of politics in research utilization', Working Paper No. 62, Young Lives, Department of International Development, University of Oxford, Oxford, November.

Sabatier, P. (1988) 'An advocacy coalition framework of policy change and the role of policy-oriented learning therein', *Policy Sciences* 21: 128–68.

Sabatier, P. (1991) 'Toward better theories of the policy process', *Political Science and Politics* 24(2): 147–56.

Sherlock, S. (2010) 'Knowledge for policy: regulatory obstacles to the growth of a knowledge market in Indonesia', diagnostic for AusAID's Tertiary Education and Knowledge Sector Unit, Canberra, June.

Stone, D. (2005) 'Think tanks and policy advice in countries in transition', paper presented at a seminar on How to Strengthen Policy-oriented Research and Training in Vietnam, Asian Development Bank Institute, Hanoi, 31 August.

Suryadarma, D., J. Pomeroy and S. Tanuwidjaja (2011) 'Economic factors underpinning constraints in Indonesia's knowledge sector: final report', diagnostic for AusAID's Tertiary Education and Knowledge Sector Unit, Canberra, 7 June.

Sutmuller, P. and I. Setiono (2011) 'Diagnostic on evidence-based public policy formulation under decentralisation', diagnostic for AusAID's Tertiary Education and Knowledge Sector Unit, Jakarta, 30 April.

TTCSP (Think Tanks and Civil Societies Program) (2011) 'The global "go-to think tanks"', International Relations Program, University of Pennsylvania, Pennsylvania PA, 18 January.

9 PROBLEMS OF IDENTITY AND LEGITIMACY FOR INDONESIA'S PLACE IN THE WORLD

R.E. Elson

> 'Our foreign policy must be in accordance with our own internal strength.'
> *Ruslan Abdulgani (1957)*[1]

Over the last half-century or so, the Republic of Indonesia has enjoyed some notable diplomatic successes in its international dealings. Among them can be counted its feat in 1949 in securing formal recognition of the sovereignty it had proclaimed over the territory of the former Netherlands Indies state on 17 August 1945; its capacity to bring early substance and energy to the yearnings of decolonizing nations for proper recognition and to assert their own unique role in international affairs; its success in securing recognition of its sovereignty over West Irian; its persistence and, eventually, astonishing success in securing international acknowledgment of its assertion of territorial rights over the waters of the archipelago; and its central role in the Cambodian peace process.

But it is fair to say that Indonesia - vast in size and large in population, gifted with immense natural resources and boasting a strategic political and economic location at the intersection of two continents and two oceans - has achieved much less in the international arena than might have been expected over the longer course of its modern history. Indeed, its influence in world affairs has for the most part been minimal. Dewi Fortuna Anwar (2010) has remarked that 'it is sometimes said that Indo-

1 Ruslan Abdulgani (1914–2005) was Indonesia's foreign minister from March 1956 to April 1957.

nesia is the most important country that the world knows least about'. Indonesia possesses little by way of threatening armaments (its army has generally played the role of a kind of neocolonial internal police force), has no energetic and influential diaspora, has no modern record of significant intellectual acknowledgment or athletic achievement, and has long had a subdued international diplomatic profile. In short, Indonesia has usually troubled the world – in the various meanings of that verb – very little. The world might have heard of Bali, or more vaguely of Krakatau or even of Jemaah Islamiyah, but it is seldom conscious of and knows little about Indonesia as either civilization or nation-state. The point of this essay is to explore the reasons, over time, for this continuing, sometimes embarrassing, sometimes debilitating – but at times useful[2] – Indonesian failure of global projection and engagement.

In sharp contrast, those young Indonesians in the early part of the twentieth century who first seized upon and then developed the idea of Indonesia, that is, that the territory of what was then the Netherlands East Indies should be ruled by and in the interests of its own people, were deeply internationalized. Not coincidentally, the Netherlands Indies had itself only recently taken on something of an individual 'legal personality' and a measure of financial independence in international matters in place of the old purely colonial, subservient identity (Fievez de Malines van Ginkel 1924). Those Indonesians were generally deeply disenchanted with the humiliating servitude that had befallen their own once-glorious histories and societies – something variously attributed to the coming of Islam or the coming of the European – and they were profoundly captured by the sense that the West provided the single viable means of resurrection. That meant 'becoming modern' – at first in economic and technological terms, and later in the political arena – by creating and energizing a modern nation-state of their own: Indonesia. That notion/nation of 'Indonesia' was almost immediately accepted by the small elite of educated Indonesians with an astonishing equanimity and lack of internal contestation (Elson 2006).

For the most part, those young Indonesian leaders were the products of modern Western education; they were multilingual, cosmopolitan and intellectually open. Moreover, they recognized the importance of commanding a strong sense of international tendencies and movements if they were to realize their dream of making 'Indonesia' a reality. Thus they understood the significance of Japanese reform and spirit in the nineteenth century in coming to grips with the imperial West, they

2 Australians, among others, have reason to be grateful that Indonesia has seldom seen itself in a position to throw its weight about in the international arena.

were particularly attuned to indigenous political developments in India and China, and they appreciated that Indonesia's size, natural endowments and geopolitical location promised a prominent role in world affairs.[3] Some of them, such as Mohammad Hatta, Iwa Kusumasumantri and Tan Malaka, had studied overseas, travelling extensively in Europe and making numerous international contacts. Similarly, the leaders of the Indonesian Communist Party (PKI), through their association with the Communist International (Comintern), were deeply international in spirit, even if characteristically nativist in domestic political action. Indigenous political leaders and intellectuals kept abreast of European politics in the 1930s and took part in it as well, as when a delegation of Indonesian students in the Netherlands attended the International Peace Congress in Brussels in 1936.[4] Some of them held deep misgivings about the rising tide of fascism, although others welcomed the emergence of Japan as a world power and, later, the arrival of the Japanese in 1942, as the means to rid themselves of European colonial rule. In short, for these early political leaders of what was to become the Republic of Indonesia, the international dimension was one in which they were comfortable, practised and even, in their own way, accomplished.

That style of outward-looking cosmopolitanism came to a sudden end in 1942. The Pacific War broke the back of Dutch colonialism in the Indies, and for much of the next decade Indonesians were to be totally consumed with the national struggle to assert and defend the independence proclaimed in August 1945. The war itself had cut the Indies off entirely from anything but the Japanese empire. Dutch efforts at recolonization following a brief Allied post-war interregnum saw serious limits placed on the capacity of Indonesians to engage internationally, even if the preamble of the 1945 Constitution spoke of a deep moral sense of Indonesian mission in contributing 'to the establishment of a world order based on freedom, lasting peace and social justice'.

Nonetheless, the republic's efforts to woo international support for its cause - expressed most clearly in Hatta's manifesto of 1 November 1945 (Hatta 1953) - were disproportionately successful. They included the 'Black Armada' episode of 1945 when Australian dock workers took the side of Indonesian freedom and refused to handle Dutch ships; the astounding capacity of the republic to gain widespread international support for its struggle, expressed in Indonesia's enthusiastic participation in the New Delhi Asian Relations Conference in March–April 1947; and, most starkly and crucially, the successful effort of India and Australia to persuade the United Nations to involve itself actively in what

3 See, for example, Douwes Dekker (1914: 16–18) and Anonymous (1924).

4 See *Soeara Roepi*, 1936, 3: 1–5.

was then termed 'the Indonesian dispute'.[5] Indeed, Indonesia's success in achieving formal recognition of its independence by the Dutch in late 1949 was to a considerable extent a consequence of the play of international opinion, and notably of a late-found American determination to press the Dutch to concede, in the United Nations and elsewhere. Despite its sacralization in the state myth of Suharto's army-backed regime, the exercise of Indonesian arms played a much smaller role, its effectiveness compromised by frequent military inadequacy and incompetence and, more broadly, by the savage internal violence unleashed by revolutionary tumult.[6]

The formalization of Indonesia's independence, then, was in significant measure a function of the success of Indonesian leaders – often those same cosmopolitans of the pre-war era – in engaging fruitfully in international diplomacy. That in turn was based on a strong Indonesian sense of the centrality of the United Nations in international affairs and on an Indonesian preference for multilateralism over bilateralism in the international arena. Despite this promising beginning, the following four decades were to prove much less successful in advancing Indonesia's interests internationally. The major cause was the direct and total subordination of international relations and international diplomacy to the always pressing, and often chaotic, demands of domestic politics.

That much became evident in the years following the formal recognition of Indonesian sovereignty. In the early 1950s the country was beset by grave domestic political and economic troubles, among them gathering problems with the institutionalization of democratic governance and challenges to the legitimacy and authority of the new state. The uprisings included an attempted coup d'état by the Legion of Ratu Adil (APRA) in which Bandung was captured and Jakarta threatened; a revolt in Makassar against incorporation into the Indonesian state, led by Andi Azis; the attempt to proclaim an independent Republic of South Maluku; and the PRRI/Permesta rebel movement in Sumatra, and in Manado and adjacent parts of eastern Indonesia (in which the republic's role was perceived by some to be that of a new colonizer). There were international dilemmas as well, but they played themselves out most strongly on the domestic political landscape rather than internationally. They included

5 Anthony Reid noted in the sixth Herb Feith Lecture that 'It is increasingly clear to me that the post-war generation in Australia and New Zealand had a particular idealism about Indonesia which did not apply in quite the same way to other corners of Asia' (Reid 2010).

6 The 3 July 1946 affair and the Madiun rebellion of 1948, both armed attempts to change the republic's leadership and the mode of its struggle for independence, were perhaps the most serious examples of internal disputation.

the speed and depth of Dutch decolonization, the Dutch refusal to allow any change in the political status of West New Guinea, tensions over war reparations and the furore over Indonesia's being drawn under the umbrella of the American Mutual Security Act by a secretive foreign minister, Achmad Subarjo.[7] The result was that Indonesia perforce focused on itself. Notwithstanding the development of a 'free and active' (*bebas-aktip*) foreign policy, Indonesia receded from the international stage to attend to its multiform internal challenges.

That situation changed, though, as Sukarno sought to free himself from the restraints imposed on him by the 1950 Constitution. Chafing at his lack of executive power and his political marginalization, the president employed foreign relations and international visibility as a means (although not the only means) of again thrusting himself to the forefront of the Indonesian political scene. In a deepening Cold War context, his apparently leftward foreign agenda, which aimed to give life and substance to Indonesia's free and active foreign policy, enlarged his international profile enormously. It also echoed the national rhetoric of seeking international peace by ending colonialism, and a refusal to side formally with the two contending Great Power blocs. That tactic materialized most spectacularly in the Asian–African Congress held in Bandung in 1955, which saw the formalization (if not yet the realization) of what would later become known as the Non-Aligned Movement.

That the Bandung Conference achieved so little in real, as distinct from symbolic, terms was a function of the fact that Sukarno – while purporting to look to the world outside, while personally manifesting the attributes of the sophisticated cosmopolitan (including multilingualism and a more than casual command of Western learning) and while being ever more deeply seduced by the international spotlight – was deeply focused on the problems of independent Indonesia, or, more precisely, on the problem of inserting himself once more in the driver's seat as the indispensable leader of the republic. That task was achieved by mid-1959, when the union of Sukarno with a now united and more purposeful army was sufficient to overcome a divided and pusillanimous party system and restore the 1945 Constitution, which enshrined vast presidential powers.

Thereafter, Sukarno's apparently revolutionary rhetoric gradually became more climactic, manifesting itself not just in the (highly popular) Trikora campaign to wrest West Irian from the Dutch, but in stranger efforts, such as the confrontation with Malaysia, the discourse of 'new emerging forces' (NEFOs) against 'old established forces' (OLDEFOs) to

---

7 On the Mutual Security Act controversy, which led to the fall of the Sukiman cabinet, see Feith (1962: 198–205).

defeat 'neocolonialism, colonialism and imperialism' (NEKOLIM), the decision to quit the United Nations, the ambition 'to build the world anew', the idea of 'living dangerously' and the creation of a Jakarta–Phnom Penh–Hanoi–Beijing–Pyongyang 'axis'. The most interesting aspect of all these efforts is that they had almost no strategic or tactical consequences of an international kind. That was because their intended audience was a domestic one. Confrontation, for example, was aimed not at crushing the very notion of Malaysia but at improving the domestic political balance in favour of the rapidly emerging PKI and at enhancing Sukarno's own domestic repute. Accordingly, it found little support within the armed forces. Fearing the capacity of the PKI to use Sukarno's rhetoric to its advantage, the army refused any but the most symbolic exercises of armed force in support of confrontation.

In fact, then, Sukarno's foreign policy involved little real and effective engagement with the rest of the world. Rather, it played an important symbolic role in assisting, then highlighting and further promoting, his return to the central position in Indonesian politics. The kind of Indonesia that Sukarno wanted to construct required his controlling pre-eminence, and foreign policy was purely a deeply turned-in tool to achieve that outcome.

His successor as president, Suharto, was very unlike the loquacious, charismatic, cosmopolitan and much travelled Sukarno. Suharto did not leave small-town Central Java for the first time until he was almost 20, did not leave Java until he was almost 30, did not travel overseas until he was 40 and did not take a further foreign trip until he had been formally sworn in as president in 1968. He spoke only Javanese and Indonesian with any fluency and had no background in Western learning. But although scholars rarely see much similarity between Sukarno and Suharto, both were masters of employing foreign relations to their own domestic advantage, especially in the quest to create their own sense of what Indonesia should be.

After the anti-PKI bloodbath of 1965–66, Suharto began his long reign by ending the confrontation with Malaysia, arranging Indonesia's re-entry to the United Nations, freezing relations with the People's Republic of China and, most important of all, establishing Indonesia as part of the anti-communist sphere, politically but especially economically, by re-engaging with the capitalist world as a means of promoting domestic economic development. All these efforts were consciously chosen to promote Suharto's sense of Indonesian identity, along lines that became increasingly strongly organicist or integralist, and that attempted a kind of homogenizing of Indonesia's social, cultural and especially political diversity. All were meant to advance the president's deeply felt desire for technocrat-led economic development.

Until the time of Suharto's unchallenged supremacy, the mid to late 1980s, Indonesia maintained a low-profile foreign policy. Its major achievement was the creation of the Association of Southeast Asian Nations (ASEAN), which, like the rest of Suharto's foreign engagements, had an involuted purpose, notably the achievement of regional security and the consequent absence of external distraction from internal problems. Indonesia played a low-key role in ASEAN, to avoid dominating the organization as a whole through its relatively large size. In that sense, ASEAN long remained an institution devoted essentially to national rather than regional interests and concerns.

It was not until the 1980s that Suharto began to engage more energetically with the world outside. That engagement often took the form of an avuncular presence at world meetings, such as those of the Non-Aligned Movement and the Organisation of the Islamic Conference, where his advice, especially on matters of economic development and political security, was eagerly sought. Suharto's encouragement (after initial Indonesian diffidence) of the Asia-Pacific Economic Cooperation (APEC) process – especially the Bogor Declaration of 1994 – marked the pinnacle of the president's program of engagement. It went as well to such matters as the need to redress and restructure North–South political and economic differences and to change the focus of the South from anti-imperial antagonisms to addressing the problems of social and economic development;[8] involvement in mediating the Cambodian problem in the late 1980s; and a role in developing a peace agreement between the government of the Philippines and the Moro National Liberation Front in the mid-1990s. Suharto, now safely and apparently permanently ensconced in the presidency, finally felt free to indulge in world affairs. But that engagement was always on his terms, and usually framed around others needing and calling for his advice as masterful political actor, or rewarding him for his domestic triumphs. It was no accident that Suharto's invitation to address the UN Food and Agriculture conference in Rome in 1985 came as recognition of his contribution to developing Indonesian rice production, or that he chose that event as the opening point of his long, lonely and intensely self-regarding autobiography (Suharto 1989: 1–2).

Suharto's New Order regime collapsed in violence and chaos in 1998, and the transitional *reformasi* governments, notably that of Habibie, were perforce focused on domestic political repair, economic rehabilitation and the urgent construction or recasting of social and governmental institutions. Accordingly, Indonesia's international profile remained relatively subdued, and in the global popular imagination, the country

8 See, for example, Departemen Luar Negeri Republik Indonesia (2005: 801–3).

was represented by the graphic images of military/militia violence as Indonesia retreated from East Timor, and the equally dramatic ones of terrorist outrages in Bali, the wreckage of places and lives in the 2004 tsunami and the damage caused by a number of catastrophic earthquakes.

Only recently, with the advent of a more or less established democratic regime and continuing economic development,[9] has Indonesia once again deliberately sought – as in the high Suharto days – a more prominent role in world affairs. That development is sketched in other chapters in this book, and includes Indonesia's holding a seat, for the third time, in the UN Security Council (in 2007–2008) and its important and still emerging role in the G20. It was most clearly signalled by President Susilo Bambang Yudhoyono's keynote speech to the 2011 World Economic Forum, where he made clear that Indonesia must play a more energetic role in world affairs.[10] Indonesia's dutiful efforts to play a lead role in managing tensions in the South China Sea may be a sign that it plans to play a similarly industrious, if determinedly modest, role in larger affairs. That outward engagement has been encouraged by Indonesia's enhanced performance, and consequently enhanced reputation, in a number of areas, including its democratic successes (and all that they entail in terms of freedoms of various kinds), its anti-terrorism actions, the marriage of so-called 'moderate' Islam with modernity, and some (admittedly halting and indecisive) moves against corruption. With greater 'performance legitimacy' has come greater confidence.

In summary, to speak of Indonesia's place in the world over the longer term is to speak with a much muted voice, since the Indonesian impact on world affairs has been, in most respects, modest. There are any number of possible explanations for Indonesia's relative absence from the world and its generally low profile. The most obvious of those is that for much of the twentieth century Indonesia remained very poor (Table 9.1).

That enduring poverty – a consequence, among other things, of colonialism, war, civil unrest, wrong-headed economic policies and rampant corruption – crippled Indonesia's capacity to address its deep-seated economic, political and social problems. As a consequence, its education system remained deeply underdeveloped, its armed forces lacked

---

9 Growth was around 6 per cent in 2010, fuelled by a huge commodities and consumer boom and a very rapidly growing middle class.

10 Yudhoyono (2011) remarked that 'Asia is of course more than China, Japan and India. When you think of Asia, also think Indonesia and ASEAN. Indonesia is the world's third largest democracy, the largest economy in Southeast Asia, a key growth area in the world economy, and soon we will have one of the largest productive work force[s] in Asia. Indonesia will feature prominently in Asia's renaissance'. He also noted that 'what we need is a 21st century globalism'.

Table 9.1 *Indonesia's GDP per capita compared with several other Asian countries, 1900–2000 (in 1990 dollars)*

	Indonesia	Philippines	Thailand	Japan
1900	745	1,033	812	1,180
1913	904	1,066	835	1,385
1950	840	1,070	817	1,926
1973	1,504	1,959	1,874	11,439
1990	2,516	2,199	4,645	18,789
2000	3,041	2,385	6,335	20,084

Source: Touwen (2008: Table 1).

any serious capacity to project power internationally (and especially to police the vast maritime regions of the archipelago), while its social institutions – such as its legal system, its capacity to maintain the rule of law (and a credible practice of respecting human rights) and its machinery of political accountability – remained weak and poorly rooted. Indonesia's abiding economic and social weaknesses might indeed go some way to account for the continuing disregard internationally for Indonesia's civilizational experience. In the United States, for example, the study of Asia has meant, for the most part, the study of China, Japan and, to a lesser extent, South Asia, and the serious study of Indonesia has remained badly marginalized.

But it is clearly not enough simply to assert that Indonesia's impoverishment and incapacity across many fields have necessarily resulted in its failure to register significantly in the international scheme of things. Other countries that once experienced significant economic and governance failure have managed to drag themselves up through persistent reform to become influential international exemplars of 'good practice'; one might mention Singapore, of course, and more recently China, Brazil or even India. China, weak and despised for most of the twentieth century, has managed to marry astounding economic growth to its immense size and ambition in ways that threaten to reshape global patterns of international power.

One might point, as well, to other explanations for Indonesia's muted international engagement. The lack of an aggressive and influential diaspora to champion its cause might be one, a function of the fact that diasporic Indonesian communities have generally been in flight from the Indonesian nation and state rather than serving as its distant supporters. But that alone is insufficient to carry much of the burden of explanation.

Another might be an absence of dangerous neighbours, but that again explains little. Many states in peaceful zones – one thinks of Canada and even little New Zealand – have played a more enduringly effective role in international affairs than has Indonesia.

Why then has Indonesia performed so poorly? In my view, one needs to examine the intersection of two crucial categories in Indonesia's modern history: identity and legitimacy.

Indonesia's identity – by which I mean the ways in which the Indonesian nation defines itself – has been deeply fraught and violently contested for much of the past century. We need to remember here that – in contrast to other nations that like to define themselves culturally and civilizationally – 'Indonesia' is a very modern idea that only began to materialize significantly in the minds of some indigenous inhabitants of the then Netherlands Indies in the 1920s. The relative youth of the idea of Indonesia, as well as the remarkable skill, tenacity and effectiveness of the Dutch in discouraging it, meant that the content of the idea remained relatively undeveloped and not accepted benignly and unquestioningly across the archipelago. An important consequence of the lack of sustained indigenous contestation about the idea of Indonesia was that the persistent, energetic championing of the idea of a free Indonesian nation and state was accompanied by deeply fraught and ambiguous differences about what the idea represented and how it might best be manifested. Thus secularist and inclusivist concepts of Indonesia rubbed against emerging Islamist ones; egalitarian and broadly democratic impulses endured alongside elitist/conservative and pseudo-fascist ones; and modernist understandings of what it meant to be Indonesian jostled, mostly gently, with nativist/traditionalist ones. Cipto Mangunkusumo put it very neatly as early as 1918: '[W]hat we mean by the Indies nation has still to be formed, that is to say, it does not yet exist. The first spade has just been put into the ground, the seed has still to be sown' (Mangoenkoesoemo 1918: 60).

The capacity of the tiny Indonesian elite to capitalize on the political opportunities presented by the Japanese occupation was truly remarkable. But because the framing of content for the idea of Indonesia had been so immature and inconsequential, the leaders of the republic, having created a functioning Indonesian state, then had the task of making an Indonesian nation and – even more difficult – building legitimacy for the nation among the huge and socially differentiated peoples of the archipelago.

That was to prove demanding. Around 1950, the notion that the republic was the only legitimate successor to the old Netherlands Indies was not nearly as well accepted among many who are now Indonesians as we might now like to think. One 'Federal' newspaper, for example, remarked in 1948 that 'we have protested for the thousandth time that the republic has no right to speak in the name of the whole of Indonesia'.[11] The task meant defining in some purposeful and meaningful way what Indonesia was and what it stood for, and then legitimizing that idea across the vastnesses of the archipelago. It is fair to say that Indonesia, for much of its history, has done rather a poor job in both those areas, although it has proved to be remarkably successful in maintaining the existential status of the nation and its state. As I have noted elsewhere, 'the whole was not created *ex nihilo*; rather, from the outset it was a Java-centred state to which things were added from the inside out' (Elson 2006: 269). The making of the 1945 Constitution bears witness to the confusions about identity that abounded; the resultant document was a strange marriage of snippets of Western-inspired liberalism, anti-imperial moralizing and deeply suspicious and heavily centralizing authoritarianism. Where there were deep uncertainties about what Indonesia meant, there were correspondingly deep uncertainties about its reception or, to put it another way, its legitimacy.

Sukarno's recasting of the nature of the Indonesian polity in the late 1950s was made in response to the uncertainties about identity that had only strengthened when independence, framed under an order of liberal democracy, failed to deliver its promised fruit, and when social and political tensions were becoming increasingly patent. That remaking was loud, pseudo-nativist in kind, rhetorically ambitious and superficially busy, but empty of meaningful content. The vain attempt to 'rediscover' the 'Indonesian essence' had a containing, blunting, debilitating effect on cosmopolitan thinking, at first on the right but eventually on the left as well. What was much worse, it provided the essential conditions for increasingly inward-looking political sectarianism to become inflamed to murderous heights in the mid-1960s.

The consequence was the army's inevitable political triumph. It marked the beginning of yet another effort to remake Indonesia, this time by reference to an entirely different template that privileged social and political conservatism and twinned it with technocratic economic acuity in an attempt to produce a homogeneously flattened Indonesia with little sign of cosmopolitan engagement, no sign of ideological rent or social division – and certainly no classes.

That model, of course, could not endure over the long term, all the more so because the New Order's economic and social policies produced not just the kind of development that Suharto craved but also the

---

11 *Mestika*, 3 August 1948, as reported in Rapportage Indonesië 1945–1950, No. 71, Nationaal Archief, The Hague.

unlooked-for side effects of a much better-educated and increasingly affluent society that chafed under the tedium of New Order flatness and constraint. The collapse of the regime in 1998 – even now breathtakingly sudden and total – produced the *reformasi* movement, and a new attempt, the fourth of its kind, to escape from the shame of the Suharto period and to define and redefine the meaning of Indonesia.

In general, then, Indonesia's identity has been fundamentally and episodically recast throughout the history of its independent existence. That remaking has involved deep social tumult, but also a persistent effort at both delegitimizing the abandoned template of what Indonesia might mean and what values it might represent and legitimizing a new one. In the doing, the predominant tendency has been to seek the construction of conservative, self-regarding, self-contained and defensive solutions, rather than open and cosmopolitan ones. The result is that Indonesia's identity has been the subject of continual fundamental reworking by different generations of leaders, perhaps far more than has been the case in comparable decolonized countries. More specifically, that serial reworking has created a consistent sense of internal frailty, an awareness of the danger of outside threats (and externally sponsored internal ones) and a general mistrust of the agendas of the world outside.

That process has had deeply damaging effects not just on identity but also, and necessarily, on the perceived legitimacy of the state, which long remained shallowly rooted and precarious. Sukarno was concerned above all with asserting and consolidating the essential political unity of the vast, ethnically diverse, weakly ruled and poorly institutionalized archipelago. 'The essential point', he once related to George Kahin, 'must be the building up [of] a nation – a strong national state' (Sukarno 1949). He did that with the only tools at his disposal, showy rhetoric and an unrivalled command of symbol and imagery, which effectively delegitimized the previous democratic regime. When the conflagration of 1965–66 destroyed that insubstantial contrivance, Suharto, similarly obsessed with national unity, replaced it with the steel of the army and a narrow, homogenizing, constraining ideology, different in content to Sukarno's but similar in intent and consequence, aimed at creating a flattened and controllable edifice free from competing ideas.

The means employed by Sukarno and Suharto were effective for a time in their own way, but they were ultimately unconvincing in legitimating their regimes, both to their own citizens and to the world outside. That helps to explain how the ideological, ritualistic and constraining aspects of both the Old and New Orders disappeared so rapidly, totally and without trace or legacy almost immediately upon the collapse of the regimes that had fathered them. As Clifford Geertz once remarked more generally, Indonesia had been left 'without a predictable system of civic discourse' (Geertz 2001: 15). That lack of comfortable legitimacy was reflected in a lack of self-assurance, of confidence in itself.

It should be no surprise, then, that one of the major aspects of Indonesia's foreign engagement, especially during the Sukarno and Suharto periods, was its flavour of obsessive suspicion at the machinations of the world outside, particularly the West – with quickly emerging outrage and loudly asserted (but often empty) protestations against any perceived attempt to belittle or impugn Indonesia's sovereignty or integrity. Thus we had, for example, Sukarno's repudiation of Western aid and his exit from the United Nations; the overblown Indonesian reaction to a newspaper piece on Suharto's business interests by David Jenkins in 1986; Suharto's unilateral dismemberment of the Intergovernmental Group on Indonesia in 1991 following criticism by its chair, Jan Pronk, of Indonesia's human rights failings, and especially its policy and record on East Timor; Indonesia's reaction to Australia's change of policy on East Timor; and its repugnance at efforts by the IMF to bludgeon it into particular modalities of economic reform. More recently, of course, Indonesian wrath soared again when Australia granted temporary protection visas to several Papuan asylum seekers, with an ambassador withdrawn and the president warning the offending government not to 'toy with' or 'insult' Indonesia (Fitzpatrick 2006).

From the point of view of the outside world, Indonesia's distracted obsessiveness with its identity, and the questionable means it has often invoked to bring that into a state of legitimacy, has meant that international interest in the country has never remained consistently strong over the long term. Only when that obsessiveness has provoked international turbulence (as with the Malaysian confrontation and East Timor episodes) has the world much noticed it. But provided Indonesia remained more or less benign in international terms – economically as well as politically – the world was satisfied to leave it more or less to itself. Under the fearful ideological jails of both Old and New Orders there was little Indonesia stood to offer the international community, and there was little on offer that might draw the world's interest, apart from its environmental diversity and its tourist landscapes. Because of its poverty and frequent bouts of governmental and social incapacity, it was not a source of weighty or influential ideas. Indeed, when I was invited recently to review a new book by Andrew Goss (2011) on the failure of Indonesian natural science, my response was cast in terms of how one might have expected things to work out any differently (Elson 2011).

The face that Indonesia has long presented to the world is, then, one that over the long term has made it difficult for the world to take the country as seriously and significantly as its size, position and potential might otherwise have demanded. More recent developments, however, indicate that at long last Indonesia is beginning to contest on the international scene in a weight commensurate with its intrinsic importance. Its economy has been growing steadily, and apparently sustainably, for over a decade; it now ranks as the eighteenth-largest economy in the world.[12] Its democratized and generally stable political system seems increasingly deeply rooted and now serves, in some eyes, as an exemplar of desirable practice for other nations as far apart as Egypt and Bangladesh.

As the analysis above might suggest, the keys to this incipient international advance are important improvements in Indonesia's overall performance, its sense of its own identity and, consequently, its sense of legitimacy. That is best achieved by the creation and constant refurbishing of institutions that allow a country to believe in itself, and to project itself as internationally credible and responsible without recourse to the imposition of empty grandiosity or of state-sponsored thuggery. That process is seemingly under way, although it is by no means complete; there is still some way to travel on the road from ambivalence to equanimity. Indonesia has sought and received international assistance from ASEAN and the European Union in monitoring the implementation of the Aceh peace agreement. It is an increasingly respected member of the G20. It has begun to project itself as a positive force in world affairs, as when it hosted the International Conference of Islamic Leaders for Reconciliation in Iraq in April 2007, and in its recent efforts as ASEAN chair to moderate tensions in the South China Sea. That expanded sense of international engagement and solidified identity and legitimacy was acknowledged and endorsed by the visits to Indonesia of Hillary Clinton and Barack Obama.

The strengthening of Indonesia's democratic identity and legitimacy should become evident in the firmer rooting of the non-arbitrary exercise of the rule of law, a gradual decline in official corruption, an acceptance that universal norms of human rights are to be taken seriously and enforced, and the growth of a more vibrant civil society.[13] It will become evident, too, in the development of a more relaxed, rational self-confidence, in the capacity of Indonesia to receive international criticism of its legal system, its modes and methods of governance or its strategic

---

12 See the GDP figures for 2010 in the World Development Indicators database, available at http://data.worldbank.org/sites/default/files/gdp.pdf.

13 Indonesia reportedly possesses the second-largest number of Facebook members in the world and the third-largest number of Twitterers, although it is not entirely clear whether this is an indication of civil society advance ('Indonesia's middle class: missing BRIC in the wall', *Economist*, 23–29 July 2011: 25).

policies without resort to defensive, obfuscating, strident outrage that sees a dark, disintegrating conspiracy in every critique.

The cautionary adage with which this essay begins – 'Our foreign policy must be in accordance with our own internal strength' – was uttered by Ruslan Abdulgani in 1957. He made this remark in the context of asserting that Indonesia must make its own interests and capacities the guide and measure of its foreign relations. But it seems to me a useful motif in attempting to explain the apparent flaccidity of Indonesia's long-term engagement with the world. That weakness has been a result of Indonesia's own internal weaknesses, themselves in significant degree a consequence of its leaders' failures to create a broadly accepted and legitimate sense of what Indonesia meant and what it stood for, installing instead a contrived and blanketing uniformity that its citizens endured but never confidently owned. That weakness, that lack of 'internal strength', has been internationally debilitating for Indonesia for too long. As that strength gathers, as it currently promises to do, Indonesia will take a more purposeful and outward-looking view of its place in the world.

REFERENCES

Abdulgani, Ruslan (1957) interview with George Kahin, Jakarta, 13 June, Kahin papers (private), held at George McT. Kahin Center, Cornell University, Ithaca NY.

Anonymous (1924), 'Indonesia in de wereld gemeenschap' [Indonesia in the world community], in Indonesische Vereeniging (ed.) *Gedenkboek 1908–1923: Indonesische Vereeniging* [Commemorative Book 1908–1923: Indonesian Association], no place of publication given.

Anwar, Dewi Fortuna (2010) 'Indonesia, the region and the world', East Asia Forum, 28 May, available at http://www.eastasiaforum.org/2010/05/28/Indonesia-the-region-and-the-world/.

Departemen Luar Negeri Republik Indonesia (2005) *Sejarah Diplomasi Republik Indonesia dari Masa ke Masa* [The History of the Diplomacy of the Republic of Indonesia from Age to Age], Buku IVB, periode 1966–1996, Jakarta.

Douwes Dekker, E.F.E (1914) *Het Jaar 1913 en Zijn Beteekenis Voor de Indische beweging* [The Year 1913 and Its Significance for the Indies Movement], De Toekomst, Schiedam.

Elson, R.E. (2006) 'Indonesia and the West: an ambivalent, misunderstood engagement', *Australian Journal of Politics and History* 52(2): 262–71.

Elson, R.E. (2011) '*The Floracrats: State-sponsored Science and the Failure of the Enlightenment in Indonesia* by Andrew Goss', *American Historical Review* 116(5): 1,469.

Feith, Herbert (1962) *The Decline of Constitutional Democracy in Indonesia*, Cornell University Press, Ithaca NY.

Fievez de Malines van Ginkel, Henri (1924) *Overzicht van de Internationaalrechterlijke Betrekkingen van Nederlandsch-Indië (1850–1922)* [Survey of the International Legal Relations of the Netherlands Indies (1850–1922)], Gebrs. J. & H. van Langenhuysen, 's-Gravenhage.

Fitzpatrick, Stephen (2006) '"Don't toy with us": Jakarta', *Australian*, 18 April.

Geertz, Clifford (2001) 'Soekarno daze', *Latitudes* 8: 10–15.

Goss, Andrew (2011) *The Floracrats: State-sponsored Science and the Failure of the Enlightenment in Indonesia*, University of Wisconsin Press, Madison WI.

Hatta, Mohammad (1953) 'Haluan politiek pemerintah' [The direction of government policy], in O. Raliby (ed.), *Documentaria Historica: Sedjarah Dokumenter dari Pertumbuhan dan Perdjuangan Negara Republik Indonesia* [Historical Documentation: Documentary History of the Development and Struggle of the State of the Republic of Indonesia], Bulan-Bintang, Jakarta, pp. 525–8.

Jenkins, David (1986), 'After Marcos, now for the Soeharto billions', *Sydney Morning Herald*, 10 April: 1, 7.

Mangoenkoesoemo, Tjipto (1918) 'Een slotwoord' [A concluding word], in R.M.S. Soeriokoesoemo, A. Muhlenfeld, Tjipto Mangoenkoesoemo and J.B. Wens (eds) *Javaansche of Indisch Nationalisme? Pro en Contra* [Javanese or Indies Nationalism? For and Against], Semarang Drukkerij en Boekhandel H.A. Benjamins, Semarang.

Reid, Anthony (2010) 'Indonesia at 65: the alchemy of nation building and the formation of modern Indonesia', sixth annual Herb Feith Lecture, Monash University, Melbourne, 27 October.

Suharto (1989) *Pikiran, Ucapan dan Tindakan Saya* [My Thoughts, Words and Deeds], Citra Lamtoro Gung Persaida, Jakarta.

Sukarno (1949) Interview with George Kahin, Pangkalpinang, 2 May, Kahin papers (private), held at George McT. Kahin Center, Cornell University, Ithaca NY.

Touwen, Jeroen (2008), 'The economic history of Indonesia', in R. Whaples (ed.) *EH.Net Encyclopedia*, posted 16 March, available at http://eh.net/encyclopedia/article/touwen.Indonesia.

Yudhoyono, Susilo Bambang (2011) 'The big shift and the imperative of 21st century globalism', keynote speech to the 2011 World Economic Forum, Davos, 27 January, available at http://www.presidenri.go.id/index.php/pidato/2011/01/27/1571.html.

INDEX

D

F

G

H

M

N

INDONESIA UPDATE SERIES

1989
Indonesia Assessment 1988 (Regional Development)
edited by Hal Hill and Jamie Mackie

1990
Indonesia Assessment 1990 (Ownership)
edited by Hal Hill and Terry Hull

1991
Indonesia Assessment 1991 (Education)
edited by Hal Hill

1992
Indonesia Assessment 1992 (Political Perspectives)
edited by Harold Crouch

1993
Indonesia Assessment 1993 (Labour)
edited by Chris Manning and Joan Hardjono

1994
Indonesia Assessment 1994: Finance as a Key Sector in Indonesia's Development
edited by Ross McLeod

1996
Indonesia Assessment 1995: Development in Eastern Indonesia
edited by Colin Barlow and Joan Hardjono

1997
Indonesia Assessment: Population and Human Resources
edited by Gavin W. Jones and Terence H. Hull

1998
Indonesia's Technological Challenge
edited by Hal Hill and Thee Kian Wie

1999
Post-Soeharto Indonesia: Renewal or Chaos?
edited by Geoff Forrester

2000
Indonesia in Transition: Social Aspects of Reformasi and Crisis
edited by Chris Manning and Peter van Diermen

2001
Indonesia Today: Challenges of History
edited by Grayson J. Lloyd and Shannon L. Smith

2002
Women in Indonesia: Gender, Equity and Development
edited by Kathryn Robinson and Sharon Bessell

2003
Local Power and Politics in Indonesia: Decentralisation and Democratisation
edited by Edward Aspinall and Greg Fealy

2004
Business in Indonesia: New Challenges, Old Problems
edited by M. Chatib Basri and Pierre van der Eng

2005
The Politics and Economics of Indonesia's Natural Resources
edited by Budy P. Resosudarmo

2006
Different Societies, Shared Futures: Australia, Indonesia and the Region
edited by John Monfries

2007
Indonesia: Democracy and the Promise of Good Governance
edited by Ross H. McLeod and Andrew MacIntyre

2008
Expressing Islam: Religious Life and Politics in Indonesia
edited by Greg Fealy and Sally White

2009
Indonesia beyond the Water's Edge: Managing an Archipelagic State
edited by Robert Cribb and Michele Ford

2010
Problems of Democratisation in Indonesia: Elections, Institutions and Society
edited by Edward Aspinall and Marcus Mietzner

2011
Employment, Living Standards and Poverty in Contemporary Indonesia
edited by Chris Manning and Sudarno Sumarto

2012
Indonesia Rising: The Repositioning of Asia's Third Giant
edited by Anthony Reid